Insiders, Outsiders and Others

Gypsies and identity

Insiders, Outsiders and Others

Gypsies and identity

Kalwant Bhopal and Martin Myers

University of Hertfordshire Press

First published in Great Britain in 2008 by
University of Hertfordshire Press
Learning and Information Services
University of Hertfordshire
College Lane
Hatfield
Hertfordshire AL10 9AB

© Kalwant Bhopal and Martin Myers 2008

The rights of Kalwant Bhopal and Martin Myers to be identified as the authors of this work have been asserted by them in accordance with the Copyright, Designs and Patents Act 1988.

All rights reserved. No part of this book may be reproduced or utilised in any form or by any means, electronic or mechanical, including photocopying, recording or by any information storage and retrieval system, without permission in writing from the publisher.

British Library Cataloguing in Publication Data
A catalogue record for this book is available from the British Library

ISBN 978-1-902806-71-6

Design by Mathew Lyons
Cover design by John Robertshaw, Harpenden, AL5 2JB
Printed in Great Britain by the MPG Books Group, Bodmin and King's Lynn

*To Dylan, Yasmin,
Deva and Sachin*

Contents

Acknowledgements	ix
1. Gypsies and their identities	1
2. Gypsy identity and culture: foundational accounts and the Academy	29
3. Gypsy identity and culture: misrepresentation, misrecognition and deception	61
4. Recognising the 'other'	87
5. Case study I: Inside the school gates: Gypsy families' experiences of education	117
6. Case study II: Media representations of Gypsy life in election year	145
7. The outsider in multicultural society	175
8. The outsider in racist society	201
Bibliography	227
Index	235

Acknowledgements

We would like to thank all the schools, parents, pupils and teachers who agreed to participate in our research. We would also like to thank the Traveller Education Services who have made time to assist us with a number of different projects. We are particularly grateful for the continuing advice and support we have received for our work from Felicity Bonel, John Clay, Sue Harry, Paul Frith and Thomas Acton. Thanks to Javier Hidalgo of Bodegas Hidalgo and to Jethro Perkins for their quick responses to our queries. Many thanks to Damien Le Bas for agreeing to the use of his artwork on the cover. We would like to thank Derek McGhee and Colin Clark for reading earlier drafts of the chapters and for providing useful comments. At the University of Hertfordshire Press we would like to thank Jane Housham both for taking on this project and for her close reading and insightful comments regarding an early draft of the text. Sarah Harrison's copy editing has made for a much more readable and intelligible text. Thanks also to Sarah Elvins at the University of Hertfordshire Press for her continuing professionalism.

We would like to acknowledge the funding received from the University of Greenwich (School of Education and Training) and the London Borough of Greenwich (Ethnic Minority Achievement Service).

Kalwant would like to thank her former colleagues at the University of Greenwich (School of Education and Training) for all their support during the fieldwork stages of the research and for providing valuable time in which to conduct the research. Thanks specifically to Patrick Ainley for his support. She would also like to thank the participants at various conferences from 2004–6 where earlier thoughts on the chapters were presented. Many thanks to colleagues at the University of Southampton School of Education for their support during the final writing stages. Huge thanks to Janet Ramsdale and Jean Rattray for their continued support.

Martin would like to thank Ben Gidley, Michael Keith and Bridget Ward at the Centre for Urban and Community Research, Goldsmiths College for making his time at Goldsmiths such a positive experience. My thanks to Kath Woodward at the Open University for her support throughout the last year. I would like to offer a huge vote of confidence to KaitO, the pop band, you are sorely missed; a ULU gig was in many ways responsible for my own change in career, thanks also to Clive, Alec, Martin and Keith who were (probably) all at the same gig and who remain great company. Love and thanks to my parents, Maureen and Peter Myers, who have always supported me.

This book is dedicated to our children, Dylan, Yasmin, Deva and Sachin, we hold them collectively responsible for any errors in the final text.

1. Gypsies and their identities

This is a book about Gypsies in the United Kingdom and in particular it is a book that provides an account of the formation of Gypsy identity/identities. Whilst it would be palpably untrue to suggest that providing such an account of any other group or community is a simple or straightforward business, there is still a clear sense of greater complexity and wider scope for misunderstanding when considering Gypsy culture. This should not be surprising; although Gypsies are recognisable figures within rural and urban landscapes, the representations that are made of them tend to reflect an imaginary sense of the Gypsy which is configured, in general, from a non-Gypsy perspective. In many ways this is a hugely confused perspective. Within the wider population there appears to be little knowledge or interest in the history and culture of Gypsy communities (little is known, for example, of the likely links between Gypsies and India); there is apprehension and distrust of many cultural aspects associated with Gypsy lifestyles and there is a historic feeling of dividedness, of an uncrossable borderline between Gypsy culture and non-Gypsy culture. What is more, the miscomprehension by the wider population, of Gypsies within the UK, reflects prevalent attitudes across Europe and further afield. It is within this context that Gypsy culture has shaped itself and continues to shape itself. The recent and historic tendencies to either misrepresent or misrecognise Gypsy culture provide the background against which this account of Gypsy identity is situated. Often such misrepresentation or misrecognition comes from anticipated sources: the sloganeering of tabloid headlines, for example. Sometimes, however, it appears more unexpectedly, in the voices of the Academy or in thoughtful and supportive articles in liberal broadsheets. In these cases such misrepresentation might take an altogether different tone, countering the tabloid tales of dirt and idleness with a romanticised version of hardworking and long-suffering families. In these more liberal accounts is the tendency to reinvent, in contemporary terms, historic dualisms in which Gypsies are portrayed in a positive and a negative fashion at the same time. It is perhaps ironic that liberal and illiberal accounts often seem to be as inaccurate as each other.

Such accounts, both liberal and intolerant, say much about the wider community and its need to place Gypsies in relation to itself. One strand of the thinking behind this book is intended to unravel that placement by society and the understanding of Gypsies that follows in its wake. Georg Simmel (1950; 1971) and, more recently, Zygmunt Bauman (1991) have raised many interesting questions about the role of the '*stranger*' in society, identifying in particular immigrant groups who come to a society from elsewhere, or, as Simmel famously put it, 'the man who comes today and stays tomorrow' (Simmel 1971, 49).

The power of the *stranger* is his ability to disrupt the ordinariness of everyday life. He is unsettling because he is not understood and yet he remains: the *stranger* is not an exotic visitor passing briefly, who strays from the tourist map and brings a little colour into our lives; but, rather, an exotic visitor who moves into the house next door, walks our street, plies his trade and lives within a distinct and different cultural milieu. This *stranger* and the baggage that he brings with him becomes a source of anxiety for wider society. In the UK today we see many clear signs of the functioning of multiculturalism and if we look closely we may also be aware of its various failings. In many respects one result of multiculturalism, in either its difference-blind or difference-celebratory manifestations, should be an overcoming of issues around the stranger; we either become blind to difference or learn to understand it. The strangeness should dissipate, the anxiety be relieved and *Daily Mail* readers should sleep a little more easily in their beds. This does not appear to happen in real life, however, and the figure of the Gypsy remains a significantly unsettling figure within contemporary accounts. This book will examine whether there is a sense of the *'stranger'* within the positioning of Gypsies in society. Related to this, and particularly to ideas of how 'otherness' is created, is an examination of the ways in which 'white' culture differentiates itself and the extent to which understandings of Gypsy identity fall within and outside notions of 'whiteness'. We might expect on the basis of well-established racism towards immigrant communities in the UK that skin colour is a dependent characteristic for such racism. It might be anticipated that the element of public opinion swayed by sloganeering demanding to 'keep Britain white' would materialise in a groundswell of right-wing thinking that is largely sympathetic towards Gypsy culture in the UK because of their long-established presence and skin colour. Within less extreme political agendas – the ascendancy of free-market thinking in the governments of Margaret Thatcher and John Major, for example, or more recently Tony Blair's slightly more fuzzy promotion of individual choice and its associated responsibilities – we might also anticipate a more affirmative embracing of Gypsy culture. With its emphasis on self-employment and family and community bonds, Gypsy culture surely has the potential to be seen as a positive model for society. None of these interpretations have materialised within wider society and there are probably very few amongst us who are in any way surprised by this. There is a general and unwritten understanding of the role played by Gypsies within society that anticipates negative accounts of their lives. Even within liberal agendas and multicultural institutions there is a clear sense that the understandings being constructed have deep roots within such negative accounts. By examining the production of representations of Gypsies and their culture it is possible to understand something of how multicultural society reproduces many of the same aspects of misrecognition and misrepresentation of Gypsy culture that might be more generally equated with less liberal regimes.

The Gypsy diaspora, Gypsies in Europe and the United Kingdom

There is no accurate account of how Gypsies came to exist as a largely nomadic group within Europe, partly because different groups of Gypsies share different histories and partly because there are few accurate records of the foundational account of the Gypsy diaspora, described below (Acton 1974; Kenrick and Puxon 1972; Okely 1983). The most generally accepted accounts suggests that Gypsies originated in northern India and moved west across the Middle East and Europe 1,000 to 1,500 years ago, possibly in response to incursions by Islam and the threats of war. There is no definitive link between Gypsies in Europe and a specific nomadic or sedentary group in India; however, linguistic studies have established a great deal of commonality between Romany and Hindi and Punjabi (Fraser 1992). Kenrick and Puxon (1972), amongst others, have noted the similarity between the Hindi *Dom*, describing nomadic Indian groups, and the word *Rom*, used by Gypsies to describe themselves. The main criticism of this foundational theory was articulated by the anthropologist Judith Okely (1983; 1997), who suggests that the linguistic theory is overstated. She argues (1983) that there is a racial group who are defined as Gypsies, whose origins are based on linguistic and cultural traits derived from India; however, she suggests that European Gypsies also originate and develop from numerous different and often indigenous groups. She further suggests (1983) a twofold tendency by *gaujo*[1] academics on the one hand and Gypsy politicians on the other to overstate the Indian connection. The academics, she suggests, are over-enamoured by the exotic nature of the connection, and Gypsy politicians have often found it expedient to suggest that Gypsies share a specific ethnicity, something that becomes more readily accepted by the establishment of a direct link to a particular place. Whilst Okely's dismissal of the Indian connection flies in the face of much established research, she rightly demonstrates the importance of other indigenous communities and cross-fertilisation of cultures in the make-up of contemporary Gypsy cultures. Most importantly, Okely stresses the need to engage with contemporary identities of Gypsies rather than with an exotic mythical group who may or may not represent an accurate historical reality.

The debate around Gypsy identity is confusing in many respects because of the understandings that are generated by academic interest in the area. The connections to India might well exist and be understood in terms of both relatively objective evidential accounts and more subjective attempts at providing reasonable accounts of where Gypsies originated. However, as Okely argues, this may not relate to the direct experiences of Gypsies themselves, for whom the place of origin may not be so important. Such a relationship to place of origin, however, flies in the face of much academic writing about identity. So, for example, Stuart Hall's (1990) description of a twofold construction of cultural identity, which emphasises on the one hand 'belonging' and on the other 'becoming', does not fit the Gypsy experience in the neat manner in which a reading of the diaspora of African people might be explained within academic discourse. In particular, the sense of 'belonging' and of sharing a 'oneness' with a single group who left India 1,000 or more years ago does not ring true, certainly not in the sense of being informed by an association to that place or those people. It is also a sense of 'belonging' that does not feed into wider, more popular, understandings of Gypsy culture. Hall's analysis, based on the experiences of the African diaspora, suggests an enormous and politically conscious body upon which an individual black person can call as political capital; and, more importantly, this allegiance is recognised within wider cultures (even in places where it is actively disliked there is still a recognition of the history and linkages of the African diaspora). Such a unified understanding is not part and parcel of how Gypsies are viewed and one consequence is a weakening of their political strength; the individual Gypsy cannot summon up within popular understandings a similar constituency with a shared and understood heritage.

Hall's parallel process of becoming sits more comfortably with Gypsy experience, recognising as it does that one result of diaspora is that amongst groups of people there are 'critical points of deep and significant *difference* which constitute 'what we really are'; or rather – since history has intervened – "what we have become"' (Hall 1990, 225). This sense of cultural identity, which in Hall's description is one that is shaped potently by the effects of diaspora, 'is a matter of "becoming", as well as of "being"' (Hall 1990, 225). It places the idea of cultural identity within a narrative framework; it senses how an individual's own history has a shaping effect on identity. For Hall, 'belonging' and 'becoming' work in tandem, although inevitably providing grounds for ambiguity and complexity in understandings of who we are. At the end of the day both aspects rely on the sense of belonging to establish a solid foundation, to anchor the individual to his identity. If this is not a neat fit with Gypsy experience, and there is no innate sense of belonging to a single diasporic people, then there is a need to explore how Gypsies remain classed in many ways as a single group of people.

Nomenclature

One indication of how Gypsy culture is classified in populist understandings as a single culture can be found in the use of terms that tend to suggest a single homogeneous group. Ironically, there is a proliferation and confusion of different terms implying homogeneity that can be applied to Gypsies. The use of the word Gypsy/Gypsies is itself loaded with difficulties because it may well not be a term used by the people being described to describe themselves; and yet its use within wider society may be considered both normal and unquestionably valid. Describing the naming of people as Gypsies in America, Hancock notes that 'the word "gypsy" is often applied to any people who conform to the perceived image, whether they are ethnic Romanies or not' (Hancock 1987, 145).

What makes a term such as Gypsy/Gypsies even more problematic and contentious is the way that it is often loaded with highly pejorative meanings in many contexts. Within the school playground the use of the word 'Gypsy' will often carry overtones of a derogatory nature, the word becoming interchangeable with overtly racist terms such as 'gyppo' or 'pikey'. In other contexts, as when used by communities to describe themselves or in scholarly accounts of Gypsy identity, for example, it may well reflect an altogether different and positive meaning.

Within academic writing various terms are used that are derived generally from two different approaches: on the one hand, there is the generic Gypsy-Traveller axis and, on the other, there are more specific identifications (such as English Romanichal). Within the first of these groups various permutations are differently used, with 'Gypsy/Gypsies' (Acton 1997; Clark and Greenfields 2006; Mayall 2004; Okely 1983) and 'Traveller/Travellers' (Belton 2005; Clark and Greenfields 2006; Okely 1983) being the most common manifestations, and 'Traveller-Gypsies' (Okely 1983) and 'Gypsy-Travellers' (Bhopal 2004) used less often. In some cases, the term 'Traveller' has been used to refer to communities who are associated specifically with a nomadic lifestyle. These communities can include Gypsies/ Romanies of English, Scottish or Welsh heritage; Gypsies and Travellers of

Irish heritage; Roma/Gypsies mainly from Eastern Europe; Fairground/Show people; New Age Travellers; and Bargees.

In our work we have chosen to use the term 'Gypsy' primarily because those groups we refer to and spoke to in our research choose to define themselves as such. Many of the people we spoke to did not choose to define themselves as 'Travellers' as, they argued, they no longer travelled. They also suggested they would always be seen as Gypsies by society at large and would always remain Gypsies regardless of their economic circumstances. Despite a recognition of the pejorative associations linked to the use of the term 'Gypsy' by non-Gypsies, the people we spoke to understood the term as having positive associations with their communities and culture. Our use of this term may be seen as 'giving voice' to and legitimising the viewpoint of those people who informed our research. Here we agree with Okely (1983), who has argued that self-identification is the means by which ethnic identity is achieved and maintained. In order to legitimise the experiences of the group we have studied we have chosen to use their own self-ascription, rather than defining them ourselves. Our work considers material from wider contexts, such as media reports and government policy documents, that utilises different terminology, sometimes simultaneously, when describing Gypsies. In particular, the use of the word 'Traveller' has entered common currency throughout many of these sources (it is interesting, also, to note the increasingly negative connotations associated with the term 'Traveller' within media reports, and the way in which this term is increasingly becoming associated with the same kind of pejorative use as Gypsy). We have understood the usage of such terms within the media or policy documents, unless explicitly noted otherwise, to express generic understandings of Gypsies. It is also important to be aware that the use of some of the terms is being insisted upon by communities themselves and that none of these terms imply homogeneity. We have tended to avoid using the generic term 'Traveller' partly, as discussed, because it was not generally used by our respondents when they described themselves and also because it does not add to attempts to distinguish individual ethnic groups. Like 'Gypsy', the word 'Traveller' is a generic term and one that assumes a link to nomadism that does not necessarily hold true for all groups identified as Gypsies. The majority of families and family members interviewed in our research were from English Romany backgrounds, and an alternative approach would be to refer to specific ethnic identities, such as 'English Romany', but we felt this would detract from an examination of the predominant constructions of Gypsy identity within society, which are essentially based upon generic understandings. There is a continuing evolution of the terms used and within this book it should be noted that the use of the term 'Gypsy' does not contribute to any stereotypical or inaccurate definitions.

The use of terms can be fraught with many different tensions generated both from within and outside different Gypsy communities. At a recent postgraduate conference at which one of the authors presented a paper looking at theoretical approaches towards understanding relationships between white working-class families and their Gypsy neighbours, of the thirty minutes set aside for questions twenty-five were spent in a debate about the use of terms, in particular whether or not it was possible to use the word 'Gypsy' without causing offence. It was a subject that clearly raised interest far beyond those people directly engaged in work with Gypsy themes:

> Postgrad: I always thought the word Gypsy was terribly offensive. Where I'm from, in Ireland, I think everyone says Pavie now, because that's what people call themselves.
> Martin Myers (MM): Well I think you have to be very careful. There's very different usage of the word Gypsy. When someone

outside the culture calls someone a 'dirty, thieving Gypsy' it's obviously offensive. But there are plenty of people who call themselves Gypsies and are proud to do so. I don't think they regard it as offensive.

Postgrad: I wouldn't think anyone would voluntarily call themselves 'Gypsy'.

What seemed notable about the discussion was that the participants were not experts in the field (and were making no claims to be), but seemed incredibly attuned to the tensions surrounding such nomenclature and to the flaws that could be exposed through inappropriate usage. In one respect they were absolutely correct: there is a need to establish exactly what context and what understandings are being generated by the use of certain nomenclature, particularly where in other contexts (the school playground for example), the term may be loaded with entirely different and offensive connotations. However, returning to the postgraduate's discussion about terms, there was also a hint of wider academic consciousnesses developing, and the need for almost competitive approaches to ownership of acceptable terminology. In many ways this also seemed to be driven by wider conceptions of 'how we name' cultures outside of the dominant culture. A slightly bizarre conclusion that might have been drawn from some elements of the postgraduate discussion was that use of the word 'Traveller' by *The Sun* newspaper as part of an ongoing campaign against Gypsy rights was more acceptable than use of the word 'Gypsy' by Gypsies:

Postgrad: It's better to say 'Travellers'? It hasn't got the same connotations as 'Gypsy'.

Within the same debate it was also suggested that Gypsies calling themselves 'Gypsies' was perhaps within the same register as black people calling themselves 'niggers', and thus reflected the reclamation of an insult, which could be seen as empowerment. Now, whilst it would be silly to attach much significance to a group of largely uninformed students talking freely and sounding out ideas for which they held no evidence, such conversations do tend to sound the alarm. They suggest half-understandings (the evolution of the meanings attached to the word 'Gypsy') linked to strangely confident pronouncements that might reflect liberal-minded tendencies to identify problematical issues through the eyes of dominant parts of society on behalf of minority groups. Listening to the postgraduate discussion it seemed hard to imagine a similar debate taking place about the legitimacy of any other ethnic group's long-established name.

Race, ethnicity and racism

Although there have always been physical differences between groups of human beings, it is only within the last two centuries that these differences have been conceptualised as racial (Banton 1997). During this time there have been many problems associated with defining and understanding the concept of race. Miles has argued that the continued use of the term is misleading, because it refers to and gives credibility to the notion of naturally occurring populations when in fact it constitutes a false representation of reality. Instead, he argues, we should abandon the term and utilise the concept of 'racialisation' to refer to the 'process of defining an other in terms of biological characteristics' (Miles 1989, 75). An alternative position, however, has been put forward by Mason (1994): that race does not refer to categories (even socially defined ones), but to a social relationship. This 'relationship presumes the existence of racism', which for Mason means ideas and beliefs 'which emphasise the social and cultural relevance of biologically rooted characteristics' (Mason 1995, 11). Expanding on this definition of racism, Pilkington suggests that it is a discourse that operates through a number of identifiable steps:

> identifying groups, which reproduce themselves over time, on the basis of physical markers; seeing essential differences between them; associating 'others' with negative characteristics and visualising the dissolution of boundaries as undesirable. (Pilkington 2003, 189)

Early notions of race and racial difference were based upon classification systems that indicated the relative superiority and inferiority of particular groups generally with white being construed as the superior race. In addition, because race was associated with distinct hereditary characteristics, traits such as differences in intelligence, for example, were understood as being racial (Cornell and Hartmann 1998). Although the terms 'race' and 'ethnicity' are sometimes used together or even interchangeably, more generally race is associated with biological or physical difference and ethnicity with cultural difference. Both terms, however, involve drawing boundaries between and around people. In this sense they can both be regarded as socially constructed, rather than naturally occurring, dividing lines.

Bulmer (1986) has argued that ethnicity is a more inclusive term than race, because while race is based on biological membership of a particular group, ethnic groups are seen as having more fluid and blurred boundaries. Members of ethnic groups can change the boundaries of ethnic group membership as these boundaries are socially constructed and negotiated (Song 2003). Recently, the concept of ethnicity has become commonplace within academic thinking in the understanding of differences between groups in society. Anthias and Davis have indicated that ethnicity refers to the sense of 'belonging to a particular group and sharing its conditions of existence' (Anthias and Davis 1992, 8). What distinguishes an ethnic group from most other groups is the belief shared by its members 'in their common descent' (Webber 1997, 18). What is important is the notion that members of the group believe they have a common ancestry and so can claim a common identity (McGhee 2005; Pilkington 2003; Ratcliffe 2004). An ethnic group can therefore be defined as 'a population whose members believe that in some sense they share common descent and a common cultural heritage or tradition, and who are so regarded by others' (Smith 1986, 192), or as:

> a collectivity within a larger society having real or putative common ancestry, memories of a shared past, and a cultural focus on one or more symbolic elements which define the group's identity, such as kinship, religion, language, shared territory, nationality or physical appearance. Members of an ethnic group are conscious of belonging to the group. (Bulmer 1986, 54)

Ethnicity is therefore a more fluid boundary that is culturally negotiated, unlike race which tends to be more prescribed and refers to fixed understandings.

Gypsy ethnicity

In many ways the sense that Gypsies cannot be named or at least do not sit comfortably within a single generic group name reflects the complexities attached to an understanding of how Gypsy ethnicity is constructed. It reflects both the divergences that have shaped Gypsy culture over many hundreds of years and also the scholarly wrangling over definitions and terms.

There are a number of ways in which a claim for a Gypsy ethnicity can be made. These include language, nomadism, self-identification and the relationship between Gypsies and wider society. Whilst these individual defining elements of ethnicity occasionally diverge, they mostly overlap, providing recognisable patterns of groups identified as Gypsies. However, quite often within different interpretations and accounts of Gypsy identity each element is loaded with greater or lesser significance, which might suggest greater or lesser degrees of divergence. So, for example, the use of specific elements of language may be interpreted differently depending upon assessments of the importance of linkages to Indian languages. This, in turn, will have an impact on the account of the relationship of Gypsy identity to India and the emphasis placed upon the importance of the diaspora from Asia to Europe for understandings of Gypsy groups in the present day. Such loadings, it should be noted, might not necessarily impact greatly on the group of people being identified as Gypsies. Within the UK, for example, it is quite feasible to construct separate accounts of Gypsies in which one case emphasises the importance of the connection to India and another argues that it is of minimal importance, and yet both accounts would still be talking largely about the same cohort of people. Such ambivalences perhaps begin to explain some of the problems identified within some academic accounts of identity, such as Hall's description of 'belonging' to an identifiable, well-established, historically situated people. Some of the markers used to identify who is and who is not a Gypsy are quite fluid and are situated not within Gypsy communities but outside of them. These markers of identity and the interpretations placed upon them tend, therefore, to be critical in understanding society's construction and perception of the boundary lines between who is and who is not a Gypsy. These boundary lines are always in flux, sometimes at 'ground level' because of changes within society and its relationship to Gypsy culture, but also at another level, where the flux results from shifting emphasis on what constitutes Gypsy culture among academics and policy-makers. Movement on both levels reflects the actions and thinking of both Gypsy and non-Gypsy constituencies.

According to Okely (1983), there are well-defined ethnic boundaries between Gypsies and non-Gypsies. She argues that a set of traditions or 'rites' very specific to particular Gypsy communities ensures a high degree of cultural separation between these groups. By remaining true to such behaviours Gypsy society is able to maintain and develop its own system of beliefs. Not only do they not subscribe to a range of beliefs and values that are commonplace within wider society, they are actively seen not to do so. This largely explains why both Gypsies and non-Gypsies see themselves as distinct communities and begins to identify behaviours that may be considered symbolically important within Gypsy culture but regarded as subversive by other parts of society. Despite the high degree of separation in terms of culture, the relationship that remains between Gypsies and the non-Gypsies among whom they live has an impact on the construction of both groups' identity: it is inevitable that Bauman's *stranger* has the effect of unsettling the dominant population's self-belief. In contrast, the relationship between Gypsy communities and wider society may actually strengthen the former's cultural identity; both Liegeois (1987) and Belton (2005) argue that a sense of opposition to the dominant culture is an important factor in shaping Gypsy identity.

Liegeois suggests that diverse Gypsy communities share a cohesive political understanding of their oppositional relationship to society. This state of affairs is far from unsettling; in contrast, it works to create a sense of solidarity in the face of hostility. The 'otherness' of Gypsies, whilst important in maintaining strength within the community, plays out very differently in the context of wider society. Belton describes this process as 'The identification of the other, [which,] seen in a positive light, marks out uniqueness and difference that can easily be reinterpreted as strange and/or alien' (Belton 2005, 23). The identification of 'otherness' is one very critical stage in the process of creating racisms. For both Gypsies and non-Gypsies the identification of their difference from each other is an important step in creating a robust identity. The insistence on difference by the non-Gypsy world also creates an unsettling understanding of Gypsy identity and is the seed for much of the racism that surrounds perceptions of Gypsy culture.

Commonly cited markers of Gypsies' ethnic identity include language and nomadism, despite the fact that no clear-cut claim can be made that either have universal or comprehensive importance to the historic conditions of all Gypsy communities. Clebert (1963) has argued that one of the most distinct features that unites and distinguishes Gypsies is their identity through language, which is Indian in origin. The importance of this claim is that it establishes a common link between scattered and distinct groups of Gypsies throughout Europe, America and the rest of the world back to a single location. Acton (1997) further argues that the significance of a shared language is the key argument in confirming the distinctiveness of Gypsies. However, not all the evidence suggests that all Gypsy communities share a common language; for example, *Gammon*,[2] the language used exclusively by Irish Travellers, bears no resemblance to Romany or other languages based on Indian characteristics (Binchy 2000). Fraser (1992) has also argued that the history of language cannot be used to establish the ethnic and racial roots of ancient Romany speakers.

The nomadic lifestyle of Gypsies is also often seen as an indicator of their ethnic identity. Whilst this is important in understanding some aspects of the socially constructed notions of ethnicity that might be relevant to some Gypsies, it is not necessarily as obvious or definitive a marker as has been suggested. Liegeois (1987) points out that many European Gypsies are not nomadic and that travelling is not central to their particular lifestyle. Within the UK there are Gypsies who are nomadic and some who are not; there may well be differently shared understandings among those non-nomadic Gypsies of the importance of such nomadism within their own histories and their daily lives. Discussing wider European experiences of Gypsies, Acton forcefully makes the point that some of the assumptions of Gypsy nomadism are completely misplaced: 'Anthropologists have tended to present the Rom as primordially nomadic, building their theories around this, ignoring the fact that many of their 'subjects' are only four generations from slavery' (Acton 1987, iii). Such authors, Acton suggests, tend to ignore well-documented historical facts, preferring instead to 'maunder on about their "mysterious history"' (1987, iii).

There are strong arguments that self-identification is the means by which ethnic identify is achieved and maintained; within this context many of the characteristics and traits discussed above would, unsurprisingly, be given as important cultural markers by different groups of Gypsies. Okely (1983) suggests that self-ascription is a more acceptable means of identifying Gypsies than a search for an inventory of objective traits and characteristics that could be used by non-Gypsies to distinguish Gypsies. For Okely the importance of this approach is not so much that it ignores the existence of specific characteristics or traits associated with Gypsy culture, but rather that it allows Gypsy communities to define themselves using definitions generated within the community and not from the outside. Within this context she states that it is primarily the nomadic aspect which defines Gypsies, followed by language, dress, ritual, cleanliness, shared values and a separation between Gypsies and non-Gypsies. Family and kinship relationships are also distinguishing features of what it means to be a Gypsy, and Gypsy identity is ascribed by birth. She argues that:

> the principle of descent provides a method both for inclusion and exclusion. Thus Gypsies, like any ethnic group, have

procedures for releasing or absorbing a number of individuals without weakening their boundaries. (Okely 1983, 30)

Ethnic minority status

Another account of ethnic identity emphasises both the ethnic and the minority status of Gypsies. Whilst identity is still marked out by shared characteristics such as common origins, lifestyle, culture and experience, greater emphasis is placed on aspects of diversity and difference within the group and, most importantly, upon the historical positioning of Gypsy communities. This approach suggests that the defining characteristic of Gypsy identity is the oppression faced by Gypsies, including the persecution and victimisation of groups who are identified as Gypsies. Such a definition examines groups with low socio-economic and social status who possibly adopt the label 'gypsy' rather than Gypsy, Rom or Romany. This group may be defined by its nomadic way of life, typified by travelling family groups who pursue itinerant occupations and live in movable or semi-permanent dwellings at a distance from the settled population.

Boundaries and identity

The creation of boundaries works in a number of different ways, sometimes emphasising the cultural baggage that relates to the group or groups and sometimes emphasising their difference from society. Often this difference may reflect the sense of Gypsies as a victimised minority who fall outside the boundaries of respectable society. Mayall describes Gypsies who are seen not as a separate race but:

> simply as outcast from society, a people living on the margins of criminality and at the bottom end of the class hierarchy. The sense of threat, nuisance, danger, conflict and confrontation runs throughout each element of this portrait. (Mayall 2004, 2)

He also argues, however, that there are two distinct ways of defining Gypsies – the ethnic definition and the socio-historical perspective – and that such distinctions are prevalent in the types of work being produced by academic communities. He suggests that 'The need to define, redefine, group and separate the various itinerant groups has been a continuous feature of the state's legislative response to nomadism' (Mayall 2004, 2).

The processes by which Gypsy groups are categorised and labelled affects how they are treated in society and how they are seen and represented. Mayall outlines five key variables in the process of shaping group relations:

> the fixing of boundaries; the use of labels and the meanings given to them; the nature of information and knowledge about the group, derived from stereotyping and experience; characteristics of the group itself, in terms of size, location and visibility; external factors such as the socio-economic and political environment. (Mayall 2004, 12)

As Mayall argues, it is the distinction of boundaries that separates groups and leads to the establishment of insiders and outsiders. The wider boundary that defines who is and who is not a Gypsy may well form the basis for racism and discrimination by society generally. Perhaps more insidiously, internal racial classifications can be used ambiguously to justify acts of discrimination by the state, working around legalistic definitions of who is an authentic Gypsy. In such cases, rights may be withheld on the basis that particular communities are identified as not being authentic Romany Gypsies. We discuss a recent manifestation of this categorisation at greater length in Chapter 6; various newspapers and politicians identify and categorise Irish Travellers as being dirty, itinerant, difficult and invasive, as opposed to English Gypsies who, in this context, are typically categorised as well established, clean and settled.

Another characteristic associated with boundary forming is the use of labels to define groups by shaping and determining particular meanings which are then attached to the group. For example, some groups do not accept the label 'Gypsy' because of the negative connotations attached to it, and may prefer to use the term 'Traveller' instead (see Bhopal and Myers 2005). Typically, the term 'Gypsy' becomes transformed into a label such as 'dirty thieving gyppo', such labels effectively being used to define the characteristics of the group (see Chapter 5 for a wider discussion of these processes within our own research in schools).

The use of these identifying terms outside the Academy may not be considered quite so scrupulously, and, particularly within elements of the media hostile to Gypsies, there is likely to be little care taken when assigning labels to groups or identifying ethnicity. The use of the word 'Gypsy' and also, more recently, 'Traveller' in some media coverage portrays a stereotypical image of a type of person and associated behaviour (see Chapter 6). Such usage tends to be compounded by the often highly contrasting ways that Gypsy groups are represented. If, on the one hand, the idea of the Gypsy is a romanticised and exoticised image, on the other it is associated with dirt, idleness and disruption. These images and stereotypes contribute to the negative ways in which Gypsies are seen.

Hancock (1992) has argued that it is the continuous appearance of specifically negative images of Gypsies that undermines their position in society: their representation within society is the source for much of the discriminatory treatment received by Gypsy communities. Liegeois (1987) also discusses how damaging stereotypes of Gypsies contribute to discrimination within wider society; however, he also notes the pernicious effects of more overtly romanticised stereotypes of Gypsy lifestyle. The stereotyping of Gypsies, be that in a very hostile manner or in a highly exotic or romanticised fashion, works to demarcate the boundary between Gypsy and non-Gypsy society. Whilst it remains apparent that hostile representations feed into a cycle of racial stereotyping and discrimination, there does not appear to be a positive impact generated by exotic or romantic representations. Mayall notes that:

> The processes of categorisation, labelling and representation are at the very heart of majority-minority relations, both shaping and being shaped by popular responses as well as official or state attitudes and policies. (Mayall 2004, 18)

It appears that stereotypical assumptions about and stereotypical representations of Gypsies simply outweigh any available evidence of their actual lifestyles.

Inventing Gypsies

Much of the wider understanding of Gypsy culture and identity in the UK is informed by a hostile society that lacks real knowledge of the culture. Often this is reflected within media portrayals of Gypsy life, which seem inevitably to focus on issues of conflict with wider society. The most overt evidence of this hostility is to be found in research work that has looked at Gypsy experiences and details a wide range of racist prejudice. One response to the very negative media portrayals and hostility faced by Gypsy communities has been the noticeably campaigning stance adopted by many researchers working to document prejudice towards Gypsies. This materialises within the tone of much of their published work and in their engagements with policy-makers at national and local level. There also tends to be strong and established links between researchers and professionals working with Gypsy communities in the fields of housing, healthcare and education. One benefit of such associations is to focus some clearly motivated voices, beyond the communities themselves, who are well-placed to challenge many of the prejudices held about Gypsies.

Since the 1960s there has been a small but growing interest in the world of Gypsies, both inside and outside academia. Some of this interest has arisen from the perspective of Gypsy politics and is driven by Gypsy pressure groups that emerged in the 1960s; these have become progressively more successful in influencing government policies. Some has also been driven by the increasing concerns of government departments; for example, the education of Gypsy children featured prominently in the Plowden Report (1967). These successes are also linked to the growing agendas of multiculturalism within society generally and within institutions such as schools more particularly. There has been a significant growth of interest in minority ethnic groups, particularly concerning their interaction with the indigenous population and the inequalities they often face. The identification of Gypsies as such a minority has led to a greater understanding of the racism and discrimination they face in society, and the need to further such understandings.

Mayall (2004) has noted the increasing body of academics and researchers producing work that seeks to raise awareness about Gypsy culture within academic thought. He also makes clear that much of this work remains undervalued beyond those with a specialist interest in the subject matter. Our own research has shown how the relationship of such academics to this area of study can be fraught with difficulties. Unsurprisingly, this partly reflects difficulties generated by the hostility historically faced by Gypsy groups and their responses to outsiders as a result of such hostility. It can often be difficult to establish and build trusting relationships with Gypsy groups in order to take forward any research. In addition, it can feel at times as though something of the wider hostilities felt about Gypsies also surfaces in the academic world. This can often be hard to pin down with accuracy but it is possibly felt in the lack of funding available to carry out research in the area and in the marginal acceptance of some findings within mainstream academic contexts. More surprising, perhaps, is the impact such hostility has had amongst those working within the field itself, that is academics and professionals working with Gypsies. This seems to materialise in ways that almost amount to the building of additional barriers between Gypsies and those outside their worlds. One area to be examined at greater length in Chapter 2 is the extent to which academics studying Gypsy lives attempt to claim ownership of the group being studied, as opposed to being simply protective of them; the impact this has on how representations are made of Gypsy culture is also discussed there.

Acton has argued that there must be an end to the 'marginalisation of Romani Studies in the world of knowledge' (Acton 1997, 24), and in some respects this does appear to be happening. The last twenty years have seen a noticeable increase in the diversity of work on Gypsies being generated within a wide range of academic disciplines (sociology, anthropology, education and health studies all spring readily to mind, but there is also interesting work going on in geography, international relations, economics and art departments). It should also be noted that, as this area of study has become a more acceptable topic for discussion and debate, growing numbers of academics have identified themselves as Gypsies.

Whilst such enthusiasm should not be stifled, it is worth noting Barany's (2002) criticism of the poor scholarship associated with some work in this field, which he characterises as the 'poverty' of Gypsy studies. There is a suspicion that by becoming too close, too sympathetic or too determined to fight the cause of their subjects, some researchers find the objectivity of their work and their findings sorely tested. Chapter 2 examines the relationships between Gypsy communities, academics and other professional organisations that provide the conditions under which potential researchers have to negotiate their initial access to communities. These relationships are, of course, also the conditions within which accounts of Gypsy culture are then produced. The 'objective' knowledge produced under these circumstances is in many ways the only viable retort to the ever-present voices maligning Gypsy culture, and it is this knowledge that, most often, will be used to inform policy-makers when they shape their responses to the needs of Gypsy communities. In particular, this chapter will ask questions about how academics shape their accounts of Gypsy identity and to what extent their accounts are bounded by their personal relationships with the subject. It will draw on the authors' experiences of conducting research work with Gypsy groups in the UK and with our various engagements with academic processes and institutions. In this respect we are, of course, as situated amongst the topics we wish to discuss as are other researchers working in this field. Like other researchers too, we are almost certainly driven to draw out positive rather than negative messages from our work, and this chapter will examine that process. The other important element to this account of the production of knowledge is an examination of the structures that govern such work, including the relationships between established and unestablished researchers working in the field; between established researchers and professionals working closely with Gypsy groups (the latter may themselves be sources or, more likely, potential gatekeepers); and, finally, between researchers and Gypsies themselves. Again, the aim in examining this area is to establish what barriers and constraints operate within these relationships to influence the construction of knowledge of Gypsy identity.

In Chapter 3 we turn to a wider examination of the representation of Gypsies in the UK over the last fifty years.

Gypsies and their identities

Developing the theme of deliberate misrepresentation examined previously within academic accounts, this chapter highlights how such distorted accounts are not a unique set of circumstances. In fact, the misrepresentation of Gypsies by the state and the media has been a consistent factor in the lives of Gypsies, and this has an important impact on the construction of Gypsy identity. Gypsies tend either to be represented as an exciting or exotic 'other' or, alternatively, as dirty vagrants. Neither of these accounts is particularly accurate, but such representations have been used to disadvantage Gypsy communities historically. There are many occasions where the state can be seen to have refused communities certain rights or privileges because they do not conform to an inaccurate stereotype. This chapter will compare such historic misrepresentation with the more recent work of academics and consider the ways in which these often very different accounts are related.

Building on the discussion of Gypsy identity and the processes by which it is constructed, Chapter 4 will place the materialisations of identity within a theoretical framework. Taking as its starting point the particular attributes of Gypsy culture that mark it out from dominant cultures, this chapter will place the Gypsy experience within the context of debates about whiteness, racism and the 'other'. Comparisons will be drawn with the experiences of 'white trash' in America, and the matter of how such a labelling of one part of society relates to the demarcation of space and boundaries more widely will be addressed. Such boundary drawing around groups seen as at or near the bottom of registers of class and respectability has clear parallels with Mayall's (2004) description of Gypsies' socio-historic plight as victims of prejudice. The other side of this debate – the construction of Gypsies as an ethnic group – is more overtly developed through an examination of Bauman's (1991) work around the *'stranger'* who is recognised for his difference. Bringing these two lines of thought together will demonstrate the manner in which Gypsies are recognised as a different culture to the norm while at the same time they are demarcated as occupying a demeaning zone or space. They both fall beyond society's boundaries and also exude a hugely unsettling presence within society.

The following two chapters will be devoted to case studies that translate the theoretical thinking about Gypsy identity into real-life examples. These will examine not only the processes that are at work in producing identity but also the effects such processes have on everyday life. The first case study will examine an aspect of everyday social life, the school. Based on the authors' experiences from a longstanding piece of ethnographic research in schools in a large metropolitan borough, it examines Gypsy families' experiences of education, as well as the difficulties faced by a school which offers a multicultural approach to education that is sympathetic to the needs of its largish Gypsy community. It will describe problems encountered around claims of favouritism towards Gypsy children, the impossibility of keeping the racism outside the school gates from entering the classroom, and the clash of cultures in terms of the expectations of both Gypsy families and teaching staff. Even within the multicultural school, it is suggested, elements of misrecognition of Gypsy culture persist and the sense of being an 'other' remains and, if anything, is made more concrete by the multicultural approach.

The second case study looks at the political climate as expressed through the media, and examines a brief period during the 2005 General Election campaign when Gypsy rights and planning legislation were challenged by the Conservative party, who placed advertisements in the national press suggesting that Gypsies were receiving favourable treatment. These advertisements appeared in the context of a hostile campaign being run in the pages of *The Sun*. This chapter will examine two representations of Gypsies made on a single day by *The Sun* and

The Independent newspapers. Whilst *The Sun* remained hostile, *The Independent* portrayed a very positive image of a 'good' Gypsy. This chapter will argue that both representations were acutely flawed and represented little more than the editorial line of both papers. As a result, both newspapers reproduced misrepresentations of Gypsy culture and perpetuated the historical inaccuracies outlined in the earlier chapters. In both case studies the notion of boundary lines being drawn will be examined with a view to identifying how both Gypsy and non-Gypsy constituencies define their space.

The final two chapters will consider, firstly, the position of the outsider in multicultural society and, secondly, the position of the outsider in racist society, in doing so picking up on the running theme of how misrepresentation and misrecognition of Gypsies by both their detractors and their allies play out within different contexts. Chapter 7 argues that Gypsies remain 'outsiders' within multicultural contexts despite and because of multi-cultural society. In some part, this is a consequence of the roles that outsiders and, more specifically, recognisable strangers have within society, one of which is the demarcation of the boundaries between acceptance and non-acceptance. It is also a consequence of the Gypsy relationship to a multiculturalism that is a product of non-Gypsy culture's attempts to be more liberal in ways that non-Gypsy culture understands. Within multiculturalism there is an expectation that other outsiders (immigrants, refugees or asylum seekers) will become more accepted over periods of time as recognition becomes familiarity for some groups. This chapter will examine why this does not happen for Gypsy groups. It will also suggest that where there is familiarity and identification between Gypsy communities and other parts of society, it is parts of white society that are themselves close to the boundary lines that would isolate them from acceptable society. This can be interpreted to some degree as the historic engagement of Gypsy groups in the UK. Finally, in Chapter 8, the book concludes with an examination of the role of Gypsy representations within parts of society that do not subscribe to a multicultural vision. This chapter will again draw on strands of thinking from earlier chapters to provide an analysis of the particular role Gypsy representations have within society. It will consider the impact of 'whiteness' and the linking of Gypsy culture with dirt, and suggest that this is another response to the overt recognition of Gypsy culture as 'strange' and 'other'. Despite different processes of recognition within multicultural and racist society, the end results of such processes often appear quite similar; the book concludes by discussing why this should be the case.

Notes

1. *Gaujo* is the Romani word for a non-Gypsy.
2. *Gammon* is the name used by Irish Travellers for a secret language that possibly dates back over 2,000 years. It is also known as *Cant* or *Shelta*.

2. Gypsy identity and culture: foundational accounts and the Academy

As outlined in Chapter 1, there has been a historic rupture within Gypsy academic circles over the construction of Gypsy identity. On the one hand it is argued that Gypsy culture is the sole preserve of a self-contained and fixed group of peoples who came to Europe from Asia around 1,000 years ago. On the other it is suggested that Gypsy communities have been constructed in a much more flexible fashion, often encompassing indigenous groups. This chapter will argue that a critical understanding of both accounts is necessary in order to reach a better understanding of Gypsy identity and that in many respects both accounts contain much that is accurate. It will further argue that academic accounts are often charged with meanings that are shaped by academics' own attempts at stating their 'ownership' of the culture. Often this 'ownership' is created through a process of identification with the Gypsy communities studied by academics. Although academics are arguably better placed to produce understandings of Gypsy culture, there is a suspicion that the kind of misrecognition about the culture that is prevalent throughout wider and less well-informed parts of society also features within academic work. Just as accounts in the tabloid press often appear to be deliberately skewed towards painting a stereotypical picture of Gypsies that undermines their acceptability within wider society, something similar, though driven by a more sympathetic approach, materialises in some academic work. In academic accounts there is often an inherent desire not to undermine the already difficult social position of Gypsies amongst wider society. Some aspects of Gypsy culture that may not sit happily within the established norms of liberal society are suppressed in such accounts. Within the wider context of multicultural society, therefore, the engagement of Gypsy and dominant culture can be seen as a failure both in terms of liberal approaches such as multiculturalism and the politics of recognition. Gypsy culture remains on the outside of mainstream culture and needs to be understood within contexts that take account of its 'otherness'. An honest engagement with the culture is likely to open up not just a more honest and open dialogue between different communities but also a dialogue in which some uncomfortable things can be spoken about.

Gypsy culture in the UK

Gypsies first arrived in Britain around 1500. At that time they were involved in trade, metalwork and entertainment. In the mid-sixteenth century Henry VIII made it a capital offence to be a Gypsy and by the mid-seventeenth century Gypsies were being transported as slaves to Caribbean and American plantations (Acton 1997; Hancock 2000; Kenrick and Puxon 1972). In part this persecution reflected common prejudices and practices towards foreigners and vagrants at the time. Many early Gypsies in Britain claimed to be Egyptians (hence the derivation of the word Gypsy) and travelled in nomadic groups similar to other groups of wandering vagrants. The Egyptian claim was seemingly concocted to substantiate Gypsies' exotic credentials and abilities as fortune-tellers; however, these practices resulted in conflict with the church. Folk-tales describing a Gypsy smith making the nails for Christ's crucifixion and as a result damning them as a race have persisted for the last five hundred years. The Gypsy version suggests a Gypsy discovered what the nails were to be used for and swallowed one, hence Christ was only crucified with three nails and Gypsies have been pursued for the missing nail ever since. Within these brief examples can be seen patterns that emerge throughout later accounts of Gypsies and persist within contemporary representations of Gypsies and their culture. There is the association with vagrancy and connotations of idleness and dirtiness; a perception of an exotic and exciting 'other'; and an association with evil often tied to the folklore of the dominant religion. As a group they fall outside the dominant culture and are misrepresented and persecuted by that culture.

In Britain today there are, loosely speaking, four groups of Gypsies: Romanichals (English Gypsies), Nawkens (Scottish Gypsies or Travellers), Kale (Welsh Gypsies) and Minceir (Irish Travellers or Pavees). Of these, roughly half maintain nomadic or semi-nomadic lifestyles; the remainder are settled often on caravan sites and increasingly many are also housed (Acton 1974; 1997; Okely 1983). Whilst many Gypsies retain links to rural economies – for example, seasonal crop picking and trading at horse fairs – few rely on the rural economy for their main income. Many Gypsies are settled in urban or semi-urban settings, generally campsites provided by local authorities. Gypsy identity is closely tied to self-employment as opposed to wage labouring and urban economies, which have in recent years provided greater opportunities for generating income. Okely (1983) argues that contemporary Gypsy culture is inextricably linked to the dominant culture because of the need to trade and generate income. She also rightly notes that historically Gypsy culture has been dependent on an engagement with non-Gypsy culture in order to survive. It could be argued, therefore, that the idea of a Gypsy 'nation', one that was not bounded by national borders, could still be understood in economic terms that are not greatly different to those of other 'nations'. In this respect Gypsy nomadism differs significantly from standard types of nomadism, as hunter-gatherers or pastoralists living isolated and self-sufficient lives. Discussing the international heritage of Gypsies, Acton (1987) also suggests that nomadism associated with Gypsies is a relatively recent, twentieth-century phenomenon.

Attempts to identify a racially pure group of Gypsies existing in self-contained rural isolation have been perpetuated either to satisfy *gaujo* yearnings for authenticity or used by the state to brand the actual Gypsies they encounter as neither 'pure' nor 'authentic' but rather 'dirty' and 'half-caste'. This supposed impurity, linked to a perception of dirtiness, is then used as grounds to persecute these Gypsies or fail to honour wider state policy for the provision of sites or education (Okely 1983). As stated above, a twofold misrecognition of Gypsies as 'dirty' or 'exotic' persists in many contemporary accounts (Holloway 2003; Okely 1983). However, the perceived 'dirtiness' of Gypsy culture generally disguises a system of taboos around cleanliness adopted by Gypsy culture and the exoticisation tends to ignore the routine involvement of Gypsies within the wider economy.

There are a number of specific fields of cultural practice that identify themselves as specific to Gypsy culture. These include behaviour and attendance at social functions and events as well as more general norms of behaviour amongst other community members and in relationships and dealings with outsiders. Weddings, in particular, are occasions when extended family groups gather together and shared understandings of culture are strengthened and reaffirmed. The celebration is an event, often lasting several days, in which links and alliances between families and their extended networks can be forged or restated. It is also an occasion when long-standing rivalries may resurface and be resolved through fighting. Okely (1983) notes how often families not directly associated with the wedding may regard it as prudent to withdraw from the vicinity until after the celebrations are complete so as not to become entangled with any fighting that may turn upon them as outsiders. Clark and Greenfields draw interesting parallels between Gypsy and non-Gypsy weddings, making a comparison between:

> Travellers [who] bring their homes when they come together for community celebrations, instead of moving into a hotel with some suitcases for a few days, which would be the equivalent for a house-dweller attending a similar event. (Clark and Greenfields 2006, 34)

This highlights the lack of comprehension surrounding Gypsy weddings and other similar events that sometimes makes them occasions when there can be conflict with the state and wider society. Enforcing regulations that restrict the numbers of trailers permitted on a site, local authorities sometimes use forceful measures to stop all families' trailers from entering the site for the duration of a wedding. Media reporting of such occasions inevitably focuses on conflicts of this sort and as a result portrays the Gypsy families as disruptive elements. The gathering of families for social events is often regarded as a manifestation of the threat of Gypsy culture towards society at large. The appearance of trailers from distant parts of the country is regarded not as a demonstration of strong family ties and celebration, but rather as a cause of great apprehension amongst the local non-Gypsy community that the families might remain. Almost inevitably this fear fails to reflect the actual motivations and commitments of the various participants.

Weddings are one of the occasions at which the importance of family and community within Gypsy culture is most clearly stated. This is reflected not only in the physical presence of the extended family, who may have travelled long distances to attend the celebration, but also in the choice of spouse. There are strong pressures to marry within the community rather than outside it. Such pressures are not binding, but are understood within the same sort of contexts that are common to many minority groups. Marriage outside the ethnic community carries with it a degree of uncertainty for a number of different reasons. These include concerns around how well different families may get along with each other and how effectively cultural values and practices will be passed on to children. For this reason marriage between families who are acquainted with each other over long periods of time is often favoured, principally because such unions ensure that there are understood and shared cultural norms. A degree of trust in the reputations attached to different families is important in predicting good future relations between families linked by any marriage. Reputation within the community is a very important factor in determining social relationships and standing amongst different families. This includes the reputation of individuals and the reputation of the family, both of which have a direct effect upon each other. Kinship obligations are therefore taken very seriously and are important markers of reputation and cultural capital within the wider community. The physical gathering of family members at weddings is important not least because it provides an environment in which reputations and knowledge can be discussed and tested.

Marriage between different ethnic groups of Gypsies or to a non-Gypsy, although not the norm, does increasingly occur, although such marriages may be regarded with disapproval for a number of reasons. As discussed, the building of stable relationships between families is an important factor and any move away from families who are already closely linked and well known suggests the introduction of an element of the unknown that may threaten future stability.

In our research it has been noticeable that *gaujo* wives of Gypsy husbands will make very clear their own status as non-Gypsies whilst at the same time also clearly defining the overwhelming degree to which their lifestyle falls within the cultural practices and values of the Gypsy community. As with reputation, there are some clearly demarcated understandings of how much of a Gypsy some family members were and how much of a *gaujo*. One mother made a clear distinction that her eldest two children from a previous marriage to a non-Gypsy were *gaujo* whilst her youngest child, whose father was a Gypsy, was described as being a Gypsy. The *gaujo* mother herself was openly very proud of the cultural aspects and heritage of her family's current life.

The distinctions drawn between a *gaujo* and a Gypsy way of life, like an individual or family's reputation, are important markers not just of cultural identity that is understood by family members but also of status within the wider community. Aspects of behaviour that might be regarded as indicative of a *gaujo* mentality are actively disapproved of (for example, placing elderly relatives into care rather than looking after them within the family). This places obligations upon the wider family network, who would be expected to participate in childcare arrangements or to look out for elderly relatives if direct family members had to go travelling. Failure to live up to such cultural values reflects badly both on individuals and the wider family.

Gender roles in the Gypsy community are divided along very traditional lines, with men working and taking responsibility for providing for the family whilst women are responsible for looking after the home and the children. Many personal matters, such as pregnancy, are considered the sole preserve of women. Whilst in general women stay at home in the role of homemaker there have been some shifts in cultural expectations which may continue to develop, largely depending upon the impact of changing economic conditions. Many younger women, for example, are encouraged by their families to acquire enough qualifications in order to be able to gain shop work. Vocational training to work as hairdressers or florists is also popular. Men continue to want to work within their own businesses and to teach their sons to follow in their footsteps. The division of gender roles also materialises at social functions; so, for example, at a wedding 'men and women will always split into their separate gender groups' (Clark and Greenfields 2006, 41).

When a family member dies the family will leave the place of death and often go travelling for a period of mourning. Generally possessions of the dead person are not retained by the family but more likely destroyed. If it is not also destroyed, the deceased's trailer will usually be sold, as will land belonging to the deceased. Other Gypsies would not wish to live in a trailer or on land associated directly with death. Funerals, like weddings, are times when extended families and friends gather, in this case to pay their respects to the deceased. Unlike weddings, however, there is a greater latitude about who is welcome at such occasions and it is generally felt that anyone who wishes to pay their last respects should be allowed to do so, even sworn enemies; it is a time when peace can be finally made and disagreements put to rest.

Staking claims of ownership: the Academy

> You clever academics befriend us for a few months, they come down to our site, eats our food and drinks our tea. Some of them even lives among us. Then they disappear to their nice homes and university libraries. Next thing we know, they're giving lectures on us, writing books about us ... what do they know about our struggles? How can they know our pain? We live it all the time. Our persecution lasts a lifetime not just a few months. Give us the tools to say it right and we'll tell it like it is. You know what we call them on our sites? 'Plastic Gypsies'. (Quoted in Scraton 1976, 76)

Foundational accounts and the Academy

These words were spoken by Roy Wells, the president of the National Gypsy Council, in 1975. Speaking at the launch of an academic report on the deterioration in relations between housedwellers and Travellers, he explained in part why he refused to be the 'token Gypsy' for academics and policy-makers. In many respects the quotation above is an uncomfortable statement for researchers; it raises some difficult questions about what research generally, and research into Gypsy life in particular, should look like. It opens up a debate about whose meanings and understandings are actually being generated within the research process – those of the researcher or the researched – and what implications that should have upon who conducts the research in the first place. It makes us question the researcher's role and, as researchers, makes us question *why we do research*. As a critique of ethnographic practice it makes for interesting, although slightly unsettling, reading. Poor ethnographic practice typified by the dubious credentials of researchers who describe how they *lived amongst the community* for short periods of time are called into question. One cannot help but wonder if the alleged cleverness of the academics in question is, for Wells at least, evidenced less by the fruits of their intellectual labours and more by their abilities to engage for a short period of time with their subject, take the food and drink on offer and then vanish back to a comfortable life. And if the idea of being 'on the take' at the same time as being engaged in poor practice wasn't bad enough, Wells offers a final, quite devastating broadside describing potential researchers as 'Plastic Gypsies'. It is almost as though the researcher has been playing a part, pretending for the duration of the fieldwork that he or she is actually a Gypsy, only to be inevitably found out and revealed as inauthentic. Wells's words raise two important issues that need to be examined here: firstly, does he touch on something specific about those academics whose careers are founded on work that looks at Gypsy lives? Do they identify so closely with their subject that they almost wish to become a part of the communities that they are studying? Is three months living in a van on a site really an attempt at living the life? And, secondly, why does Wells identify this level of identification as being such an insurmountable problem, particularly bearing in mind the historical evidence suggesting there has been movement between Gypsy and non-Gypsy communities? Wells himself would surely be acquainted with individuals who had inter-married? Is a degree of identification with subjects a seriously problematic approach? Does Wells subscribe to a closed-community argument or are his words a recognition of the type of people involved in academic study and the type of people outside Gypsy groups who can become engaged in the movements across boundary lines?

It could be argued that all sociological research involves a relationship between an outsider (the researcher) and insiders (the subjects of the research). However, even where there is a great deal of shared cultural capital between both parties, the research process still entails a distancing of the person describing themselves as a researcher. Often what is being described as 'the research process' is something that is quite ordinary and represents patterns of behaviour that are not exclusive to academics. It is, after all, an activity that derives much of its validity from skills such as observation and engaging people in conversation, all of which are necessities of everyday life. One point that distinguishes the research activity is the acknowledgement of what you are doing; so if, as a Millwall Football Club fan, for example, I observe and engage with other fans and non-fans on match day, this is not necessarily behaviour that distinguishes me from everyone else at the game. However, if I metaphorically take a step back and acknowledge that I am observing from a different position, one where I have distanced myself from the people around me, this begins to suggest that I am creating a new role as a researcher. This distancing is done entirely within the realms of an interior voice: it is a personal acknowledgement of the creation of distance and it is a useful means of making more calculated judgements of the world. In circumstances such as the development of an account of Millwall Football Club by a Millwall fan, an academic audience would require an acknowledgement and an outline of both the membership of the subject group and the processes used to distance the research, as well as evidence of an awareness of those locations where an ambiguous relationship between researcher and subject matter might still exist. However, this is still a perfectly reasonable standpoint from which to develop a valid account of Millwall Football Club. Similarly, research on Gypsy communities conducted by a Gypsy does not present particular problems; if anything, it is an area that would potentially benefit from researchers with a depth of knowledge about the communities being studied.

More often, however, academic researchers find themselves researching subjects from which they are more concretely distanced. The sociologist who is a Millwall fan may well want to produce work that examines the lives of his or her fellow fans, but the realities of academic funding mean they are likely to be engaged in unrelated work. Again, there is nothing too problematic in principle in these circumstances; such disjunctures between subject and researcher are evident in many projects and reflect a basic human motivation to be interested in people other than ourselves. A degree of self-awareness is still obviously required and the need to question what baggage the researcher brings to the research is always a helpful part of the research process. Roy Wells seems to suggest a relationship between researchers and subjects (admittedly in the mid-1970s) that is perhaps less positive than this ideal; and, rather more significantly, he also suggests a breakdown in these readily understandable relationships. According to Wells such research is driven by a researcher role that is essentially a sham, based on a passing or temporary identification between researchers and Gypsy communities. He clearly believes better work could be generated only by the deeper understanding of someone wholly identified with the community.

The anthropologist Judith Okely (1992) argues that knowledge acquired (in this case through photographic evidence) during the fieldwork can be a bodily experience, by which she meant that she had noted that, in a photograph, she had adopted the same bodily posture as the Gypsy woman (one of her respondents) next to whom she was standing. While adopting her posture, Okely had also replicated her 'stance' towards life – her attitudes. 'Positioning' is a term used by researchers and scholars to recognise and make apparent the types of relationship they develop with respondents; quite often it is a means of acknowledging power relations between different parties and the impact these might have on their findings. The question of posture that Okely uncovers relates closely to the relationship of power between researcher and respondents. Okely argues that her body expressed a certain kind of (anti-) power relationship between the subject and the object (Okely 1992, 17). Rather than imposing her own substantial claim to power, derived from her professional standing within an academic institution, it appears she privileges, and to some extent shoulders, her respondent's world view. In this case the power relations are seemingly expressed unconsciously, thus appearing to work in a highly empathic fashion; the suggestion of mimicry seems to indicate a particularly sympathetic identification with the subject.

If, as Wells's account would suggest, the engagement of the academic researcher with Gypsy life is a difficult and quite possibly flawed relationship, it is worth bearing in mind the significance such engagements may have. From the foundational accounts of the Gypsy diaspora to studies funded by government departments aimed at influencing policy on all aspects of Gypsy life, including education, health and housing issues, the Academy is involved. Its engagement with Gypsy culture has inevitable political, cultural and economic impacts on the lives of Gypsies and those they live amongst. At the most basic level, the work of academic researchers funded by local and central government will shape policies that affect the everyday lives of Gypsies. Policy reports on subjects as diverse as health provision, 'community cohesion' or changes to planning law will all, almost inevitably, contain references to academic work intended to demonstrate the thoroughness and validity of such documents. There is nothing overtly suspicious about this process; it reflects longstanding and very visible working practices amongst politicians, civil servants and academics, and is a process that is present in all aspects of policy-making, be they high or low profile, controversial or not. It should also be clearly noted that the academic input might not be the determining factor in final policies; ministers and their civil servants all have their own agendas. These agendas might well be fed into the research process at an early stage; the cynical amongst us might suspect that government only ever wants validation of its own position, whilst those with a less pessimistic frame of mind might not consider it contentious that government policy be driven by an essentially democratic process in which the political voice of the minister should be heard by the researcher as well as *vice versa*. For the academic, an awareness of these relationships and the likely impact of any work on policy and on the lives of the people he or she has studied will (or maybe should) colour the research process.

Caught between being Wells's 'Plastic Gypsy' and a contributory voice to policy-making processes, the researcher is entwined within a very complex set of worlds and understandings. He or she might well want to subscribe to Denzin's

(2001) 'seventh moment' in ethnography, in which politicised ethnographers overtly recognise and position themselves as having taken a side. Such work, inevitably, is about more than just the research subject; it is 'that form of inquiry and writing that produces descriptions and accounts about the ways of life of the writer and those written about' (Denzin 1997, xi). Taking such an approach and engaging in the different networks of people that surround work on Gypsies may well produce some interesting and very honest accounts of the work, but it may also disappoint the researcher, who may be neither as engaged with his or her subjects as hoped for, nor as effective a champion of their cause as might otherwise be possible. Instead, he or she may be contributing work that is almost as inescapably locked into the worlds of interested parties as it is into the experiences of subjects' everyday lives.

In our work we have discussed how the conduct of research projects with Gypsy communities and the processes of working with colleagues in the Academy and professionals working closely with Gypsy communities suggests that representations made within a scholarly field are often compromised (Bhopal and Myers 2005). There is a need for the researcher to negotiate not just with the Gypsy communities to whom one might hope to speak but also with a close-knit group of professionals and academics who, to some degree, operate a level of control over access in their role as gatekeepers. Research nearly always has to be negotiated within this network and amongst the biases exhibited by its members; these can include antagonism towards new researchers, particularly researchers who are not already known within the network and who have not demonstrated their commitment towards a pro-Gypsy body of work. When one of the authors (KB) first started work on a project funded by the Department for Education and the Environment (DfEE) examining Gypsy experiences of the education system, a startling level of hostility was expressed towards someone who, at that stage in her career, was considered an outsider within the world of academics and professionals working around Gypsy issues (see Bhopal 2005). It was apparent that her status as a newcomer to the field aroused a great deal of suspicion amongst established academics, who made it very clear that any work with Gypsies was rightfully theirs. In quite stark language and in a public forum (a conference attended by academics, education professionals and government officials) it was suggested that, because this unknown researcher did not have an established pedigree, she was regarded as suspicious and was considered to be possibly working against the interests of Gypsies. In other words, there is a clear positioning by the Academy: academics working on Gypsy issues are over-whelmingly sympathetic to the Gypsy cause and it appears that any approach other than a fastidious alignment to promoting the interests of academics' subject matter is considered at once alien and threatening to the *status quo*. Whilst this approach does (bearing in mind the appalling historic treatment of Gypsies) commend itself for its passionately liberal engagement with a genuine cause of social justice, at the same time it leaves itself open to criticism by its suggestion that any independent, objective approach to producing understandings of Gypsy culture is not acceptable. One effect of this is that new interpretations of Gypsy culture, engagements by the culture in new circumstances, or new approaches by the culture towards society are liable to be overlooked or ignored. The need to be positioned and accountable for that positioning has been successfully argued since the publication of *Writing Culture* (Clifford and Marcus 1986). However, Denzin (1997) argues that all attempts to create new paradigms within which ethnographic texts can be cons-tructed have become outdated and are bound to fail in rep-resenting truthful accounts of the subjects studied. Ethnography has become 'messy', and there is a real need to produce a process of validation that informs the reader. Denzin suggests replacing validity with *values* and *politics*: 'Such criteria would flow from the qualitative project, stressing subjectivity, emotionality, feeling, and other antifoundational criteria' (Denzin 1997, 9). Such an approach would undoubtedly suit much of the work produced in relation to Gypsy culture; however, its use is never overtly stated in this context.

Other economies: research, hard cash and the Academy
Whilst the outright hostility generated towards some researchers without a proven pedigree of sympathetic interest and involvement in Gypsy research is clearly an excessive and unprofessional response, there are also some good reasons why those working around Gypsy issues do feel the need to maintain a certain wariness. In particular the persistence with which stereotypical representations of Gypsy lives and culture appear within academic contexts gives cause for concern. In 2005 both authors were approached to become involved in a research project concerned primarily with healthcare issues and Gypsies. What rapidly became apparent was just how opportunistic this project was. A partnership of interested parties had gathered behind the closed doors of a well-established red brick university to discuss 'strategy'; an important topic was the dilemma of a local healthcare provider, which had long identified a problematical set of relationships between itself and Gypsy families and had, as a result, set aside a sum of money to 'do something' about it. This money was sitting in the limbo of the account books and little interest or imagination was being expressed from within as to how it might be used. Its existence had, by chance, come to the attention of two academics at the university in question whilst they were engaged in another project. During the strategy meeting it became apparent that the academic institution concerned had no knowledge and perhaps little interest in the

Gypsy side of things; they did, however, have a good track record of attracting funding. At one point the conversation turned to the use of the word 'pikey':

> Academic: So you know all about this 'pikey' stuff then?
> MM: Yeah, a bit. You shouldn't use 'pikey' though. It's a term of abuse, like name-calling.
> Academic: But travellers call themselves pikeys?
> MM: No, no. It's a very offensive term.

The discussion of Gypsy issues that followed was brief, ill-informed and based upon a number of quite specific and dubious assumptions about why research might be difficult: Gypsies would typically be problematic patients who would be abusive to staff and other patients; their extended families would be likely to take up residence in hospital car parks, in the process creating large amounts of rubbish; these family members would be involved in criminal activity and irresponsible behaviour; any attempt at engaging with such Gypsies for the research process would therefore involve engaging with a difficult cohort of subjects who would be largely hostile to the work. Such difficulties were considered surmountable but an awareness of them needed to be built into the project. These assumptions were in part those fed through from the healthcare provider in question (which, in truth, appeared to have realised that its assumptions were part of the problematical relationship it had identified) and in part reflected more widely held views about Gypsies. What seemed at odds with the academic process was the lack of interest in challenging such stereotypes. If the research subjects had been gay parents or Somali families it seems likely that the stereotypes would have been challenged. Similarly, there would have been more well-established understandings of the bigoted terminology that might be associated with such groups, and the level of offence that its use can generate. The meeting only became animated when a discussion of possibilities for matched funding cropped up on the agenda.

Such a discussion may be unusual within academia, but it seems unlikely that it is the only case of such opportunism. It is interesting to consider the main drivers behind the creation of these circumstances, however: firstly, the healthcare provider, who, taking baby steps towards its responsibilities under the CRE General Duty (Commission for Racial Equality 2000), had managed to identify a problem but was being less than pro-active about taking it forward; secondly, researchers who carry the status and reputation of their institution and are pro-active and expert in securing funding, but who are also willing to engage in a set of stereotypes about Gypsies that abound in wider society. This situation seems to speak of the difference in how Gypsies as an ethnic minority are generally viewed. It is also the sort of engagement between academics and Gypsies and those working with Gypsies that could lead to hostility and suspicion on the part of the latter group when faced with a request to meet with another researcher in the future. We both declined to take any further part in this particular project, as did a number of other agencies who were approached as potential partners.

Staking claims of ownership: gatekeepers and experts

Throughout our research projects, gatekeepers have been used to obtain access to communities. The Gypsy community can be a close-knit community, and has its own social norms of conduct and behaviour. Outsiders who do not identify with the group are often regarded with suspicion. It would be extremely difficult, therefore, simply to walk onto a site and ask to conduct interviews with parents and children about their educational experiences; smartly dressed researchers with pens, notebooks and tape-recorders may well be assumed to be from social or educational welfare services. As a result of these factors, access is typically negotiated via the development of close links with the Traveller Education Service (TES). The TES has regular contact with families and is trusted; it is known to assist families in many ways, from filling out forms to attending meetings with them. If the TES was comfortable with a research project it would agree to provide access; it acts as a 'gatekeeper', allowing access and entrance into the community or, alternatively, blocking access. Whichever decision is made has an impact on the community, who may or may not meet with the researcher, and on the researcher, who may or may not meet his or her intended respondents. The gatekeeper is not only endowed with 'expertise' about the community, therefore: he or she is also in a powerful position regarding the exercise of interaction between the Gypsy and non-Gypsy community. Compared with the experiences of many other groups who find themselves the subjects of research, this access, channelled through very specific individuals, is unusual. It could also be an unsettling experience for the researcher, who suddenly has to negotiate not within the community and its sensitivities but within the sensitivities of an 'expert' class which, although it is almost without exception both sympathetic towards the needs of the community and aware of issues affecting it, is still not a member of the community itself. Rather, the gatekeeper is positioned in a symbiotic role – outside, although close to, the community – and is also positioned within a specific set of highly nuanced relationships with other members of institutions that have dealings with the Gypsy community; specifically, TES members have day-to-day dealings with colleagues working in schools, in local government and within the academic community. Their position is at once an all-powerful one (they control access) and yet at the same time it is a weak position; *their* community, the Gypsies, is often regarded as being difficult and undeserving, never a priority issue when the allocation of funding and resources is discussed. Like those academics specialising in Gypsy issues, they have a clearly defined and sympathetic stake in the interests of Gypsy communities. At times this may be expressed as hostility towards the unknown researcher or anyone outside the community or the various classes of experts. In one early encounter with the TES in the DfEE project mentioned previously, the open hostility that was felt towards the author's involvement in the project was made very clear from the start (this hostility was almost certainly initially generated from the conference discussed above). The member of the TES opened the conversation with the question 'Who are you and what do you want?' The baldness of this question slightly undermines its wider context, which was to establish the researcher's background, the experience she had of working with Gypsy communities and the intentions behind her current piece of work. The antagonistic approach is partly understandable; the fears of members of the TES about misrepresentation of Gypsy families and potential future reductions in TES funding were all genuine concerns at the time of the project. However, the direct hostility expressed by the TES member to the researcher was deepened by further comments that seemed to make a deliberate play on issues of Gypsy aggression with regard to Asian ethnicity. The TES member made the following warning about the racist reception that might be awaiting an Asian researcher:

> Kalwant Bhopal (KB): Do you think they'll open up to me and talk to me about their experiences of education and also how they experience racism? Because I think that's going to be one of the fascinating things about the research.
> TES: Well, it depends, but I think because we're taking you and introducing you they should do. They might not at first, but then if you go again they might. Also they can be a bit funny with some people, so I don't know.

KB: What do you mean a bit funny? With me?
TES: Well some of them are a bit racist, I don't know if you know that.
KB: Do you think they might be racist towards me?
TES: I don't know, you'll have to wait and see. They could be very racist.

What seemed implicit in this encounter was the sense of the expert 'protecting' their community, in an admittedly cack-handed fashion, by instigating a conversation apparently designed to scare off an unwelcome intrusion into their private world. At best it might be read as an attempt by the TES member to protect a vulnerable community which does undoubtedly suffer at the hands of outsiders. At worst, it can be read as protective of the world of the TES, itself at times a vulnerable and insecure world, but one whose problems are more accurately paralleled with those of many other worthy but underfunded arms of local government.

Whilst working with both academics and experts in the field, one becomes accustomed to constant references to Gypsies as 'our subjects' and to the subject matter as 'our area'. This sense of ownership leads to statements such as the following (by a member of the TES, about the education of Gypsy children): 'the Gypsy children are our children and we can help them'. This reinforces an attitude within many schools that Gypsy children are the sole responsibility of the TES and so are 'your children and you can sort out their problems'. The school effectively relinquishes responsibility for problems associated with Gypsy children (Bhopal 2004). This shifting of responsibility towards the community and those working with it is reflected widely in other areas, such as health and housing. That some institutions, such as schools or housing associations, should be content with this state of affairs is understandable; it is an effective 'get-out clause' that reduces their workloads. What is less clear is why organisations working closely with Gypsy communities should also be content to go along with such practices.

The relationship between academics who are engaged in work around Gypsy issues and organisations like the TES seems to be one in which both parties validate each other's work. The academics consider the TES as their gatekeepers to their subjects about whom only they can speak positively and reliably. Academics with specialist backgrounds in Gypsy work obviously represent only a tiny handful of all academics working in the UK. Within the wider ranks of academics, however, there are many with specialisms that although not directly concerned with Gypsy issues could have a useful, interesting or enlightening bearing on such work. Many have very specific relevant knowledge that could be harnessed to improve understandings of Gypsy lives; an expertise in planning law or inclusive education, for example. On occasion, something more general might also be relevant: an expertise in migration and diaspora, possibly. We are left, however, with a suspicion that in circumstances where wider crossovers of academic knowledge might be anticipated, the tendency is in fact for a small number of academics who identify themselves as the experts in Gypsy work to close ranks to protect the subject matter for themselves. Just as the professional groups working with Gypsies may be open to question about their motives, so too these academics perhaps need to consider whether they are merely driven by a desire to protect Gypsy communities from opportunistic or misinformed researchers or whether their intention is to preserve their own expert status and their own private world.

In effect, the academic community constructs boundaries of ownership and knowledge over which only certain members can cross in order to join the group. It is this membership that becomes privileged; these academics become the 'select few' who advocate the legitimacy of their academic 'knowledge' and professional discourse. Outside the community they study, they preserve an insider status with professionals in the field.

It could be argued that this sense of ownership, which permeates the ranks of academics and professionals working in the field, is both unhealthy and inappropriate. If the work of newcomers is actively discouraged by those already established within the field, we can surmise that the existing networks of academics and professionals are keeping alive a very specific and unchallenged approach to work around Gypsy communities. This is worrying, not least because it begins to mirror some of the processes by which misrepresentations made about Gypsy culture that appear in other places, such as the tabloid press or amongst policy makers, also often go unchallenged. It is not the case that society does not have high expectations of standards for the media and government; but such standards are limited perhaps by the exigencies of the commercialism of the former, and by politics in the case of the latter. Within academia the expectation is that a critical and questioning approach would be the only acceptable standard. Worse still is the sense that the repetition of such an approach across recent decades has to some degree compromised the work of researchers and stymied original approaches to such work. Any newcomer intending to produce academic work about Gypsy communities who speculates about how his or her work will be conducted in the first place and how it might later be received, may well conclude it is altogether easier to work within the established parameters of existing academic approaches. Also compromised is the ability of Gypsy communities to engage as successfully as could be imagined with parts of liberal society that embrace multi-culturalism and more particularly with the dialogues generated around multiculturalism. If Gypsy culture does not necessarily lend itself to the overarching experience of multiculturalism in society, there is a sense in which within certain institutions or environments such as schools, Gypsy culture should thrive to a greater extent than it actually does. Instead, it appears that any such engagement has been at best partially successful and that both Gypsy and dominant cultures have been the losers in this process. A theme that will be returned to throughout the later chapters of this book is the sense that Gypsy culture remains outside mainstream thinking, including that surrounding the politics of recognition and its related impact on the engagement of minority groups with a multicultural state. There is almost a sense of a missing dimension to the discourses around Gypsy culture, a tangible space in which debate is muted and knowledge frozen, and this seemingly occurs at the intersections between state, Gypsy communities, professionals and academics, and wider public spaces. It is an uncomfortable reality that media stories and political speeches that in the first place pander to stereotyped attitudes about Gypsies, and secondly work to sediment such attitudes are often driven by opportunistic motives (selling newspapers to, or buying votes from, 'middle England', for example). Such motivation might not be pleasing to behold but it is understandable. What seems altogether less clear is the motivation behind other more sympathetic and intellectually-driven voices remaining reticent about the subject.

Some clues to such reticence are discussed in Chapter 5, where there is a more detailed analysis of the experiences of school life encountered by some Gypsy children. In our research overt racism by Gypsy children towards other more recent immigrant groups is clearly noted. This plays out within contexts such as wider white society, in which racist language and behaviours are in many respects commonplace. In some respects it appeared that the verbalisation of racist points of views by Gypsy children reflected an ability to go further than their white peers might openly go, and that their views about non-white immigrants in the locality were in fact more widely held. There were, for instance, greater discrepancies between what non-Gypsy children would say in private and what they would say openly. Teachers in the schools we researched were aware that racism existed amongst children at the school but was, more often than not, expressed beyond their hearing. A set of learned behaviours that reflected an awareness and a need to conform to the demands of a multicultural institution was in place within the general school population, leading to the suppression of racism, which remained unspoken in front of staff members (and academic researchers). The Gypsy children seemed less constrained by these easily understood and enacted rules of behaviour; they were more open in their use of racist language about, for example, black children. This manifested itself during our interviews with the children and also during discussions of the experiences of teaching staff at the schools.

The racism of Gypsy children, which is symptomatic of more widely held views within Gypsy communities, is a topic that is noticeably absent from academic accounts of Gypsy culture as well as from accounts in the media. Our own research has picked up a number of consistent accounts of such racism in different locations, in different contexts and amongst different parts of different Gypsy communities. The views expressed by the Gypsy children in London certainly reflected very similar attitudes to those of their parents. We have also encountered openly racist comments about non-white groups (particularly black families) elsewhere in the country. Often this is discussed in the context of marriage or other associations with a black or non-white person:

> My sisters all live on the site and we're always here for each other. And we know each other well ... we like our kids to marry people we know. It's like if Sarah wanted to marry someone else, like say a black man or something, her dad would go mad and it's just not right. (Gypsy woman)

Apart from racism expressed towards non-Gypsy groups, we have also regularly encountered racist and derogatory language used about different Gypsy groups. In 2007, while interviewing English Romany families, we were consistently given accounts of Irish Travellers as being dirty, unhelpful and potentially violent.

TES members and other professional groups have all openly discussed with us concerns about racism and the impact it might have on our projects. Such discussion generally occurs when the conversation is with both of us, or exclusively with Kalwant (who is obviously an Asian woman), and is less likely to arise when talking exclusively to Martin (who, equally obviously, is a white man). We have both concluded that the different emphasis placed on the likelihood of potential interviewees expressing racist sentiments is generally done out of concern for Kalwant's feelings. The account given above of Kalwant's early contact with a TES member, whilst clearly raising an awareness of perceived racist behaviours, seemed loaded with the personal agenda of the individual concerned. More recently, while conducting an unrelated piece of research looking at Gypsy education in rural environments and medium-sized towns, a member of the TES expressed her relief that, of the two of us, it was the white man who would be conducting most of the interviews. She was concerned that some of the respondents would express openly racist views and that this might affect our response to the research itself. It is important to note that in practice almost all the examples of racism that we have encountered have been directed at other people rather than at ourselves.

As noted, relations between organisations such as the TES and academics working on Gypsy issues are very close, so there can be some assumption that most academics working in this area will have some experiences of the racism expressed by Gypsies, or will have heard accounts of it from those working closely with Gypsy communities. That such racism does not figure prominently in wider academic work seems to speak of a desire to protect Gypsy communities. There is perhaps a well-founded fear that, by openly discussing such issues, anti-Gypsy lobbies will be given further ammunition with which to attack Gypsy communities. One problem with this approach is that it undermines the wider academic work, which needs to consider these unpalatable factors in order to generate better and clearer understandings of Gypsy culture and its engagement with British society. We discuss in Chapter 5, for example, some aspects of multiculturalism and the education of Gypsy children that do not appear to work as well as might be expected. An important part of understanding why this should be the case is a recognition of the impact that expressions of racism by Gypsy children have within the school, particularly as regards the way in which these expressions affect the sympathies of teaching staff towards these children.

If it is understandable that academics might seek to cover up examples of Gypsy racism, it is less apparent why the press should also appear to take so little interest in the subject. In principle, we might anticipate that some newspapers who are overtly unsympathetic towards Gypsies might find it very useful to accuse them of racism (not least because it might leave some of these newspapers' more liberal critics feeling rather uncomfortable). It may be that within those elements of the media that find it useful to attack Gypsy communities and portray their lifestyle in a derogatory manner we also find work that often edges close to other expressions of racism. Much of the racism expressed and the undermining attitudes it reflects represent a shared sense of communal values between newspapers and their readerships. In other words, readers of particular newspapers identify with the standpoints offered by those newspapers and expect such standpoints to be reinforced rather than challenged by the stories they carry. Newspapers which attack Gypsy lifestyles on a regular basis may also attack a variety of other groups identified as alien and undesirable. The identification of these groups changes over time according to shifting cultural values that reflect changes in society's understandings about different groups' standing. Fears of Black and Asian immigration from forty years ago, for example, have given way to newer, although similar, stories; sometimes these identify specific subgroups, such as 'bad', potentially fundamental Muslims, as opposed to 'good' hard-working Indians; or they might identify entire new groups, such as Somalis or asylum seekers. A suspicion remains, however, that locked within the current discourses of hatred towards these newer groups is a more generalised dislike towards all groups of outsiders. Its public voice, the stories printed in daily newspapers, toes the line in order to avoid identification as an overtly racist voice, but at the same time it picks away at the edges, hinting at the underlying discourse which contends that non-British and non-white people are a dangerous, unwanted 'other'. It is in this context that the newspapers have perhaps to be very careful in their portrayal of Gypsy culture; if they were to run stories suggesting that Gypsy communities were racist this would possibly create an uncomfortable situation for the newspaper and its readers. They would be confronted not by Gypsies who were explicitly an 'other' and different from them, but who in fact shared degrees of similarity with them. Even more uncomfortable for the reader, these similarities would be the half-hidden traces of racism; that is, attitudes that are spoken only very carefully and in ways intended not to fully express the magnitude of racist beliefs held.

Compared to their peers, and in particular compared to other white children, Gypsy children's expression of racism is understood differently. It is an understanding that is shaped by the lack of well-understood or accurate accounts of Gypsy culture in the UK. This happens in a very direct sense with Gypsy children in some part responding to sensitivities around the undervaluing of their culture. Perhaps more importantly it happens indirectly at times when an interpretation of such racist behaviour may be anticipated but does not materialise There are a number of explanations why this should happen. For academics and professionals it might seem these children are more sinned against than sinning and that any highlighting of Gypsy children's racism could only make life harder than it already is. The same academics are also aware that there is a highly speculative element involved in predicting the consequences of making overt reference to such racism: it will not be received within the context of an understanding of Gypsy culture but within a non-Gypsy misrepresentation of Gypsy culture that has historically been overwhelmingly hostile to such culture. The point at which an acknowledgement of racist behaviour in Gypsy culture is made is thus fraught with fear of the possible repercussions. For white peers and their families, there may be recognition of the racist sentiments expressed, and even a fundamental identification with beliefs that are normally expected to remain behind closed doors.

It is clearly demonstrable that Gypsy communities are positioned outside wider society and that their culture is misrepresented within society. Under these circumstances accounts and understandings of Gypsy lives, particularly in media stories, will always need to be interpreted closely and carefully in order to pick apart exactly what is and what is not being said. This is one juncture where we should expect academic interest to surface, producing work which enlightens our understandings. If within media accounts of Gypsy culture one of the unspoken topics is the sense of similarities between Gypsy and non-Gypsy people's lives and attitudes, this is worth exploring, even if such similarities seem based upon unpalatable sets of racist beliefs. Elsewhere in this book we examine more positive aspects of Gypsy culture and how they might have an appeal to society at large (and we discuss how there appears to be an inability by society to recognise such potential strengths). In essence, there appears a willingness on the part of many different interested parties to maintain a status quo in which Gypsy culture is never fully revealed.

These are all very difficult paths to navigate, let alone to speak openly about. The best of intentions contest with moral standpoints; mutual recognitions fly in the face of established credos of difference; and the recounting of stories is stymied by knowledge of what is and is not capable of being spoken. These, and other similar junctures, are the grounds on which much of the discussion about Gypsy identity needs to be debated, and it is very obviously unsettling territory that does not easily allow any debate to take place. It is, however, equally obviously a space that is occupied by Gypsies and non-Gypsies in their everyday lives; it is part of a discourse in which all the main participants seem so unsure of themselves and others that there is a near impossibility of moving forward. It is also a discourse that simply entraps its participants within a closed, circular engagement.

It is this unspoken space within public discourse that should necessarily be viewed as an area of challenge for academic understanding. If the Academy is seen to be complicit in not trying to unravel these understandings then this raises questions about the value of its work in the area. Simply working towards the improvement of a community's position in society is commendable but seems to fall short of generating a more encompassing understanding or a greater engagement between different communities. This engagement is something that can perhaps be drawn out from a further analysis of Roy Wells's comments about outsider researchers and the feeling that they are engaged in an inauthentic self-identification with the subject. The opening up of an alternative engagement, one that acknowledges the differences between researcher and subject and seeks to create understandings within that dialogue, may be more fruitful to all parties concerned.

Roy Wells is almost certainly wrong to suggest that an outsider cannot usefully carry out research amongst Gypsies (or any other group of insiders: the white middle classes, perhaps). But he latches on to something very important when he describes the researchers as 'Plastic Gypsies'. It is the sense of an inauthentic created subject; it is the researcher inventing themselves as a representation of the Gypsy, identifying themselves with the community. We know it cannot be true. We can delineate the lines of difference between the researcher and the subject. What is more, it is unhelpful; the research process needs to understand something of the Gypsy experience, not that of the recreated 'Plastic Gypsy', and that is what we suspect is being produced when we hear Roy Wells's account. It would be far more helpful to hear the highly positioned voice of the researcher rather than the pain of identification with the subject. If we are told 'I am a white, middle-class researcher working for a red brick university; my work is based upon an engagement with the historic oppression of Gypsy communities and seeks to remedy this past injustice by influencing policy-making to improve social provision for the communities I work with', then we know, more or less, where we stand. Similarly, if a researcher states 'I am a contract researcher of twelve years' standing and am researching Gypsies on behalf of a local council health delivery unit', we understand a different positioning. What should also be clear is that neither of these two (here, fictional) positionings would necessarily produce work that was not of value.

    An engagement between the Academy and Gypsy communities based on a clearer positioning of the academic researcher and an acknowledgement that the outsider role of the researcher is a useful tool could be the means for opening up the terms of dialogue between Gypsies and non-Gypsies. In many ways it seems absurd that, despite the daily and longstanding engagement of Gypsies with the economies of non-Gypsies and the regular interventions of the state to engage Gypsy communities with the obligations and legal requirements of everything from schooling to planning law to housing provision, much of this engagement is conducted in a mute, dumbstruck fashion. Chapter 5 will consider what appears to be a lack of engagement between Gypsy families and the multiculturalism of many schools; one reason behind this seems to be the current failures (sometimes, admittedly, these are near-misses) of dialogue between schools and families. The idea that relations between Gypsy and non-Gypsy communities would magically improve dramatically were both parties simply to 'talk to each other a little' is an idle fallacy. However, there are some very clear recent examples where dialogue between Gypsies and their non-Gypsy neighbours has produced some interesting developments. In 2004 the BBC reported a story about the residents of Cottenham in Cambridgeshire who initially opposed the expansion of a local Gypsy site quite vociferously. Dialogue between the different Gypsy families on the site and the residents led to a degree of understanding between all parties and joint statements were issued condemning government policy and its failings rather than each other (BBC News, 16 September 2004). Such dialogues tend to concede the differences between different communities and accept there will be continuing difference between them that does not have to be reconciled, allowing a position where difference can be spoken about within a framework of greater cultural understanding and tolerance. The Academy is already positioned and has the clear potential to engage in similar dialogues; that is, dialogues that engage with differences honestly and openly.

3. Gypsy identity and culture: misrepresentation, misrecognition and deception

Browsing for sherry amongst the wine racks of Sainsbury's it becomes clear that marketing gurus have established two tried and tested means of branding their product. On the one hand there are the restrained and slightly old-fashioned bottles, warm and inviting and adorned with a flowing antique script; ad men, we guess, envisage them sitting on the sideboards of grandparents or maiden aunts. On the other hand there is something that appears to represent a 'shock of the new', enticing the next generation of young foodies with clear angular lines and bold typography. Amongst them all one bottle stands out as slightly different. *La Gitana* from Bodegas Hidalgo is a mid-range, distinctively labelled Manzanilla. The image used is a slightly florid picture of the Gypsy girl in question, hair tied up and a shawl around her shoulders, a hint of cleavage and a faraway look on her face. It resonates with a particular kind of image of Spain and Spanish flamenco dancers that is both exotic and alluring. It might be suspected that the image works in different ways for different sherry consumers in the UK.

It is clearly presented as an attractive image of a romantic figure. It is also, plainly, not a contemporary representation of what we in Britain might understand by Spanish culture. More than anything it seems to resonate with memories that are perhaps slightly fading now, of package holidays to Spain in the

1960s and 1970s; posters, ashtrays and souvenir trinkets adorned with bullfighters and flamenco dancers. The direct resonances of such an image are probably only felt by cohorts of the population of a certain age, whose family holidays were changed irrevocably by the availability of cheap package deals to the Balearics. The notion of an exotic encounter in the guaranteed sunshine and heat of the Mediterranean has perhaps been thoroughly overtaken by newer meanings of Spain: the ex-pat world of Brits abroad mimicking suburban life back in the UK.

More than anything the image of *La Gitana* is old-fashioned; according to personal taste it might be charming, gaudy or tacky, but the manner, expression and portrayal of the Gypsy girl belong to an earlier time. It represents a set of comfortable engagements with the everyday and the exotic. At its heart it is also very representative of one image of Gypsies that remains fixed in the popular imagination; that is, an exoticised image, tied to dancers and guitarists and open fires. It is an image located in understandings of what it means to be foreign and links this to the suggestion that the Gypsy in question is exciting and different from what we are used to in our own homes; in its own way it is so attractive that it can be brought into the homes of non-Gypsies as a means of bringing a particular kind of glamour into their lives.

Now it is very clear that within the dominant discourses of British people there is little or no desire to bring Gypsy people into their homes. There is a clear understanding of difference and separation. This state of affairs reflects not a shocking and sudden engagement between Gypsies and non-Gypsies but a longstanding relationship built up over many centuries. If anything, there is a degree of familiarity on the part of both Gypsies and non-Gypsies despite the fact that their relationship includes notions of maintaining separate and discrete communities. Such familiarity exists in large part only because Gypsy communities are not exotic new arrivals to the British Isles;

they have been around for centuries. What seems perverse, in this light, is that an image that holds a certain currency within the popular imagination should be quite such a *foreign* image of 'the Gypsy'. It's not that exotic and alluring Gypsy flamenco dancers do not exist in the UK; it is more that within engagements between Gypsies and non-Gypsies in the UK the appearance of quite such a Gypsy is a relatively rare occurrence, whilst engagements with many other wholly different Gypsies are relatively common. This very specific image is, however, one that is constantly alighted on; so *The SunWoman* fashion pages, for example, can suggest that their readers should:

> *Get the gypsy look*
> Put some passion into your fashion with the wild gypsy look. Lovely Jennifer Lopez was among the first to wear the revealing style but other celebs were quick to follow suit. Aussie pop princess Kylie Minogue and supermodel Claudia Schiffer have both showed off ruched 'n' raunchy gypsy tops by Yves Saint Laurent.
>   J-Lo's became a trend-setter when she wore the wild-at-heart look to the premiere of her hit movie *The Wedding Planner*.
>   The bad news is that her Dolce & Gabbana top costs an eye-watering £800.
>   Luckily, you don't have to splash out a fortune because the High Street is full of catwalk copies at bargain prices.
>   Stores such as Topshop and Morgan are bringing the frilly fashion to the masses.
>   This summer cleavage is out and shoulders are in – so show them off in these romantic styles.
>   Finish off with hooped earrings and a subtle smile for that hint of gypsy mystery.
> (Fatima Bholah, *The Sun*, 16 April 2002)

Here, then, is at least one well-established reading of what the figure of the Gypsy represents which could be read in a positive fashion. The constraints on reading this in a positive light are, however, many and manifest, not least because in the context of the many other less positive representations of Gypsy lives in the pages of *The Sun* our jaws are still firmly agape. Here, in contrast, we learn that the Gypsy look might be associated with passion and romance; it is raunchy, wild-at-heart and mysterious; it is also affordable, something we can all buy into. Bholah summons up an image of the Gypsy woman that has already been written in popular imaginations and flags up all the attractions of an exoticised 'other'; the language used is the language of titillation, the reader is being excited and encouraged to lose some reserve. There is a sense that what is on offer here is a little sniff of freedom that cannot be found in our own safe homes. Readers of *The Sun* can have an air of mystery about them if only they can shake their shoulders free and beat a path to Topshop.

It is an image, however, that probably has little resonance with the lives of Gypsies in the UK. Even the reference to hooped earrings needs to be embellished with a 'subtle smile', an indication perhaps that the author has an image in her mind of the fairground fortune teller rather than a mother in a playground or some other mundane encounter of everyday life. It is also an image that starts to explain some of the difficulties that may arise when non-Gypsy society encounters Gypsies. Within these descriptions there are a number of constants, one of which is the romanticised nature of such portrayals, something which seems linked to the exotic nature of this Gypsy's foreignness. The image bears, perhaps, more similarity to the types of image we might find in holiday brochures pitched at couples looking for a romantic trip abroad. When the journalist demands her readers 'put some passion back into their fashion', she is using an understanding of an image of Gypsy womanhood that relates to a very particular kind of sexuality, one that seems to be distanced from stereotypes of British women and anticipated expectations of their sexuality. Nonetheless, the adjectives used to describe this fashion are oddly counterbalanced; on the one hand it is 'wild' and 'raunchy', on the other 'frilly' and 'romantic'. There is a distance between these two sets of description that perhaps accounts for the air of 'mystery' generated by the fashion; it also seems to suggest an alliance between, on the one hand, more exotic and foreign styles, on the other, something altogether more homely and suburban. The descriptors 'wild' and 'raunchy' are clearly used to suggest an image of a strong woman, an image imbued with a physicality that seems to belong elsewhere, perhaps in the sexually provocative dance routines of R&B stars like Jennifer Lopez, although it also evokes earlier memories, such as the leading ladies of 1940s and 1950s Hollywood movies – Jane Russell, for example. If 'wild' and 'raunchy' are not descriptions from here, 'romantic' and 'frilly' certainly seem to be grounded in something more British, although also something which is possibly slightly outdated and slightly out of fashion. There is a hint of Mills and Boon in this romanticised image that perhaps harks back to a time before J-Lo was strutting her stuff on pre-watershed TV.

Both descriptions of the 'Gypsy look' work to some degree by distancing through time and/or space. This works to ensure that however strong or positive an image of Gypsies is being suggested, it is not related by the journalistic account to the real lives of Gypsies, and it places the understanding of what it means to be a Gypsy beyond the boundaries of Gypsies and non-Gypsies alike. It is an image that is distanced by being both foreign and old-fashioned and is therefore almost meaningless in its lack of connection to physical, material lives. In this sense, the image that is being produced is generated from nowhere, because it is not intended as a gritty slice of reality but rather as a fictional account of a romantic and exotic 'other', an account which comes from, and is exclusive to, the non-Gypsy world.

If the portrayal of Gypsies within a romanticised context is a common occurrence in non-Gypsy understandings of Gypsy culture, there is another, more overtly negative, image that is probably even more commonplace. This alternative reading makes its presence felt in the media, in local and national politics and in everyday conversation, and suggests that Gypsies are dirty and unclean. The following contribution to a House of Commons debate by the Conservative MP for south-east Cambridgeshire, James Paice, is typical of many accounts:

> Fences and gates can often be broken to gain access. While the Travellers remain, they frequently desecrate the surrounding area, cutting down fences and trees for fires and then leaving piles of rubbish and detritus, sometimes including human excrement. (Paice 2006, column 130)

Paice's description is, in contrast to other accounts, relatively mild in its condemnation of Gypsy culture and seems to reflect his understanding that what he is recording is simply commonly shared knowledge of the reality of non-Gypsy encounters with Gypsies. These sentences were presented almost in passing in the introductory passage of a Bill that would make it an offence to commit criminal trespass with a vehicle. Paice develops his argument by use of some very commonly held stereotypes about how Gypsies should be understood; the first of these appears in the distinction he draws between *good* Gypsies and *bad* Gypsies. We learn that within his own constituency there is a significant population of Gypsies whose 'pitches are generally clean and tidy' (*Hansard*, 28 February 2006, column 131); he then goes on to note that a 'substantial incursion' of Irish Travellers are, unfortunately, not as respectful of the environment. As the Bill develops we are led to believe that, following more punitive legislation of trespass in the Irish Republic, there has been a great increase in the numbers of Irish Travellers entering the UK (and presumably south-east Cambridgeshire in particular). Noting that there is a shortage of sites for Gypsies, Paice stresses 'that is not the point at issue here' (Paice 2006, column 132).

Paice uses a shorthand for describing Gypsies that is easily understood within the public sphere, in the same way that Bodegas Hidalgo uses the image of *La Gitana* and *The Sun* is able to promote a notion of Gypsy chic to its readers. These images are representative of very widely held understandings of what it means to be a Gypsy and of how Gypsy culture materialises in the UK. That they are in many ways contradictory does not raise a huge problem, partly because many of us may find ourselves holding contradictory views about many difficult subjects at different times, and partly because this version of what Gypsy identity means, with its consistent accounts of *good* Gypsies and *bad* Gypsies, actually encourages and explains the holding of such contradictory views. This can be seen in Paice's assertion that the main problems he has encountered seemed to be caused by the large number of Irish Travellers who are coming to the UK; immediately there is an acknowledgement of a pecking order amongst Gypsies in which the authentic *good* Gypsy is possibly an English Romanichal and the disruptive *bad* Gypsy is an Irish Tinker.

If Paice's description lacks the romantic or exotic connotations discussed earlier, the clear distancing still exists, here through an assertion that these are people who belong elsewhere. He would seemingly be a happier man if only he had to deal with British Gypsies rather than Irish Travellers. We might guess that this is not actually the case, that in fact the Gypsy population of south-east Cambridgeshire would be problematised whatever their perceived origin, but Paice still feels the need to make a geographical distinction. In many ways this seems a useful political strategy; Paice is able to buy in to commonly held cultural understandings of Gypsies, who, at their best, are a rarely encountered 'exotic' other. Describing the problems he wants to clamp down on within his own constituency, he again uses commonly held cultural reference points about dirt and anti-social behaviour. Within the subtext of his argument is the conspiratorial nod to his audience and a whispered voice saying *'and, what's more, these people are not even real Gypsies'*. The compounding of an 'Irish/immigration problem' with a 'Gypsy problem' ratchets up tension and the fears of his domestic constituency. By making the case for his anti-trespass bill within a set of stereotypical and popularly held views, Paice manages to lay responsibility for any problems entirely with a population of seemingly invasive outsiders who need to be resisted. This allows him to dismiss the issue of a shortage of sites in his constituency almost in passing.

What Paice also does in his speech is to create even greater historical distance between Gypsy and non-Gypsy constituents. He suggests that one reason for the large numbers of Gypsies in Cambridgeshire is that at some time in the past they were engaged in casual labour harvesting fruit and vegetables; however, 'a minimal number of Travellers, if any, are engaged in such activities today' (Paice 2006, column 130). Once again there is a sense that the Gypsy is being portrayed as being 'out of time'. In the past he may have been a useful part of the rural economy but now he is a redundant resource in the face of agricultural technology and cheaper eastern European gang labour. Whilst other communities who are faced with the disintegration of their livelihoods might at least receive some sympathetic words from their parliamentary representatives about their plight, Paice does not feel the need to do this. Instead, the sense that Gypsies are 'out of time' seems to suggest something of a final – and negative – judgement on their presence within the constituency.

For Paice, the distancing of Gypsy communities clearly validates his dismissive comment about the shortage of sites and the problems that might be associated with this state of affairs; the subtext of what he says speaks very clearly of a desire to be entirely disengaged from a dialogue with Gypsy culture. His account of the lives of his Gypsy constituents seems stereotypical and flawed, but more important is the perspective into which he places their lives. The implication that they come from another time or another place takes them out of the representative process; effectively, Gypsies are not constituents and they do not belong in the constituency of south-east Cambridgeshire.

Time and space

If the difference represented by Gypsies for the non-Gypsy world could be neatly categorised simply as being a culture of an 'other', of a recognisable group that comes from elsewhere, then the Gypsy experience would mirror closely the experiences of other immigrant groups within the UK. However, some noticeable differences are apparent in the history of Gypsy engagements with non-Gypsies, and these appear to figure within the understandings of both Gypsies and non-Gypsies. The most important difference is the very fixity of much of the prejudice that is expressed towards Gypsies. The characterisations made about who Gypsies are, and what they are like, appear remarkably constant since their arrival in the UK over 500 years ago. That a group of outsiders should be misrepresented and subject to prejudice is expected, but that the same misrepresentations should continue to be made over long periods of time seems a unique phenomenon. The time spans involved suggest that this particular engagement between dom-inant and subaltern cultures maintains an equilibrium. Possibly, at some level, it is a relationship that is useful to the nation state on a grander scale, providing a fixed marker for the boundary lines of national identity. Such equilibrium is not typical of the experiences of other minority groups whose relationship with the dominant culture generally undergoes some degree of movement across time.

Different groups of immigrants share different experiences of their reception within the UK, and this reception reflects different feelings expressed about these groups by the natives. So, for example, the Windrush generation black Caribbeans in the 1960s, white South Africans coming in the 1970s, black Somalis arriving in the late 1990s and white Europeans moving from newly signed-up member states of the European Union in the twenty-first century all have different experiences of migration to the UK. These distinct groups of people are themselves differently represented within the imaginations of the UK population. All of these groups (and dozens of others) are recognisable as different and as 'other'; some are received sympathetically, but most are not and these groups probably face differing degrees of racism in their daily lives. Many groups over time become more readily understood and understanding, and many of the original understandings of 'immigrant' and 'native' change with time. There is interaction between separate communities and inevitably there are changes in their relationships with each other. This does not guarantee or even suggest any particular progress towards a more equitable society, although it is often a noticeable consequence.

Within the construction of understandings of immigrant groups there is a noticeable construction of 'types' to act as representatives of changing understandings. These 'types' materialise as soap opera characters and news story subjects and seem to underline the interaction between dominant and subaltern cultures. Jamaican culture in the UK in 2007 may well materialise in a soap opera as either a home-grown manifestation of the Yardie (intelligent, driven and violent) or as the respectable hard-working black couple (middle-aged, struggling with a mortgage and facing the same trials and tribulations in life as their white neighbours). The same figures appear within the context of state discourses such as Operation Trident, the ongoing London Metropolitan Police campaign that began in 1998 against black-on-black gun crime, in which the figure of a dangerous young black man wielding a knife or a gun engenders an appeal to the community for leadership. These are ongoing constructions and ones that have changed and developed within cultural understandings of natives and immigrants across periods of time. The 2007 incarnation of the black gangster is the knife-wielding, gun-toting, disaffected youth, a product of first-world city life that can be traced back to the Yardie of the 1990s. The Yardie appeared in the cultural imagination straight out of the Jamaican ghetto, transforming local crime waves into a global epidemic; and, in turn, had mutated out of the Rude Boy of an earlier generation, a symptom of the shift from rural poverty to urban deprivation. Meanwhile, our respectable middle-aged couple can trace a genealogy that links directly to the SS Windrush and a far less sympathetic understanding of their lives than has more recently been forthcoming. Much of this sort of gloss on the Jamaican experience of migration to the UK since the 1960s suggests a degree of stereotyping about experiences and, whilst that is true to some degree, it also reflects a degree of charac-terisation made by both natives and migrants. Characterisations that are readily understandable within *Eastenders* or the national press are thus equally at home within the books of Sam Selvon or Victor Headley, in the cinema of *The Harder They Come* or forty years of Jamaican music.

The varying imaginations around Jamaican lives suggest an engagement in cultural discourse that demands and promotes change. Thus the same hard-working couple who were expected to live in poor housing in the 1950s and to do the jobs white people felt were beneath them, and who were subjected to racist abuse on a daily basis, are now running a little shop on Albert Square. They have become beacons of respectable and ordinary lives, planning for a secure retirement just like their white neighbours. Such change is important as it suggests an interaction between outsiders and their new neighbours, an engagement in which some level of understanding is being tested out. Such understandings may well be wilfully misplaced or inspired by malicious and racist thought processes, but the process of testing out such knowledge and of entwining it within the narratives of the dominant culture ensures that engagement between foreign cultures is maintained and will continue. In a sense simply understanding different cultures is not enough to promote a better or more equitable world; what seems more effective is a willingness to enter into a dialogue between these understandings.

By contrast, the engagement of understandings of Gypsy culture with non-Gypsy understandings seems remarkably unchanging and disengaged. In newsprint, stories that repeat already well-established prejudices about Gypsies making a mess on a site or scrounging off the state continuously appear. These stories are relayed in an entirely different register to that which might be anticipated in casual assertions of national stereotypes; a joke involving an Englishman, a Scotsman and an Irishman, for example. Such a joke might be regarded as offensive but more usually it will pass within more acceptable statements that reflect a particular ingrained sense of familiarity with the world we live in and notions of sick or politically incorrect humour within that world. The stereotypes summoned up can all be quickly turned from a supposed comedic positioning to outright abuse depending on the circumstances in which, and the methods with which, they are used. More often they intimate tolerance and their comedic value is upheld because most of the population do not believe the stereotypes to be the truth.

The same types of stereotype (dirty, scrounging, layabouts) about Gypsies are demonstrably more hostile and more firmly held. Whereas many understandings of 'otherness' are reconciled within a shared set of understandings about prejudices, Gypsies are not understood as ordinary neighbours or part of the wide tapestry of our many and diverse communities; they remain, instead, subject to enormous hostility. The stereotyping used to define Gypsies and their presence in the UK is never intended as an unbelievable humorous jibe indicating some degree of affection for a perceived 'otherness'; in contrast, it is meant to be harmful. It is also meant to be believed. The dirtiness of Gypsy sites is used not just as a marker of 'otherness' but also as the grounds for action. The call for Gypsies to be removed from sites because they are desecrating the countryside, creating a danger to public health or causing the value of house prices to fall is all too common and suggests deeply held beliefs about how Gypsies lead their lives. That there is a misrecognition of Gypsy culture is all too apparent and the effects of such misrecognition need to be understood from the perspectives of both Gypsies and non-Gypsies.

For Gypsies the misrecognition of their culture suggests they are victims of a damaging and demeaning relationship with the world around them. Every facet of their lives that involves any engagement with non-Gypsies is blighted in some part by a knowledge that their culture is actively misunderstood. For the non-Gypsy world another type of damage is done; the failure to engage in the world of Gypsies is in itself an absence. It goes unrecognised, but the *gaujo* world is forever missing out on an aspect of life that surrounds them – they are blinkered to another world view. Such misrecognition is effectively damaging to all communities.

The politics of recognition

Taylor (1992) argues that within contemporary politics it has become commonplace to 'demand' recognition for various subaltern groups. A recognition of their culture is vital to recognition of their identity – that is, their most fundamental and defining characteristics. The need to recognise identity is, within the context of the politics of 'multiculturalism', the need to appreciate the worth of minority groups:

> The thesis is that our identity is partly shaped by recognition or its absence, often by the misrecognition of others, and so a person or group of people can suffer real damage, real distortion, if the people or society around them mirror back to them a confining or demeaning or contemptible picture of themselves. Nonrecognition or misrecognition can inflict harm, can be a form of oppression, imprisoning someone in a false, distorted, and reduced mode of being. (Taylor 1992, 25)

Taylor identifies two historical changes that have resulted in current preoccupations with identity and recognition. The first of these is the 'collapse of social hierarchies' (Taylor 1992, 26); that is, the flattening of social status so that (almost) everyone is 'Mr' or 'Ms', whilst the nomenclature of the nobility has been whittled away. Secondly, Taylor describes an intensification of self-awareness dating from the end of the eighteenth century: 'human beings are endowed with a moral sense, an intuitive feeling for what is right or wrong' (Taylor 1992, 28). This intuition, this sense of the individual's authentic self-understanding of personal motives, displaces traditional Christian thinking that emphasised a calculation of the *consequences* of actions; expressed politically it is Rousseau's 'le sentiment de l'existence' (Rousseau 1959, 1047). Taylor understands the creation of individuals' identity to be a *dialogic* process developed by an engagement with society, with the *language* of others:

> We become full human agents, capable of understanding ourselves, and hence of defining our identity, through our

acquisition of rich human languages of expression. For my purposes here, I want to take language in a broad sense, covering not only the words we speak, but also other modes of expression whereby we define ourselves, including the 'languages' of art, of gesture, of love, and the like. (Taylor 1992, 32)

Taylor underlines the dialogical construction of identity by reference to Herder's (1877–1913) arguments in which not only 'the individual person among other persons, but also ... the culture-bearing people among other peoples' (Taylor 1992, 31) is imbued with 'originality' or 'identity'. Identity is shaped both personally and in the public sphere by the individual's relations to 'significant others'.[1] The 'demand' for recognition is therefore not just a demand by the minority group to be recognised. It is also the demand by the dominant group of the need to recognise minority cultures and for a politics of equal recognition; it is an assertion of the identity of liberal democratic society.

It is questionable whether or not dominant society in the UK aspires towards living within a liberal democracy. It is also readily apparent that they do not 'demand' recognition for Gypsy culture. What is more, on the evidence of the prejudicial accounts that are regularly constructed within the media it would often appear that there is an active desire to 'see' Gypsy culture in a particular light, one that does not have any bearing on real lives but prefers to perpetuate a collection of prejudiced stereotypes. On the one hand there is a failure to demand recognition for Gypsy culture and on the other there is misrecognition of Gypsy lifestyles. The implication is, therefore, that without finding a means by which such recognition is universally applied, we all live in a world that does not fully benefit from different cultural values. One part of this equation of misrecognition is the feeling that within the dominant population there is a belief that Gypsies have very little to offer wider society. This is challenged in Chapter 4, with an examination of Gypsy culture's maintenance of a recognisably strong tradition of community in the face of a changing world. The strength of such culturally produced social frameworks might well be attractive to a British culture that sometimes appears to yearn nostalgically for a lost sense of community. Ironically the misrecognition of Gypsy culture ensures that there is no real dialogue that would highlight shared values or successful strategies from different cultures that might benefit wider society in its search for a sense of community.

Arguing that society as a whole is somehow missing out on the value that could be transferred to wider society by the Gypsy community is perhaps wishful thinking. It is not evident that all parts of what could be described as 'liberal society' demonstrate an active desire to engage in Gypsy culture. Also, as already suggested, many members of wider society do not subscribe to genuinely liberal ideas, and we do not have to look too far to discover evidence of intolerant and illiberal culture. More importantly, within the context of the nation state, it may be that the presence of groups who are seen as outsiders plays an important part in defining the state itself. It does this partly in obvious ways. Within simple binaries, for example, the outsider defines natives by not being a native: the native is x, the outsider is y, x falls on one side of a boundary line and y falls on the other. More subtly, perhaps, where difference is real it acts as a useful reminder for the state to keep itself on its toes, to be able to sense and react to difference in a defensive manner in order to protect the *status quo*. This seems particularly apparent where the outsider bears a resemblance to the figure of the *stranger* described by Bauman (1991; 1997) and Simmel (1971); the very unsettling nature of this figure works to disrupt notions of safety within society. Instead of feeling comfortable within his own boundaries the native starts to feel under threat and responds by working not towards a liberal and all-encompassing dialogue with the *stranger* that might resolve potential tensions, but rather towards defending and consolidating his own position. Ahmed (2000) makes the point that the *stranger* is a recognisable figure and this highlights the disruptive effect the *stranger* can generate. Difference is recognised but seems misplaced within the lived experiences of the native; it is anticipated that 'otherness' belongs elsewhere but instead it is confronted at home. In part this explains why some of the understanding and representation of Gypsy difference becomes displaced in terms of a conjunction of space and time. By understanding the Gypsy as an alien other, *in the wrong place at the wrong time*, it seems somehow easier to both recognise difference and reconcile the familiarity of their appearance amongst the *natives*. It still remains possible to draw an absolute distinguishing line between *strangers* and *natives*, even in circumstances that at first glance seem less clear-cut.

It is not enough to simply close the borders to protect the purity of the state because there is an identifiable enemy within; a threat bubbles closer to the surface than is comfortable and that threat has to be faced. The recognisability of Gypsies is a recognition of discord within the boundaries of state and society, threatening that the *status quo* may not be reproduced and that instead the dangers of the outside may start to influence or even dominate what happens inside the boundary lines. For the state, assuming it wants to maintain and reproduce itself, the recognisability of Gypsies can be viewed as hugely beneficial. Gypsy difference becomes a tool to establish the need both to maintain safety and to do something to clarify understandings of who belongs within the state and who does not. The 'something' in question has historically been the processes by which the state has marginalised, rather than entered into a dialogue with, Gypsy culture. Simply entering into a dialogue suggests not a resolution of the threat but instead an engagement in a process through which the state would be changed. So, for example, when James Paice (2006) addressed the House of

Commons and referred to the lack of sites for Gypsies, rather than dismissing the importance of this issue, he could have entered into an alternative dialogue that included a consideration of the needs of Gypsies within his constituency. Within such dialogues possible opportunities for change could have briefly been opened up. However, the idea of a genuinely liberal state, as epitomised by such dialogues, suggests an end to the state in which we live today, and instead a world in which the Gypsy was no longer a *stranger* and the native no longer a native. In assessing the negative impacts of the status quo on Gypsy communities it is worth holding on to the suspicion that they are not the only losers in this situation.

The misrecognition of Gypsies

Whilst the lack of a dialogue between Gypsies and society at large undoubtedly has a negative effect on wider communities, the first and most obvious victims are Gypsies. It is Gypsy lives that suffer most keenly from a lack of recognition by their neighbours. Gypsies occupy a seemingly unique niche as the only group that can be disparaged in absolutely racist terms with little or no comeback upon the perpetrator. Such comeback does not materialise within a legal framework and, perhaps more importantly, it does not arise within cultural and social worlds. Whereas in many contexts the use of racist language or behaviour results in censure for the racists, the same depth of opprobrium is rarely displayed when Gypsies are the target. A limited degree of empathy for the sensitivities of Gypsy culture is a hallmark of their misrepresentation within the press and media and also within the treatment and handling of Gypsy issues by official institutions.

One example of the continuing inability of the dominant, sedentary culture to recognise significant aspects of this particular subaltern culture can be gleaned from an examination of the education system and its engagement with Gypsy communities. Acton (2004) makes clear that even where there has been some recognition of Gypsy culture there is still a considerable onus on the part of Gypsies to manipulate value from the education system. Gypsy culture is derided by racist name-calling even in schools that overtly recognise Gypsy culture and this name-calling inside the school is a microcosmic reflection of attitudes outside the school (Bhopal 2004; Bhopal and Myers 2006). Name-calling invariably marks Gypsy culture as dirty, poor and inferior to the dominant cultures; Gypsy children are referred to by their peers as 'dirty gyppo' or 'dirty pikey'. This misrecognition is reflected in wider society. For example, the frequent complaint that Gypsies are 'dirty' demonstrates a blindness to Gypsy taboos about cleanliness and hygiene.

As discussed above, the alternative common misrecognition of Gypsy culture is based around the exoticisation of Gypsies in the portrayal of, for example, quaint images of ornately decorated horse-drawn wagons, open fires and the strains of a Gypsy fiddle. This romanticised image becomes figured in the dominant culture as an idealised version of the 'real' or 'authentic' Gypsy. As few, if any, Gypsies conform to the dominant culture's ideal, the majority of Gypsies are therefore deemed 'inauthentic'. That this image of the Gypsy bears little resemblance to the actual encounters with Gypsies that non-Gypsies experience in their lives does not appear to affect the potency of this image in any way. And that it is potent is clear from the use of romanticised Gypsy imagery, such as *La Gitana*, within advertising and fashion. The impact of such imagery is partly felt in the failure, in numerous instances, of local authorities to enact their statutory duties towards Gypsies regarding issues such as site provision, healthcare or education; the failure of the Gypsies encountered by local authorities to live up to a spurious imagery is deemed grounds enough to label such Gypsies inauthentic. They may be categorised instead as vagrants or half-caste and, in so doing, the authority is able to argue that its responsibilities towards them change and lessen.

Taylor's need for groups within a liberal democratic society to be in dialogue with each other clearly breaks down when the 'other' in question is a Gypsy 'other'. Not only does recognition of cultural differences not happen, but the processes that might enable such recognition to gain a foothold, such as a dialogic engagement between different communities, never materialise. With a few notable exceptions (such as the Traveller Education Service), there is very little engagement with an active remit to speak with and understand Gypsy culture between the official world and Gypsy communities. This seems to be legitimised by the wider cultural constructions and understandings around who Gypsies are. The popular constructions of a dirty vagrant on the one hand and a romanticised, exotic figure on the other are very real parts of the understandings that shape such official worlds, at the level of both civil servants within government departments and elected officials engaged in gathering support from their electorates. Dialogues between politicians and voters, elected representatives and civil servants, and local authorities and council tax-payers understand Gypsy culture in an exclusive fashion: one that excludes dialogues with Gypsies. Effectively, such dialogues fail to recognise the nature of Gypsy culture, preferring instead to hold fast to a false set of imageries about Gypsies. Dialogues with Gypsy communities seem highly unlikely if they are inspired by the understandings that are held by the non-Gypsy world, which is, on the one hand, unable to locate a 'true' Gypsy to talk to, and, on the other, faced with the prospect of a figure of the 'dirty vagrant', and thus has little willingness to engage with such a community.

A further cause of the failure of dialogue with Gypsy culture is the mix of commonality and acquaintance that British society has with Gypsies. Gypsies are not, after all, uncommon figures, having been present in the economies and imaginations of British society for a long period of time. But this acquaintance is severely marked out by notions of strangeness. In some respects Gypsy strangeness is driven by their being a recognisable but at the same time an unseen 'other'. Not only are the stereotypical figures rarely to be found, but British Gypsies are not marked out as overtly racially different; they are a 'white other'. This subtly disorientates the process of understanding Gypsy culture 'otherness' further, as it adds to the sense that there is no appropriate niche in which an understanding of Gypsy culture can be fixed. The creation of a 'white other' suggests the creation of a figure who cannot be seen and cannot be located. A 'white other' sits beyond the pale, beyond the boundaries of acceptability, and yet still unsettles all expectations by retaining a visual similarity to the dominant culture. Again, there are implications for dialogue between different communities, particularly dialogue in a wider sense in which understandings are shaped through instinctive and gestural engagements with the world. Dialogues around Gypsies are halted by the inability to readily contextualise understandings of difference. It is not, after all, that the perceived whiteness of Gypsies indicates they are the same or share a culture; rather, the whiteness indicates a different type of difference from those normally encountered in the world. It is this particular germ of a difference that creates an unsettling 'other', one that takes on the mantle of the *stranger*.

In our research amongst Gypsy families we have consistently encountered very strong attachments to community and cultural values that are implicitly understood within Gypsy communities. The individual, the family and the community all maintain exceptionally robust understandings of their various inter-relationships and of a cultural identity determined by these relationships. Ironically, in the face of the disquiet that seems to infuse non-Gypsy understandings of Gypsy culture, there is far less ambivalence at play when the perspective is reversed and Gypsy understandings of dominant culture are examined. Often the *gaujo* world is regarded with a great deal of hostility and wariness; the reasons for this reflect the historic difficulties of the relationship between the two cultures. However, Gypsy understandings of the *gaujo* world tend to be marked by a greater fixity around understandings of who non-Gypsies are and how engagements with them should be conducted. This does not mean that every Gypsy in Britain is gifted with a special insight into the workings of the *gaujo* world, although there is an argument to be made that it is necessary for members of a particularly marginalised group to have an astute understanding of the dominant society in order to successfully engage at an economic level and maintain a degree of prosperity. It is more accurate to suggest that Gypsies maintain understandings of the communities around them that might well be disputed by those communities, but which provide Gypsy communities with a workable basis on which to interact with the *gaujo* world, and/or a solid foundation on which to construct understandings of their own culture and its difference from that of *gaujos*.

This is reflected in very different ways in Gypsy attitudes towards self-employment and care of the elderly. By preferring self-employment to employment by non-Gypsies, a relationship is created in which Gypsies maintain a distance between their culture and wider society. This works on various levels but, importantly, ensures that there is no longstanding reliance on individuals or companies in the non-Gypsy world. A degree of security is thereby generated (which to many non-Gypsies might be interpreted as a highly insecure situation) by relying on the self to generate income. Whilst self-employment is a means of engaging in a workable and self-protective manner with the *gaujo* world, cultural understandings, such as those around the care of the elderly, suggest a strengthening of community values in part by ascribing negative values to *gaujos*. The suggestion that non-Gypsies do not value or look after their elderly relatives appropriately is a cultural stereotype. It is one that ignores much of the reality of the non-Gypsy world, including those elderly people who are cared for by their relatives, those who seek more independent lives and those who have different social needs. However, by depicting a negative picture of *gaujo* culture and by doing so in a way that taps into fears about loss of community values, the strength and value of Gypsy culture is reinforced.

In some respects this feels a little counter-intuitive. We might anticipate that ambivalence and a sense of being ill at ease with the world would be more overtly characteristic of the migrant who does not belong in a community, rather than the natives. The sense of disorientation felt by migrant communities is explored by Sennett (Sennett and Cobb 1972), who firstly describes the construction of working classes in Europe through the migration from rural to urban environments. He notes how the disorientation felt in this process is hugely amplified in America, where the cultural shift is typified as a migration from European rural settings to US urban environments, creating an urbanised country where immigrants are categorised within a:

> moral hierarchy of national and cultural differences in which the Western Europeans – with the exception of the Irish – stood at the top, diligent, hard-working, and for the most part, skilled labourers, and in which Slavs, Bohemians, Jews and Southern Europeans stood lower, accused of dirtiness, secretiveness or laziness. (Sennett and Cobb 1972, 14)

Sennett could undoubtedly add Gypsies to the ranks of those at the bottom of this moral hierarchy. This apart, his analysis of what subsequently happens to such migrants, in particular the effects of working-class mobility over periods of time, shares little similarity with the Gypsy experience. He describes the gentrification of American cities and the resultant move of migrants from Little Polands or Little Italys into middle-class suburbs, where they seemingly become more settled and comfortable. Taken at face value, their lives have materially improved; financially and socially they are comfortable and secure. It is almost the American dream writ large. However, in this process the migrants appear also to lose something, suffering a psychological blow to their understanding of what constitutes their identity. Sennett notes that:

> integration into American life meant integration into a world with different symbols of human respect and courtesy, a world in which human capabilities are measured in terms profoundly alien to those that prevailed in the ethnic enclaves of their childhood. (Sennett and Cobb 1972, 18)

Sennett's interviews with working-class men who make this transition uncover an unsettling ambivalence. Although comfortably off and capable of adapting to middle-class norms of behaviour, they uniformly exhibit a sense of lost dignity, fulfilment and roots. A number of factors seem to be at play here. The very success of their lives seems loaded with negative connotations because in large part it is a success driven by absorbing and becoming part of an alien culture. Sinking into American suburban life is the antithesis of the cultural hopes and expectations that may have been defined by a European rural life. These were men who were no longer respected individually but instead had become part of a new, slightly amorphous group of middle-class, middle-aged Americans. The sense of struggle evaporated and with it most of the opportunities to take personal responsibility for determining life chances and constructing a cultural identity that remained tied to wider cultural nets of family and roots.

The Gypsy experience of a transition from rural to urban, of being rooted to a migrant identity, is different, not least because it does not result in a relegation of the culture or an integration into the dominant others' set of values or symbols. It materialises in numerous ways that signify the continuing importance of specific cultural markers, such as self-employment or living in a trailer. The values used to judge behaviour remain those inherent to and developed within Gypsy culture. It is these values, rather than behaviour patters that mirror or copy the dominant sedentary culture, that determine the respect and status of individuals within the community (Okely, 1997).

Sennett's American migrants, with the passage of time, find themselves dislocated from their ethnic roots and from their cultural values. Whilst materially their lives improve, their culture slips away between their fingers and they are seemingly unable to pass on a workable sense of their own identity. Sennett's work highlights one failure of the American melting pot in which a wider, newer group identity is forged at the expense of individual cultures. Gypsy culture appears far more resilient. By adapting its *response* to changing conditions rather than adapting its culture, the identity of individuals, families and communities gains a degree of security. The conditions are produced in which Gypsy culture can be reproduced and can survive within a fairly hostile environment. This culture is embedded within the practical responses to British society needed to make life – if never easy – at least liveable.

Note

1. The term 'Significant Others' is originally taken from Mead (1934).

4. Recognising the 'other'

If Gypsies are clearly misrecognised and misrepresented within the UK, thus reflecting the wider experience of Gypsies in Europe, America and beyond, the materialisation of these processes is to be found in the boundaries created around and between Gypsy groups. Boundaries can be drawn around individuals and groups along many different lines dictated by geographical, racial or socially constructed differences. Many of these boundaries, even those that at first sight seem specific and easily fixed, are actually quite ambiguous, porous or in a state of flux. The boundary of London is an obviously complex and probably indefinable concept made up of fixed but inexact territories (the City of London, the London boroughs), territorial allegiances that do not sit comfortably together ('I'm from London', 'he's from South London', 'they're cockneys') and psychological and subconscious understandings that are perhaps only clear to the natives (how, for example, on a summer bank holiday the boundary of south London is where the pebbles on the beach at Brighton meet the English Channel). All that is surprising about the complexities and convolutions of such boundary lines is the clarity with which they are generally understood. We rarely find ourselves wondering which side of the line we belong to and we rarely wander outside our own borderlines.

What also seems clear is that such boundary lines are

constructed internally and externally; the south Londoner has a sense of being a south Londoner and is also understood by those outside south London as belonging within such a category. The ambiguities of space are clearly apparent from the importance such boundaries have for the construction of identity, however; living within the boundaries of south London does not of itself constitute being a south Londoner, and a south Londoner who moves 300 miles north to Newcastle upon Tyne does not suddenly transform into a Geordie.

Often we are conscious of boundaries within boundaries, something which can become most apparent at moments where 'otherness' can be attributed to individuals or groups. Gypsy communities are amongst those groups in the UK who recognisably sit within a category of 'otherness', which, as we discuss in this chapter, materialises in a number of different ways. We would anticipate that some of the boundaries drawn around Gypsies would at times be ambiguous and subject to change, reflecting their lengthy presence in the UK, and therefore what is most surprising about the boundaries that seem to operate between Gypsies and the rest of the population is the degree to which they have remained constant.

This chapter will examine such boundary formation and the ways in which this is manifested. In addition, it considers an apparent intensification of the boundary between Gypsy and non-Gypsy culture and questions how this might relate to a specific and unsettling creation of the idea of Gypsies by the non-Gypsy population. In doing so, the work of Simmel (1950; 1971) and Bauman (1991) around the figure of the *stranger* will be considered, as will the ways in which a certain type of 'otherness' may be ascribed to certain groups including Gypsies. Within the construction of this particular 'otherness' a number of factors seem to play a significant role. First amongst these is the misrecognition described in the previous chapter.

This misrecognition is not a simple misunderstanding of Gypsy culture; that is to say, it is not the case that the general population construct a misconstrued notion of Gypsy culture out of, for example, laziness or ignorance. Rather, there is some deliberation in the construction of the 'otherness' of Gypsies by the non-Gypsy population. The regularity with which dirtiness, for example, is attributed to descriptions of Gypsies regardless of their personal or community lifestyles is symptomatic of a process initiated and perpetuated by non-Gypsy society. Within the various social engagements of Gypsies and non-Gypsies, the continuing misrecognition shown by much of the non-Gypsy world towards Gypsy culture appears in some part to be a proactive rather than a passive process.

One reason for the continuing willingness on the part of the dominant population to misrecognise Gypsy culture seems to be related to some of the ambiguities generated by the apparent whiteness of many Gypsy groups in the UK. Skin colour acts as perhaps the most clear-cut visual marker of difference and 'otherness' that can be ascribed to a minority group. Being a white 'other' is freighted with an uncertainty about the 'otherness' in question, unlike the seeming clarity with which a black or brown skin might be understood. Although it is possible to speculate that Gypsies in the UK may have been darker skinned in the past, reflecting their Indian origins, they are largely not discernible as 'others' on the basis of skin colour today. The fact that many Gypsies are now visibly white makes for an endless, open-ended discussion of the origins of Gypsies and their engagements with the native British population, but the visibility of white skin colour has other, more practical, ramifications. For example, it allows Gypsies, if they choose, to conceal their origins in certain circumstances, such as when attending school or a job interview. Whiteness is also a contributory factor within the unsettling relationship with the wider population; the feeling that an 'other' group should share quite such a defining insider characteristic demands the intensification of understandings of other, more ambiguous, boundaries.

White 'others'

Holloway (2005) has argued that the relationship of Gypsies to whiteness is ambiguous both in their relationship to the non-Gypsy population and vice versa. The minority status of Gypsies is not as visible as that of non-white groups, making it hard to immediately distinguish Gypsies from the rest of society. What is more, the boundaries of whiteness are not simply constructed around skin colour but also include other considerations such as ethnicity and background. Gypsies do not comfortably sit within all the interpretations placed upon the concept of whiteness despite their skin colour. Although there is clearly an overlap between the categories of 'whiteness' and of 'Gypsies', understandings of that overlap tend to be unsettling. In some respects this reflects the uncertainty that is generated by whiteness being coupled with elements of society considered disreputable.

Where whiteness becomes associated with an underclass – 'white trash' in America and, more recently, 'chavs' in Britain, for example – quite ferocious outpourings of revulsion are often generated within the wider population. Whilst this in some ways mimics racist abuse by naming the shared characteristic (whiteness) and then generating a vocabulary of hate around an imagined field of repugnant behaviours, it also does something slightly different, in naming boundaries of 'white' good taste, decency and respectability. It says more about the fields of acceptable white behaviour than does much racist language directed at non-whites because it has to. White people who generate insults aimed at a white underclass need to think more carefully and in more detail about the distinctions being made between 'respectable' white people and a white 'other'. The hatred generated towards Gypsy groups materialises both in the register of racism directed towards non-white ethnic minorities by whites that uses visible differences such as skin colour as its starting point, and also within the more nuanced racisms made by white people about other white people who fall beyond their understandings of respectability. On the one hand there is the type of abuse that mirrors an Asian shopkeeper being called a 'paki', when Gypsies are routinely called 'pikeys', for example. On the other hand there is the near-mythologising of accounts of difference: Gypsies are dirty, they lie, they cheat, they don't pay tax, their dogs are wild, they mistreat animals. There is a level of detail in these accounts that is used to identify a distinguishing line between what is respectable and belongs within the territory of white people and what falls outside that territory and constitutes 'otherness'.

The various abuses piled upon other white underclasses do not directly parallel those directed at Gypsy communities but there are similarities and commonalities that make it a useful area of research when trying to understand how a perceived whiteness has an effect upon the type of abuse that is generated towards Gypsies. When we think of Gypsies as 'others', we need to understand their status not only as 'outsiders' but as *white* outsiders, and to comprehend what this means for them as well as for our wider understanding of them as a group that remains alien and alienated.

There is a significant body of work that has sought to explore understandings of whiteness in relation to social class (Hartigan 1997; Jarosz and Lawson 2002), the underclass and social exclusion (Haylett 2001). Within the discipline of geography there has been an increased understanding of the concept of whiteness and the meanings it conveys to particular groups (see Bonnett 2000; Nayak 2003; Winders 2003). The residents of

Hartigan's (1997) ethnographic research in downwardly mobile but formerly respectable white working-class areas of Detroit identified the decay of their neighbourhoods less by the influx of black families than by that of 'white trash'. These white 'others' disrupted the residents' 'implicit understandings of what it means to be white' (Hartigan 1997, 46), and as a result the established residents resorted to name-calling in order to displace the incoming contingent of white culture; hence 'white trash' as a stigmatising insult 'constitutes more than a derogatory exchange of name calling; it materializes a complicated policing of the inchoate boundaries that comprise class and racial identities' (Hartigan 1997, 47). Hartigan notes that, whereas the use of the word 'nigger' was never acceptable in his presence (and his was obviously a very distinctively defined presence as an academic researcher), there was no hesitation about using the equally vitriolic 'white trash'. Similarly, the use of 'paki' and 'coon' is hugely restricted within British culture but the use of 'chav' as a near-equivalent post-millennium British marker for 'white trash' has become quite commonplace. Jack Dee's 2004 *Live at the Apollo* performances for the BBC regularly used the figure of the 'chav' as the butt for many of his jokes. In other contexts it would be quite easy to swap 'chav' for 'white trash'; these two different figures bear a striking resemblance to each other. The following example was reported in *The Sun*:

> Jack Dee quipped: 'Toblerones, lukewarm Bacardi Breezers and as many crisps as you could eat – it's like a chav's Christmas dinner'. (*The Sun*, 23 December 2005)

Similarly, the use of the word 'pikey', with just a hint of irony, is considered acceptable despite the obviously derogatory nature of this term. On ITV's *The Frank Skinner Show* (28 December 2004), David Baddiel was interviewed, during which he discusses his appearance (his looks and his clothes) and explains that in his everyday private life he is not overly concerned about dressing smartly or looking after his appearance. He goes on to add that when not dressed up to do a performance he 'looks like a bit of a pikey'. That both the word 'chav' and the word 'pikey' can be used fairly freely on mainstream media indicates the degree to which these terms are considered acceptable. It is not so much that they won't cause offence, but that they will not offend in a way that would bring down any opprobrium upon the performers themselves. The use of the word 'pikey', for example, will not lead to a performer being accused of using racist language or of actually being a racist. Within broadcasting there are generally well-understood legalistic parameters regarding what can and cannot be said, and clearly broadcasters do not anticipate that the use of 'chav' or 'pikey' will lead to their being prosecuted under race relations legislation. More importantly, there is a cultural awareness about what is or is not offensive, and when a performer is seen to break such taboos it has an immediate and detrimental effect on their public standing.[1] The 'whiteness' attached to 'chav' and 'pikey' allows these terms to be used in a fairly free manner, one that is obviously designed to cause offence to the subjects and yet does not, within wider cultural understandings, cause any harm to the person causing the offence. Hartigan argues this is a class issue and that the making and recognising of an 'other' matters more than racial differences:

> white trash is a cultural figure and a rhetorical identity, it is a means of inscribing social distance and insisting upon a contempt-laden social divide, particularly (though not exclusively) between whites. (Hartigan 1997, 50)

Initially this analysis of class difference seems to ring truer for 'chavs' than for Gypsies, and in any case the historical social distance between Gypsy and non-Gypsy culture barely requires any additional rhetorical device to further identify such divides. However, in the popular literature and media frenzies that materialised around the figure of the 'chav' in the early years of the twenty-first century there is a frequent linkage made between the terms 'chav' and 'pikey'. The chavscum website,[2] for example, invites amusing contributions from its readers about experiences and encounters with 'chavs' in their area, and the seeming interchangeability of the two terms is particularly noticeable in those contributions. The terms both operate in a similar fashion, identifying recognisable categories of people and casting them in terms that suggest they lie beyond the boundaries of acceptability and respectability. 'Chavs' are effectively distinguished as being poor, feckless and lacking good taste, whilst 'pikeys' are idle, dirty and ignorant. The association of Gypsies with an urban underclass floundering outside of respectable society works to produce another figure that is as much an imaginary construct as the more traditional (mis)representations of idealised rural exotics or 'dirty gyppos'.

That Gypsy culture should be equated to a white urban 'other' falling off the register of respectability is unsurprising; in many ways this process represents a useful rounding-up, on the part of dominant society, of subjects that lie beyond the boundary of normative culture. On a slight tangent, it is interesting to note that the word 'chav' almost certainly derives from the Romany word for a small child, 'chavvy'. Although speculation on how this word entered the general language is probably fruitless, it is hard not to note the irony of such intuitive linkages. It is also worth considering that in many ways the connections made between 'chavs' and Gypsies may act as a greater marker for the poor, white, working-class groups identified as 'chavs'; it appears that this connection is a part of the process whereby they are positioned outside the boundaries, joining Gypsies, who already occupy such territory.

Recognising the 'other'

In his discussion of 'white trash' Hartigan describes name-calling as 'contests over signification' in which 'the namer and the named are locked in an unending struggle where there is no neutral ground' (1997, 53). This resonates with much of the intent behind the name-calling of Gypsies, which is perhaps best highlighted in the context of the school playground. It seems clear that name-calling, which uses behaviours learned outside the school gates and from peers, is used by children to create boundaries and mark out social distance. This mirrors the wider societal understandings of difference between the respectable white dominant group and the Gypsy 'other'. The most common forms of name-calling are variations of 'dirty, thieving gyppo' or 'dirty, thieving pikey'; the associations both with dirt and with illegality are historically persistent abuses of Gypsy character and both situate Gypsies outside the wider culture. Although accusations of law breaking obviously carry with them a negative judgement about the character and respectability of the supposed thief, it is the implication of dirtiness that seems to carry greater weight when marking out difference between Gypsy and non-Gypsy culture. The enduring perception, or at least naming, of Gypsies as 'dirty' seems in some part directed at disrupting the confusing visual marker of Gypsy whiteness; it is almost as if this marker can be changed to a blackness associated with dirt. Okely notes that 'Travellers' existence is affected by the way Gorgios represent them. Travellers cannot escape the gaze of the Gorgio' (1983, 232).[3] If that gaze is determined by creating not only difference but strict dividing lines between themselves and Gypsies, any points of similarity then have to be re-interpreted and made to work against the possibility of the Gypsy encroaching inside the boundaries of society. Rather than seeing a white Gypsy, it is far more comfortable and understandable to construct and gaze upon a dirty Gypsy. The same trajectory of thought that allows an exotic representation of the Gypsy as a flamenco dancer on a bottle of sherry to be brought safely into the home is at play here. It is the imaginary Gypsy who is seen as exotic and glamorous and therefore finds a place within dominant society, whilst the lived experience of being a Gypsy is seen as dirty and out of place.

The 'gaze', the way in which dominant society sees subjects, becomes an instrument in the construction of those subjects' identities; it defines the boundaries by inscribing what sort of people belong within society. bell hooks (1997) discusses how white people assume the ability to control black people's 'gaze', in part through privileging the 'White gaze'. In America in the years of slavery and later racial apartheid a black slave or servant was not permitted to observe white people; the black servant was merely an object rather than a subject. hooks (1997) also describes white students in her classes struggling to comprehend that their black peers might observe their behaviour with 'a critical "ethnographic" gaze'. hooks suggests that the assumption that black people are unable to observe white people is a continuation of the assumption that white people cannot be seen by black people. It is almost as though black people are in some way blind to the behaviours of white people. This assumption of a lack of recognition contributes to the perception of black people as 'other'; that is, not part of the 'white' superior group. It also works to suggest that black people are therefore unable to comprehend how the white group maintains power. hooks places this analysis within Dyer's (1997) commentaries on how Judaeo-Christian society has seen whiteness to correlate with good and blackness with evil, and argues that, 'Socialized to believe the fantasy, that whiteness represents goodness and all that is benign and nonthreatening, many white people assume this is the way black people conceptualize whiteness' (hooks 1997, 169).

Various generalised and stereotypical accusations made about Gypsy culture seem to fill the ether and inform any public debate on how Gypsies and non-Gypsies live their lives. Amongst these are notions about dirtiness and illegality (already discussed), but often they materialise in more specific allegations: for example, Gypsies do not pay taxes, they do not insure their vehicles, their children caused the latest outbreak of head-lice in our local school. What is seen, and this would be 'seen' in its loosest, most imaginary sense, is behaviour that represents irreconcilable difference between different cultures. This is interpreted as behaviour that deliberately places Gypsies beyond societal norms, something which Gypsies understand to be the case. Regardless of the truth or falsity of many of the accusations that are thrown at Gypsies, behind them all is an assumption that Gypsies to some degree subscribe to the same set of values and norms as do the dominant population but choose to distance themselves from those norms. So, typically, everyone could expect to live in houses these days, but Gypsies choose not to; therefore, they are somehow failing to subscribe to normative lifestyles. From this assumption of the superiority of a particular culture comes an immediate failure to engage with a different culture. Where there are points of difference between Gypsy and non-Gypsy culture, little or no attempt is made to understand these differences; and, where there are points of similarity, these are re-interpreted in order to maintain the social distance. Gypsies are marked as 'dirty' and their culture is blackened to conform to the stereotyping of the white gaze. The Gypsy's gaze, meanwhile, goes unnoticed and the meanings that the Gypsy comprehends are unseen by the dominant society. Ironically, Gypsy society cultivates and values the ability to see and understand *gaujos*, to establish economic advantage when trading with the dominant society and, if possible, to get the better end of the deal (Okely 1983). That this is largely unnoticed by wider society is unsurprising; where it is noticed it is often re-interpreted as the Gypsy 'pulling a fast one' or reneging on a deal.

The dominant society's perception of Gypsies is largely governed by a desire to mark out a boundary between the acceptability of the dominant culture and the unacceptability of the subordinate culture. Where one is clean the other is dirty, where one is industrious the other is idle, where one is modern and urban the other is backward and rural (Bhopal and Myers 2005, 8). The perception of the Gypsy goes further than that of simply an 'other'; a neighbour can be an 'other' but still live on the same street, whereas the Gypsy is a stranger who can never live within the neighbourhood.

Gypsies and strangers

Bauman (1991) describes relationships between friends and enemies who, although polar opposites, are inescapably linked together because they define their understandings of each other and of their societies:

> The friends/enemies opposition sets apart truth from falsity, good from evil, beauty from ugliness. It also differentiates between proper and improper, right and wrong, tasteful and unbecoming. It makes the world readable and thereby instructive. It dispels doubt. (Bauman 1991, 54)

Friends are a pragmatic solution to the difficulties and fears associated with living outside of society; they provide a culture of mutual cooperation and responsibility to help ensure survival. Those who are unwilling to share responsibility and who do not participate in work directed at survival are identified as enemies belonging outside the community of friends. Bauman understands this relationship as being one of struggle. However, through engagement in this struggle the oppositional relationship between friends and enemies creates a framework in which sociation, the construction and maintenance of societies, can exist; that is, the sociation of friends and the sociation of enemies. In contrast, a third group – strangers – plays an uncomfortable and unknown other role in this binary relationship and possesses the potential to disrupt the shape of society. The stranger sits uncomfortably outside the relationship described above:

> the stranger rebels. The threat he carries is more horrifying than that which one can fear from the enemy. The stranger threatens the sociation itself – the very possibility of sociation. He calls the bluff of the opposition between friends and enemies. (Bauman 1991, 55)

Bauman draws a distinction between strangers that society can accommodate relatively easily – the tourist, for example, restricted by the boundaries of the tourist map – and the stranger described by Simmel as 'the man who comes today and stays tomorrow' (Simmel 1971, 49). This second stranger is an altogether more incongruous and unsettling figure. His continued presence demands some calls made on the notions of responsibility described above; by being amongst the society of friends the stranger is seemingly entitled to the same rights and the same level of protection afforded by society to all its members. This entitlement however is a one way street; the stranger is not accountable to society. His presence is marked by his earlier absence, his other life; for Bauman, the disruptive power of the stranger is clearly derived from his arrival. It is not, for example, a case of the stranger simply being an oddball, someone born within the society who is different; strangerhood comes physically from elsewhere:

> There is hardly an anomaly more anomalous than the stranger. He stands between friend and enemy, order and chaos, the inside and the outside. He stands for the treacherousness of

friends, for the cunning disguise of the enemies, for fallibility of order, vulnerability of the inside. (Bauman 1991, 61)

What is more, the stranger is a figure who becomes associated with space and the lived environments of communities. According to Simmel:

> his position in this group is determined essentially by the fact that he has not belonged to it from the beginning, that he imports qualities into it, which do not and cannot stem from the group itself. (Simmel 1950, 402)

The stranger is seen to be a fixed presence within a spatially located group, yet at the same time he is not a *bona fide* member of this group and does not belong within the group's cultural or social values. Sway (1981) has argued that Gypsies occupy a very similar position to that of Simmel's stranger, with settled society creating boundaries between Gypsies and itself.

The stranger represents closeness and distance at the same time and this is perhaps the most potent resonance between the figure of the stranger and the figure of the Gypsy. Being within society, certainly being within a society such as the British nation state, implies a degree of shared citizenship and associated rights. Such rights often do not distinguish between natives and strangers. The simple presence of individuals within the nation state is an entitlement to certain rights, many of which can be identified in very material ways. The right to free healthcare or primary and secondary education, for example, are not restricted to types of people or dependent upon specific behaviours by the citizenry. These are services that are provided freely to everyone. Gypsies in Britain are granted these rights just as non-Gypsies are, although there are clearly times when the granting of such rights is loaded with expressions of the dominant population's belief that they are not deserved. There are also many occasions when the delivery of such rights appears to be done in a less than equitable manner, or in a manner designed to devalue the worth of Gypsies. In these unhappy transactions the closeness:distance dichotomy is being tested and boundaries are being drawn. The potential for ambiguity in such situations is great and this seems particularly to be the case when one party is thoroughly misunderstood and misread. There is always a likelihood that the dominant society will draw their boundary lines at an inappropriate point, one that will leave a subordinate or minority group feeling vulnerable or short-changed. The drawing of boundary lines at points of contestation may in itself be a useful strategy for the dominant society because it is a means of clarifying what is distinctive about their society. Redfield (1971) makes the point that communities are often dependent on being able to understand absolutely who belongs and does not belong within their notion of community. When distinctions about who is 'one of us' and who is not become blurred, the stability of the community is threatened.

The figure of the Gypsy is that of an exaggerated stranger. Not only does the Gypsy arrive from elsewhere, the 'elsewhere' in question is hugely confusing. There is little clear sense of where the point of departure for Gypsies might be. The idea of a Gypsy homeland or a recognisable state to which they belong is not well-defined in popular thought. Within different constructions of Gypsy identity there is a mythical 'Egypt', possibly, or a fabled India. More likely in twenty-first-century Britain, however, it is an unknown homeland; unnamed and, in many respects, unimaginable. One aspect of the role of the stranger is the sense of connection to somewhere else, that is to the place from which the stranger originally came. The Gypsy seemingly retains his connection, therefore, to a strange and unknown land. The connection is made real in the eyes of the dominant population by an apparent nomadism that might take him back to this other place, possibly returning in a year's time. This somewhat nebulous and misunderstood relationship to a homeland acts in an unsettling manner; it disrupts some fixed notions of how subordinate groups come into existence. This acts to exaggerate the strangeness of Gypsies and makes their relationship with dominant society more troubling. Even more confusing to the dominant culture is the fact that Gypsies are nomads who are often, in fact, settled on caravan sites and may rarely be inclined to travel. They are, in many other cases, actual neighbours, living in the house next door.

The Gypsy is white but his culture is at odds with those around him: he is nomadic and self-employed with different skills and different taboos. There is a need for the dominant culture to mark him out not just as an 'other' but as a hugely unsettling 'other'. If Bauman's stranger sits outside the sociation both of friends and of enemies then this suggests alienation in an almost absolute form. For Gypsies this is a material realisation of living amongst a society within whose cultural boundaries they do not belong; one, indeed, whose cultural boundaries may well be drawn and redefined in order to exclude the cultural values of the Gypsy. Strangerhood is exaggerated within this context because Gypsies as a body of people have neither a physical space that is home nor any context that resembles a nation state or homeland. Unlike other immigrants, they do not come from an identifiable elsewhere; they come from nowhere. Bauman's delineation of friends and enemies suggests the physical boundaries that the nation state is going to occupy. The reality of such geographical boundaries could well prove to be porous, fluid or of dubious psychological value to friends and enemies alike, but they are mappable. Disputes over such boundaries are eventually reconciled through international legal processes that identify space and territory as lines on a map. The Gypsy nation cannot be reconciled within any such similar process.

Gypsies construct themselves and are constructed by others as not belonging to the wider community, the school or society: they are 'outsiders', never insiders. The social space occupied by many Gypsies falls outside the boundaries, both real and imaginary, of the dominant population. They are read as the worst kind of stranger: they camp illegally, they do not contribute to society, 'they are dirty, filthy, thieving gyppos' (Bhopal and Myers 2005). Their space is not their space – they are an illegitimate presence in space that does not belong to them, and, whatever the boundary line, be it a physical demarcation of geographical space (the school gates, for example) or the boundaries of imagined spaces (respectable occupations, dress or demeanour), it is transgressed when Gypsies occupy the spaces of non-Gypsy communities (Myers 2006). Their presence is without purpose to the majority population and so it is regarded as suspect.

The tone of much recent media criticism of Gypsies' purchasing land for caravan sites and subsequently ignoring planning legislation is set by the question: what if we all behaved like that?[4] This question effectively accuses Gypsies of behaving beyond the normative 'white' boundaries: they (Gypsies) are behaving in a manner that we (white people) are unable to emulate, because to do so would be to become an outcast by crossing beyond the boundaries of cultural acceptability. As a native within the nation state this would mean crossing cultural distances far greater than those travelled by ex-pats moving abroad. It is the scale of remove suggested in the construction of subjects such as 'white trash' or 'chav scum'. Within the construction of such subjects is a sense of revulsion at the idea that the subject apparently feels content to live with poverty; they are not just behaving illegally, but are also not capable of conceptualising and behaving within the moral codes of society, and are forever mired within that status, unable to change their circumstances. Whereas 'white trash' constructions are overtly connected to the meanings dominant society ascribes to its own codes and values, although they are obviously understood through the differences and gaps between them, the figure of the Gypsy is much more ambiguous. The understandings placed upon the Gypsy seem to reflect the lack of a connection between Gypsy culture and the dominant culture and represent an attempt at rationalising the unknown space between them. Such a rationalisation inevitably draws a comparison between known elements of society who are seemingly understandable and the unknown Gypsy. In this context it is clear how useful the figure of Bauman's stranger can be to understand the figure of the Gypsy, particularly in terms of the way that the figure of the Gypsy generates unease as well as hostility, unlike the figure of the 'chav', for example, which is largely reduced to a contemptible and laughable character. The discomfort that attaches to the figure of the Gypsy today is also symptomatic of earlier historic engagements going back over 500 years between dominant society and Gypsy culture. However, for all that Gypsy culture sits outside the dominant culture, the figure of the Gypsy remains firmly in sight; Gypsies engage with the dominant society as their survival depends upon creating economies with non-Gypsies.

Drawing boundary lines

The stranger is fixed within a particular spatial group whose boundaries are marked out by a certain spatial membership. As Barth states:

> If a group maintains its identity when members interact with others, this entails criteria for determining membership and ways of signalling membership and exclusion. Ethnic groups are not merely or necessarily based on the occupation of exclusive territories, and the different ways in which they are maintained,

not only by a once-and-for-all recruitment but by continual expression and validation. (Barth 1969, 15)

Barth indicates that ethnic boundaries involve social processes such as exclusion and the maintenance of discrete categories, despite a changing participation and membership within the lifetimes of group members. Over time groups may transform radically in terms of their membership, social organisation and cultural beliefs, but a 'continuing dichotomisation' ensures that the distinction between the insiders who belong and the outsiders who do not remains in place (Barth 1969, 14). Being a stranger, or indeed being a member or a native, does not imply being constrained within an unchanging identity. The terms of engagement will change and mutate and this will be reflected within groups' cultural development. However, such spatial belongings will remain in place; strangers will become different types of strangers. Gypsy engagement with the non-Gypsy world has adapted and changed to reflect changing economic circumstances, opportunities and challenges, but the historic alignment of Gypsies as an 'othered' group within society remains a potently fixed understanding. The ethnic boundary is based on a complex organisation of behaviours and social relationships:

> A dichotomisation of others as strangers, as members of another ethnic group, implies a recognition of limitations on shared understandings, in differences in criteria for judgement of value and performance, and a restriction of interaction to sectors of assumed common understanding and mutual interest. (Barth 1969, 15)

Historically, Gypsies have been referred to as a group who are strange and mysterious and who fall outside normal culture and normal society (Bercovici 1929). Today there are still many associations with this stereotype, as they are seen by wider society as a group who remain different, distinct and separate from wider society. The use of boundaries to explain both the positioning and disengagement of Gypsies with wider society has been used by some commentators (Holloway 2005; Mayall 2004) to reflect accurately how as a group they are 'othered'. We wish to take this idea of boundaries further by considering how and why Gypsies are able to create and construct boundaries in which they themselves are excluded from wider society. On the one hand the boundaries are used to give legitimation to society to exclude and vilify Gypsies, and on the other they are used as a means of self-exclusion by Gypsies themselves. In this second sense they are used as a means of protection; families and communities can insulate themselves from outsiders, effectively creating a space in which values and culture can be defended.

Whether or not boundaries are created by insiders or outsiders, they institute a notion of difference between both parties. Boundary formation and boundary maintenance are inextricably linked to a labelling process in which the upper hand lies with the more powerful dominant society. Gypsy communities may well describe themselves within sets of meanings that have a resonance for them, but within wider societal understandings it is the labelling practised by the dominant society which will have the most recognisable potency. So, for example, some communities may identify themselves as Travelling Showmen, drawing a very clear distinction between their lives and those of other groups who they might refer to as Gypsies or Travellers. However, when their lives are interpreted by dominant society there is a good chance that the distinctions drawn by specific and defined groups about themselves will be passed over and all such groups may well be seen and described as Gypsies. Such a labelling process becomes a form of power which is used to separate groups, in this case the homogenous group understood to be Gypsies, and to reinforce their difference. Ironically, this notion of difference in many respects is a misnomer: it ignores the full range of differences inherent to different communities, as the dominant culture finds it more useful to establish a blanket difference that covers a diverse but recognisable group of outsiders. It limits ideas of difference to those held by wider society.

Jenkins has argued that 'as well as being self-forming, the boundaries and identities of minority groups are decided and imposed by outsiders through "externally located processes of social categorisation"' (Jenkins 1994, 197). On the one hand, Gypsy communities remain socially excluded by society, and, on the other, they choose to exclude themselves. That there is a relationship between these two actions seems unquestionable, as does a sense that the balance of power in such processes is strongly tilted towards the exclusion of Gypsies by society, rather than towards their self-exclusion. However, the precise balance of power still seems more open to debate: the formation of boundaries is not therefore a one-way process and it is certainly not one in which all control has been wrested from Gypsy communities.

This process of exclusion and self-exclusion and the setting and maintenance of boundaries that may protect and maintain the Gypsy lifestyle and Gypsy culture can be seen within the ambiguous negotiations of daily lives and experiences. It is clearly manifested, for example, in the degrees of acceptance and engagement families may have with the education system. Many Gypsy families regard it as important to send their children to school. In so doing, however, they might also hold different expectations to those of the school and other parents as to the sort of education that should be provided for their children; in some cases, this may be limited to children learning to read and write. Beyond this basic set of criteria the school may not be accepted as a legitimate place to educate children in any wider concepts, and the additional educational requirements of children will instead be regarded as the responsibility of family and community. Therefore, Gypsy children who attend school often have limits to their involvement in school life that are different from those of non-Gypsy children. There are boundaries to their participation and consequently to their acceptance by the school; so, for example, many Gypsy parents do not want their children to go on school trips because their interpretation of what constitutes a safe environment differs from that of the parents of non-Gypsy children. On some occasions members of the Traveller Education Service will accompany Gypsy pupils on a school trip in order to provide the assurance required by the child's family that their safety and welfare is being properly addressed. Other issues that may affect how Gypsy children take part in school life include participation in PE and sports activities, which again raises safety concerns; participation in sex education lessons, around which there are concerns about *gaujo* morals; and the wearing of jewellery, which may be forbidden by school's rules but regarded as an important cultural marker. As with school trips, these are all issues that have to be negotiated between school and family in order to ensure that agreement is reached about the basis on which Gypsy children will attend schools.

Whilst many other minority groups require schools to understand the various demands of their culture, in our research we found many schools that regarded some Gypsy families' requirements as either excessive or unnecessary. This in part is motivated by the types of misunderstanding and misrecognition discussed earlier; the cultural needs of Gypsy children may not be driven by identifiably religious or ethnic values, for example. Gypsy children may instead be identified simply as white children whose parents place a large number of awkward demands upon the school.

The participation of Gypsy children in school life is therefore based on a process of self-exclusion in which their engagement in the school is limited by their cultural values. These self-exclusionary practices further inform and become a part of other processes of exclusion, in particular when families were met with an unsympathetic response from the school. The engagement of Gypsy families with schools may well be determined by the schools' misunderstandings of Gypsy culture, in which Gypsy children are branded as troublemakers with behavioural problems as opposed to being viewed perhaps as children sticking up for themselves in the face of a culture that devalues them.

An acceptance of Gypsy culture by society, alongside the maintenance of their unique identity and separateness, would be considered by many Gypsy communities, like many other communities, to be the most ethical way of coexisting with wider society. Such a desire reflects an established strand of liberal multicultural thinking that seeks to recognise difference in a positive light and accepts the need to live with difference (as opposed to assimilating that difference within the normative culture). Within our own research there was a clear signal from different Gypsy communities that acceptance rather than assimilation was the way forward. This was understood within a context of other groups appearing to assimilate more successfully, which in our research was expressed powerfully as the perceived ability of other more recently arrived ethnic minority groups to 'work the system' through perceived assimilatory strategies, as a result receiving housing and other state benefits that Gypsy communities felt was denied to them because they expressed their difference by other means (see Bhopal and Myers 2005). Although such assimilation was seen as being successfully used as a means to an end, it was also clear that Gypsy communities felt that such assimilatory tactics would be counter-productive to the maintenance of a strong Gypsy culture and should therefore be resisted. Bauman (2001) argues that the process of nation-building can work in either an assimilatory or an exclusionary manner. The assimilatory method is loaded with imagery of being consumed by the host nation, the difference between cultures being eaten away and destroyed:

> The purpose of the assimilatory pressures was to strip the 'others' of their 'otherness', to make them indistinguishable from the rest of the nation's body, to digest them completely and dissolve their idiosyncrasy in the uniform compound of national identity. (Bauman 2001, 93)

The alternative is to be excluded, an option which, in Bauman's imagery, is again loaded with a degree of violence. It is suggestive of being cast out and ghettoised, but it also suggests that the minority group have a certain strength in the face of a hostile set of circumstances which allows them to maintain an identity and not become subsumed within an assimilatory process. Under such circumstances, notions of community may actually become stronger and more resilient as groups are forced to make a choice between defending what they value or surrendering everything. Weeks argues that:

> The strongest sense of community is in fact likely to come from those groups who find the premises of their collective existence threatened and who construct out of this a community of identity which provides a strong sense of resistance and empowerment. Seemingly unable to control the social relations in which they find themselves, people shrink the world to the size of their communities and act politically on that basis. (Weeks 2000, 240–3)

Given these two alternatives, of which one is to be assimilated and have your identity obliterated and the other is to be effectively cast out of society, we might conclude that this is not much of a choice at all. The presentation of such a stark set of alternatives will not produce an easy road to perpetual happiness and contentment, but it is the sort of choice that has been faced by Gypsy communities in Britain for a very long time. One reading of 500 years of not assimilating is that these groups have defended their culture in an extraordinarily robust fashion.

The impossibilities of self-exclusion

The term 'self-exclusion' has an oxymoronic feel to it; the very notion of exclusion seems to suggest something that is done to an individual or a group. To be 'exclusive' indicates restraint and holding back; it is something that we can easily envisage when we look at the world and see dominant or powerful groups on the one hand and subordinate, less powerful groups on the other hand. If we look at the elite public schools, for example, we can see that rich and well-connected parents pay for a particular education for their children. In principle, such schools provide an education that will deliver academic and social skills that ensure that rich kids become rich parents. Such schools sell an 'exclusive' education, one that excludes on the basis of wealth and social class. It is generally not the case that families from poorer backgrounds and of lower social class exclude themselves from such public schools. Generally we anticipate exclusion to work on this basis; power, money or status distances itself from the masses because it allows a privileged existence. Royalty don't shop at Tesco, government ministers don't use public transport (unless it's a photo opportunity), and celebrities are on the guest list. Such exclusivity is easily understood because it is a reflection of our everyday lives. The most excluded groups of people are those who sit uncomfortably on the furthest margins of society, be they children in care, homeless people, or people with mental health issues or drug problems. These groups are characterised in large part by the lack of power they can exert over their predicaments. They are not well situated to challenge the actions of wider society if those actions appear to make their lives harder and if they are further excluded from the wider benefits of society. Exclusion works in practice because the victims of exclusion in its most extreme manifestations are unable to resist the actions of significantly more powerful groups. Exclusion operates along an axis that at its extreme ends suggests impossible chasms that can never be crossed: the vast majority of middle-class parents will never realistically send their children to Eton or Gordonstoun, nor will they cadge a lift in a ministerial car. They may well, however, move house in order to enter the catchment area of the best local school, and they may well be treated seriously at an MP's monthly surgery.

The issue of exclusion operates differently for Gypsy groups partly because it is a useful opportunity for them to maintain a cultural identity. In part also, by reworking the generally accepted negative connotations that attach themselves to the process of exclusion within a self-exclusionary context, it is possible to recognise how this might produce a sense of esteem that would not generally be anticipated amongst other groups who are excluded. In this latter sense exclusion, by being produced at some level on Gypsy communities' own terms, could be seen as a strength in their relationship with wider society. In the first instance it is important to recognise that Gypsies are an excluded group and that exclusionary practices against Gypsies are commonplace and well-documented. Historically these practices have often included the inadequate provision of education, healthcare and accommodation, reflecting the low social status accorded to Gypsy groups. In part this status is a result of Gypsies being relatively powerless in engagements with wider communities and their institutions and therefore being unable to broker improvements to their living conditions. However, this does not appear to be the full story of Gypsy engagement with society; Gypsy groups are also apparently reluctant to be mobilised and perceived as a single political mass. There is no 'voice' for Gypsies that is in any way comparable to the community organisations and mouthpieces that represent other minority groups in the UK. This is not a criticism of Gypsy communities. Indeed, bearing in mind the internal criticisms often levelled at community leaders that they are unrepresentative of the communities they claim to represent, it may well be that Gypsy communities have a greater depth of understanding of their own differences than many other groups. However, it still seems startling that there is not a very vocal national organisation with a recognisable (to the general public) face that is overtly engaged in public dialogues with political institutions and media outlets in the UK.

In some respects this lack of a publicly recognisable mouthpiece flies in the face of general understandings of what it means to be a 'community'. When minority groups in the UK are faced with some new crisis one of the strengths by which they are seemingly judged in media and political terms is their ability to represent themselves as a community through the statements of community leaders. Often the 'community leader' in question is simply a religious leader of an embattled minority group, but the importance is attached to his representative power as a leader of community. We hear hints of Bauman's (2001) lost paradise of community in these instances; a certain nostalgia or longing for the sense of community that seems to have been lost in wider society but which can be imagined, albeit in a fashion that is never really pinned down to a tangible reality, within the lives of the 'other'. There are surprisingly positive associations made around the idea of 'community' that is believed to exist within Asian or black society in the UK. Representations of Gypsy 'community' do not materialise in the same way and this reflects a lack of visibility attached to community representations. 'Community', as an ideal state, is understood almost entirely as an absence within UK society, something that was once a national characteristic but has long since slipped away. If it only appears as a reminiscence or is heard as an echo within someone else's culture, then it becomes important to consider how Gypsy notions of a community that is active and ongoing could be understood within wider cultural debates. As discussed, Gypsy understandings of community are very strong – individuals, family groups and community groups are bound very closely together by various obligations and responsibilities – therefore, we might expect a nostalgic glance towards the Gypsy family on the part of wider society when considering what became of community more generally. However, Gypsy communities exhibit a fluidity that does not place itself easily within the idea of community as a feature of the nation state. Such fluidity is a strength that binds individuals, families and wider networks together in the face of hostility and within a context in which the response to such hostility may involve movement, dispersal or the concealment of identity. From the point of view of the nation state the 'Gypsy community' is a highly abstract version of community – one that in local terms is not bounded spatially, for example – and, when compared to other groups of 'others', does not sit together as a comfortable whole. Gypsy community does not meet the expectations of the nation state, even though it exhibits the strengths ascribed to community.

In this relationship the exclusivity of Gypsy culture can be understood. This is a community that does not feel the need to mimic ideals of community held within the western nation state and, by not doing so, it retains a type of community that belongs wholeheartedly to a Gypsy nationhood. Just as Gypsies are excluded within society by the many means discussed, there is also a sense that Gypsy groups are excluding wider society from the world of Gypsy communities. This can be read in a number of different ways. One of these is that Gypsies have self-excluded themselves from the dominant culture. The misreading of self-exclusion is to suggest that Gypsies are therefore responsible for all the exclusionary practices directed towards them, that they have brought all their troubles upon their own heads. Such a reading plainly ignores the hostility, racism and oppression faced by Gypsies at the hands of the dominant population over many years. Another reading of self-exclusion is that it allows an abstract space to be created within which the culture and way of life can be protected outside the very tangible spaces of the nation state. One final reading that should not be ignored is the issue of whether, by excluding *gaujos* from Gypsy culture, power is being exercised and a state of affairs implemented in which *gaujos* are excluded from something valuable. This 'something' could well be the ideal of community and the ability to re-imagine community in ways that do not reflect the very bound conceptions of community that tend to be generated within the nostalgic understandings of wider society. Instead, a strong sense of community that remains firm in the face of a very fluid and changing world, and can deal with traumatic historical events, feels like a very valuable commodity.

Notes

1. Jade Goody and her sidekicks' seeming racism towards Shilpa Shetty during the 2007 *Celebrity Big Brother* had catastrophic consequences for careers and earning potential.
2. http://www.chavscum.com.
3. 'Gorgios' is an alternative spelling for *gaujos*.
4. See Human Rights Usurp Planning Law, 4 October 2004, National Farmer's Union Countryside, http://www.countryside.org.uk.

5. Case study I: Inside the school gates: Gypsy families' experiences of education

This chapter is based on an ethnographic study that the authors have been engaged with in schools in a large metropolitan borough over a period of several years. It will examine the difficulties faced by schools who offer a multicultural approach to education that is overtly sympathetic to the needs of their largish Gypsy communities. In particular, it will describe problems encountered around claims of favouritism towards Gypsy children, the impossibility of keeping racism outside the school gates from entering the classroom and the clash of cultures in terms of the expectations of Gypsy families and teaching staff. One of the core findings from this work has been that even within the multicultural school, elements of misrecognition of Gypsy culture persist. As a result, Gypsy children and their parents retain a position of 'otherness' in their relationship with the school; they remain outside much of the daily social world fostered by the school and parents in general. In some respects this 'othering' is made more concrete by a multicultural approach.

Schools, education and Gypsies

There is a long history of well-documented concern around the education of Gypsy and Traveller[1] children (Plowden Report 1967;

Swann Report 1985; Bhopal *et al.* 2000 and a number of DfES reports 2003; 2005). This literature indicates that there are issues around access, attendance and achievement for Gypsy and Traveller pupils. The work of the Traveller Education Service (TES) over many years has resulted in an increase in the numbers of children attending primary school, but longstanding concern exists regarding the numbers of children failing to attend secondary school. Recent data (Ofsted 2003) reports that there may be around 12,000 Gypsy children who are not registered with any school. Within the context of the *Every Child Matters* agenda there is a requirement for schools to make adequate provision to address the needs and expectations of Gypsy and Traveller communities.

The DfES has shown that there is a continuing need to tackle and understand the underachievement of Gypsy and Traveller pupils in schools. In 2003 the department published *Aiming High: Raising the Achievement of Gypsy and Traveller pupils*, a guide offering practical advice and guidance for schools on how to develop effective polices and practices to raise the achievement of Gypsy and Traveller pupils. From 2003, 'Gypsy/Roma' and 'Travellers of Irish heritage' were included as categories in their own right in the Pupil Level Annual School Census data (PLASC). From data published in 2004/5, the DfES has analysed the performance of Gypsy and Traveller pupils; it argues that the data show cause for concern and that more help is needed for children from these communities to achieve their potential and succeed in schools. Schools and local authorities are obliged to comply with the statutory requirements under the Race Relations (Amendment) Act 2000 to monitor and assess the impact of their policies on children from Gypsy/Roma and Traveller backgrounds.

In recent years the DfES and TES have reported an increase in the number of families who have decided to opt for elective home education (EHE), and have expressed some concerns about this alternative route towards the education of children. There has been some concern that elective home education is being used as a device to avoid school attendance without legal penalty. It has also been argued that a majority of parents are not well equipped to deliver an education that is adequate or suitable for the needs of their children (DfES 2006). According to Ofsted:

> There is a growing trend among Traveller pupils for secondary age pupils, in particular, to be educated at home. The adequacy, suitability and quality of such provision are very uneven and raise serious concerns. (Ofsted 2003, 2)

Significantly, more recent research has indicated a 40 per cent year-on-year increase in EHE (DfES 2006). This increase appears to be tied to many of the historical reasons behind the reluctance of Gypsy parents to send their children to school, including fears of cultural erosion, a lack of relevance of the secondary school curriculum, concerns for the safety of children, and racism and other types of bullying (Derrington and Kendall 2004; Reynolds *et al.* 2003). However, other research (Bhopal 2004) has indicated that parents do want their children, both boys and girls, to get an education because families do not have the same economic opportunities that they had in the past and, in addition, there has been a general decrease in the amount of travel undertaken by nomadic families. In this context EHE could conceivably become an effective answer to both the concerns about schooling and the desire for an education.

There are a number of reasons why EHE can be problematic: it is often difficult to monitor the quality, scope and delivery of education within the home environment and this may result in children receiving only a very poor level of education and alternative options neither being identified nor made available; the inspection and monitoring processes for EHE across local authorities is uneven and, as a result, problems related to some children's education are not being identified; some families may not necessarily be in a position to manage and advance their children's home schooling because of poor literacy skills; and TES staff can often be put in a difficult position when parents approach them for support for EHE. This last point is a consequence of the funding arrangements for the TES, which are aimed solely at providing support for Gypsy children in schools. Officially the TES is unable to help with home education matters and should refuse to do so, but in reality it is often hard for them to do this as they know the families, have close relationships with them and often want to help the children and the families. If children were to receive a poor-quality education this would suggest a major conflict with the *Every Child Matters* agenda and other education policies.

If EHE is delivered effectively and Gypsy children receive an education that is adequate to their individual and personal needs, rather than the formal structured education and subjects that schools offer, then it can be very beneficial for the children. Many families feel their children are able to receive an education that will be more useful and helpful to them in later life than that on offer through traditional formal schooling. Some branches of the TES have indicated that the number of families who opt for EHE will grow, especially if families feel that this option will enable them to keep their children at home and avoid prosecution over school non-attendance. Families may also feel that this is one way of avoiding contact with 'official' organisations such as schools. Within the EHE framework it is up to parents to decide *how* to educate their children at home; they are not, for example, required to follow the national curriculum, which in itself may be a significant advantage for Gypsy children. In addition, parents are not legally required to inform their local authority that they are home schooling or of their change of address should they move. Furthermore, local authorities have no automatic right of access to parents' homes; however, the local authority has to be satisfied that the child is receiving an adequate education at home.

It can clearly be argued that Gypsy families are best placed to understand the educational needs of their children. By providing an education that meets their own needs, Gypsy families are to some extent strengthening and protecting their culture and community. There is, however, a question over how strongly EHE can figure within a community framework; one fear is that EHE reflects not just an opt-out from the practices of education but also from other social and community networks, be these wider non-Gypsy communities or other Gypsy communities.

Schools in the UK receive funding for Gypsy and Traveller children, as they do for other children, through the Education Formula Spending Share. In addition, Gypsy and Traveller children also benefit from the Vulnerable Children Grant (VCG). The VCG, which came into use in April 2003, merged several Standards Funds Grants, including the Traveller Achievement Grant, and was a substantial increase on the grant that it replaced. For 2005/6 the VCG grant allowed local authorities to allocate funding based on local needs in order to provide support to a range of vulnerable children, including those from Gypsy and Traveller backgrounds. Funding for Gypsy and Traveller children (via the VCG) goes to the TES, whose staff work closely with the local authorities and schools to improve levels of attendance and achievement, and also to raise the level of understanding of these groups on the part of the educational community. Local authorities have a statutory duty to ensure that education is available to children of compulsory school age and is appropriate to their age, abilities, aptitudes and any special educational needs they may have. This duty applies to children whether they are residing permanently or temporarily within the local authority area and therefore includes all Gypsy and Traveller children.

The 1999 report *Raising The Attainment Of Minority Ethnic Pupils*

(DfEE 1999) indicates that Gypsy and Traveller pupils are at the greatest risk of underachievement. As far back as 1985, the Swann Report identified Gypsy pupils as being strongly affected by racism and discrimination and indicated the need for stronger links between parents and schools in combating this problem. More recently, the Commission for Racial Equality has identified racism towards Gypsies as extreme, pervasive and totally unacceptable (Commission for Racial Equality 2006), and Ofsted (2003) has argued that Gypsies remain on the periphery of the education system. Travellers have been recognised by the European Parliament (Resolution 89/C) as being one of the most socially excluded groups in schools and as having the highest rate of illiteracy:

> it is important that mobility and uncertainty of lifestyle do not deny children their entitlement to a full education. Each school they attend should offer them the same opportunities it does other children and if or when their education is disrupted the TES network will do all it can to maintain continuity. (DfES 2005, 4)

In 2005 the DfES argued that one of the most effective ways to promote the achievement of Gypsy children is to ensure that they gain early access to education during the foundation stage. The Foundation Stage Profile, which underpins the ongoing statutory assessment process in the second year of the Foundation Stage, supports teachers and advisory staff and should be used to build high expectations and monitor the progress of the children at this early stage. The Profile should also be shared with parents to identify areas of achievement and areas of improvement.

The DfES report *Ethnicity and Education* (DfES 2006) identifies that Gypsies consistently have lower levels of attainment than other ethnic groups across all key stages, and that Gypsies make less progress than other similar white groups at primary and secondary levels. On average, Gypsy pupils do less well on the scales of the Foundation Stage Profile than the average for all other pupils. They also continue to perform less well than similar white British pupils during secondary school, and perform consistently below the average for all pupils across the key stages. In addition, Gypsies and Travellers of Irish heritage are over-represented among many categories of Special Educational Needs (SEN), including moderate and severe learning difficulties. Gypsies and Travellers of Irish heritage are also included in those groups (along with other minority ethnic groups) who are more likely to be excluded from school (permanently or for a fixed period) than other pupils. In 2003/4 the permanent exclusion rates of Gypsy and Travellers of Irish heritage were over four times that of the average for all pupils (DfES 2006). The literature suggests that a number of factors are implicated in these failures, ranging from those associated with schools, such as negative teacher attitudes, racism and bullying, and a curriculum perceived as lacking relevance, to factors associated with Gypsy cultures, such as the desire for teenaged boys to leave school to work with their fathers and pressures for girls to leave school around puberty because of concerns about *gaujo* moral standards.

The government has recognised the marginalised position of Gypsies in society and has begun to tackle this in a number of ways, including the publication of *Community Cohesion Standards for Schools* (Department for Communities and Local Government 2004). This document recognises that Gypsy children have particular needs within the education system and that, in order to close the attainment and achievement gap, assessment arrangements for these groups must ensure students are able to attain at the highest possible level and schools must ensure that no groups are put at a particular disadvantage. *The Improving Opportunity* report (Home Office 2005) has indicated that Gypsy groups are less likely to succeed than other minority ethnic groups and achieve poorly in formal examinations. The report also states that the government feels that it must focus on improving the achievement of Gypsy young people, who have the poorest recorded levels at GCSE of any minority ethnic group. The report argues that one of the ways in which we can try to build an inclusive society is by encouraging and advising schools to develop *Active Citizens in Schools* schemes and inclusive opportunities for volunteering and participating in the local community.

What becomes abundantly apparent when reviewing the work and interest shown in the education of Gypsy children is just how much time has been spent looking at the subject by government and by educationalists. It is probably the area of Gypsy life that has attracted the most attention from outside the communities themselves. This is in many ways hardly surprising and reflects a number of factors, not least the widely held assumption that the single best means of improving the life chances of individuals from deprived backgrounds is through the education system, improved educational opportunities at a young age having the greatest impact in ensuring future attainment. The engagement of Gypsy children with schools is also an area that is readily identifiable as an easy route into conducting research on Gypsies. There is a legislative requirement for all children to partake in formal education and for Gypsy children there are specific networks in place (the TES and Education Welfare Officers, for example) to ensure and promote their engagement. Education is therefore one sphere of life where contacts are in place between the Gypsy world and the dominant culture and its institutions. The same cannot so easily be said about other aspects of Gypsy life, such as work, housing or health.

The work that has been conducted regarding Gypsy education has, almost without exception, identified a number of themes that reappear continuously. These include the comparatively poor attendance and achievement records of Gypsy children, accounts of racism and name-calling towards Gypsies, bullying, and a perception amongst Gypsy families that the school curriculum offers only a limited amount that is useful within Gypsy culture. Even allowing for the very significant improvements in attendance that have been seen in the last forty years, it still seems striking that so much work should be revealing the same messages about the education of Gypsy children (Acton 2004).

In our own work we looked at schools in an urban context and we also uncovered many of the same concerns about Gypsy children's experiences of education. Our work looked at specific and institutional examples of 'good practice' and tried to understand and situate these more widely, in particular within geographical understandings about the intersection of different communities inside and outside the school. In particular, we examined how the locality of the school – that is, the streets and neighbourhoods surrounding the school where most of its pupils lived – affected the school's approach to Gypsy families. Our aim was to understand how Gypsy children's experiences of education are shaped by both the school's multicultural agenda and the wider impacts of society beyond the school gates.

Methodology

In 2004, the University of Greenwich funded a study to explore the social exclusion and marginalisation experienced by Gypsy children in relation to school achievement and attendance. This study included research in one primary and one secondary school and involved sixty case study interviews with professional educators (heads, assistant heads, heads of year, teachers and classroom assistants), parents and pupils attending the schools. The TES was instrumental in gaining access to the schools and acted as our 'gatekeepers', and through it we were initially introduced to families and children who agreed to participate in the research. The interviews were recorded and the data transcribed. All of the interviews with educational professionals took place in the school. Most of the interviews with parents and children took place in the school, but some took place at a nearby site in families' trailers. Permission to interview children was obtained from parents via the TES and a letter to parents explaining the aims of the project. None of the parents or the children refused to participate and this was indicative of the support the project received from the TES.

In some cases, where mothers felt uncomfortable with the research process it was agreed that a member of the TES would remain present throughout the interview. The authors felt that the presence of the TES member had some impact on the nature of responses and discussion; there was a suspicion that both the researchers and the respondents were slightly stilted in their conversation because (even if only at a very low level of consciousness) we were discussing subject matter that might be deemed sensitive by the TES. In later conversations with the TES it was confirmed that they also viewed their presence as slightly counter-productive to the aims of the project. It was not felt that the integrity of responses or questions was necessarily being undermined, nor that the honesty with which these conversations were approached was called into question. There was simply a sense that all the participants may have been slightly more guarded than would have been ideal and that on occasion some things may have been left unsaid. Generally it was felt that there was a good degree of engagement in the research process.

Some interviews were not tape-recorded at the request of respondents; their reasons included a disinclination to have their words on tape and a desire that others should not hear what they had said. They were happy, however, to allow the researchers to record their responses in note form. The data analysis consisted of generating themes around issues that were discussed in relation to the project objectives; that is, issues around social exclusion, marginalisation and 'good practice'.

Case study I: Inside the school gates

As a result of this initial work the authors later secured further funding to carry out more wide-ranging research on 'good practice' in schools throughout the borough. The aims of the research were to identify schools which had large numbers of Gypsy children attending and then to examine themes of social exclusion and marginalisation as they pertained to these groups. Access to the schools was obtained through the Ethnic Minority Achievement Service (EMAS) and the TES. In addition to the core aims of the specifically funded work, a considerable and useful wider awareness was developed in the margins of both projects. In particular, connections were maintained with a number of people over a long period of time because the research process was conducted over a period of two years. Many subjects and conversations were revisited in less formal settings than the interviews and these findings also feed into the research.

Interview data was analysed using methods of grounded theory (Strauss and Corbin 1990). It was indexed in relation to particular themes and categorised under topics and headings from which to build theory. We coded data on description of text, interpretation of the relationship between text and interaction and explanation of the relationship between interaction and social context. By focusing on the ways in which respondents spoke about themselves and other groups we were able to make sense of the events that they experienced, enabling us to understand the meanings they attributed to different groups, events and contexts and to analyse the language they used to describe them.

Woodvale School[2] and its locality

The research was carried out in a large metropolitan borough where there is a large population of English Roma Gypsies. They have been in the area for over fifty years and in the wider locality for several hundred years. Although the Gypsies who participated in the research were primarily from English Roma backgrounds, other Gypsies from many diverse backgrounds, including Irish, Scottish and European Travellers, also reside in the area. Many of these other families were perhaps more isolated or distanced from their wider communities and in some cases preferred to be discreet about their ethnic origins. The same concerns were not an issue in anything like the same degree for the English Roma families, who in large part were members of an obviously identifiable community. Most of these families live on an official Traveller site in static caravans, although some were living in housing in the surrounding area. There is a long history of children from this community attending the local primary and secondary schools. Gaining access to the families provided the opportunity to explore their specific experiences of and engagement with the formal education system.

The area in which the interviews took place is predominantly a white working-class area surrounded by council estates. It is an area that can be described as socially deprived on the basis of a number of indicators: unemployment in the locality is high, home ownership and household car ownership is low.

Much of the research was completed at Woodvale School, where the majority of Gypsy children of secondary school age were enrolled. The school was situated in closest proximity to the official site and had built longstanding relations with the families living there. The school itself has a diverse ethnic mix reflecting considerable changes in the last five years, but this does not necessarily reflect the ethnic make-up of the locality. Those children from minority ethnic backgrounds (predominantly Somali, Asian and Afro-Caribbean) tended not to live in the immediate vicinity and often travelled some distance to the school. Ofsted described the school in 2001 as being:

> an average sized 11 to 16 mixed comprehensive, with 885 on roll. There are slightly more boys than girls. White European pupils

account for the majority of the school roll. There are five per cent Indian, 12 percent Black African heritage and two per cent Black Caribbean pupils. Recently a number of Kosovan and Somalian pupils have joined the school. [Woodvale] is the main receiving secondary school for Traveller pupils in [the Borough]. Objective indicators identify the area as having high levels of social deprivation. Educational aspirations, as measured by the percentage of adults with higher education, are very low. (Ofsted 2001, 7).

Findings

Some of the more interesting findings from the research related to the interactions between Gypsies and non-Gypsies, schools and communities, and localities and communities. Sometimes quite complex relationships of difference were played out in minor aspects of school life, such as the rules concerning the wearing of jewellery. As would also be expected, major issues such as racism had huge impacts on people's engagements with the school. In all cases, however, there was a feeling that it was crucial to place understandings within the wider contexts of the immediate locality and the world outside the school gates.

School rules and policies: problems of favouritism

The school has a number of policies that have very particular impacts on the experiences of Gypsy children; these include policies relating to bullying, equal opportunities and racism, and the wearing of jewellery. This last issue was the source of a surprising amount of concern for some teachers. Pupils were allowed to wear earrings no larger than the size of a ten pence piece. However, as many Gypsy children at the school made clear, the wearing of somewhat large and ostentatious jewellery is an important part of their cultural identity. The school adopted a fairly flexible approach towards the wearing of jewellery by Gypsy children and in some cases it was clear that the rules were slightly bent to accommodate them. The thrust for this approach came from the more senior members of the school (the head and deputy head in particular), and was clearly an issue for some staff. One head of year commented:

> We have a policy here that you have to wear earrings the size of a ten pence piece but for some children this is not the case. Some of the Traveller kids are allowed to wear whatever jewellery they want and this bothers some people. What happens is you get other kids saying that it's one rule for them and one rule for us and that can bother them.

Other teachers viewed the issue differently and suggested it was not a problem, just an example of the school coping with diversity amongst different pupils. One classroom teacher said:

> I think it's ok that some of the Traveller kids are allowed to wear earrings that are a bit bigger than the 10p rule. It's the same for other groups, we would let girls wear something in their nose if they said it was part of their culture or their religion and we do make many provisions. We want to make sure that we treat the children fairly and take into consideration what they say and that we respect their culture, no matter what that culture may be.

It was apparent from the energetic responses that it produced that the ten pence piece rule was an important issue. It was also very obviously an issue that spoke more widely of the understandings of culture that teachers, children and parents brought to the school. Within different discourses in the school there were a number of alternative explanations offered for the ten pence piece rule. Whilst for some the demonstration of the school's flexibility was an indication of a respect held for the culture and lifestyle of Gypsy children, a counter-interpretation argued that this was a demonstration of favouritism towards Gypsy children. In this case, rules were understood to be broken rather than simply bent.

The size of earrings permitted in schools can seem a trivial matter but to treat it as such would be a mistake. For the children involved it represented an everyday part of their lives and any prohibition would have lead to a daily sense of grievance about attendance at school. For some of the teachers it represented a daily reminder that Gypsy pupils were treated differently and that the school rules were not being upheld. The resonances of this interpretation of the school rules seep out beyond the school gates and inform wider community understandings of the school. One of the Gypsy children interviewed indicated that she respected the head of Woodvale:

> Mrs White[3] is great because really we're not supposed to wear big earrings but she lets us and she listens to us and we like that, 'cos most people don't.

And this sentiment was echoed by a parent:

> I think the school understands our culture and what that means to us and they make an effort to allow the children to do and not to do some things.

Understandings of the school institution by Gypsy families were shaped by a clear awareness of the head's role in promoting policies felt to be sympathetic towards Gypsy culture and Gypsy children in the school. This was situated in a context of wider understandings of other institutions that were considered less overtly sympathetic towards Gypsy culture. Such sentiments also materialised within the research as a sense of ownership towards the school (referred to by Gypsy parents on many occasions as 'our school') and an engagement with a locality that could be envisaged as encompassing the local authority site where many of the families lived and the school.

The corollary of these sentiments is the accusations of favouritism which themselves have very strong echoes of the world beyond the school gates. This world materialised (and is discussed at greater length in Chapter 6) most vividly in the middle of our research during the 2005 general election campaign, during which media stories and right-wing politicians suggested that the Human Rights Act was being deliberately invoked to allow Gypsies to get around planning laws that non-Gypsies were bound to abide by. The bending of rules in favour of minorities by institutions perceived as being liberal-minded carries with it a potent set of understandings about the ways in which some parts of dominant society feel they have been poorly treated. In particular, and again this is discussed in greater depth in other chapters, the sense that British white cultural identity has felt the impact of great change and uncertainty since the Second World War produces a framework in which such actions appear threatening.

Racism – inside and outside the school gates
One of the most striking aspects to emerge from the research was the issue of racism, both that experienced by the Gypsy pupils and the racism they demonstrated towards other minority ethnic groups.

Racism outside the school is perceived as being a major problem. The area is notorious for having a strong British National Party (BNP) following and at one time the BNP maintained a national office less than a mile away from the school. Woodvale School has a Race Equality Officer whose role is to record racist incidents and to deal with them with both the perpetrator and the victim. However, there are very few recorded incidents of racism within the school. Despite this, many of the teachers indicated that racism towards Gypsy pupils was a problem. Mrs Jeffries, a head of year, said:

> I think that some kids can be racist towards them they call them names like 'dirty gyppo', but I think it's not that bad in the school. It's worse outside the school gates. This area is like that and has been for a while. The people round here think it's their territory and they don't like different people moving in. That's why I think there's a problem with the Somali kids and sometimes that comes into the school. The Gypsy kids don't get on with the Somali kids and there can be problems.

And in fact parents did indicate that their children often experienced racism inside the school:

> Yeah it happens all the time. People call us names, they think we're dirty and smelly but we're not like that. We are proud and I'm proud to be a Traveller and don't care what any of them says.

The children also said they had experienced racism:

> People call us names because we're Gypsies, but they don't know what we're like and they think we're troublemakers, but we just stick up for ourselves.

The interviews also revealed the overt racism demonstrated by Gypsy children towards other groups. This was evident in some of the comments made both by teachers and by the children themselves. According to one classroom teacher, there was a suggestion that Gypsy children felt they could 'get away' with name-calling:

> I have had experience of them calling other black kids names because of their colour. They try not to do it when we are around,

but there have been times when I have heard things. I have always picked up on this and questioned them about it. It seems that they are allowed to do this. Even though they are a group who experience discrimination themselves, they are still negative towards other groups and I find that hard to understand.

The racism demonstrated by Gypsy children towards other minority ethnic groups was evidently not a reflection on the school's 'good practice'; it was something that existed outside the school and was brought into the school. As one child said:

… yeah, if I have a fight with someone I will call her a black bitch, but she'll call me a 'dirty gyppo' … my dad wouldn't let me marry or go with a black man, it's just not right.

One of the parents also echoed these feelings:

We don't really mix with them people [black people]. We don't like them and they don't like us and it's better to keep it that way. We don't want to live near them, and we want them to keep away from us.

The racism demonstrated by Gypsies seemed driven in part by the community's engagement with the local area. Other minority groups were regarded as muscling in and trying to integrate with the locality in a way that the Gypsy community has not done and in a way that they felt unable to tolerate. Although it is slightly contradictory, there is a suggestion that Gypsies wanted to both maintain their distance from the wider community but at the same time express an attachment to this community. One parent commented that:

Because they're black they're better off than us. They come here and they get more than us and they get treated good. We've been here for longer than them and have to fight for what we got.

The Gypsy children, like many of their non-Gypsy peers, were actively engaged in racist behaviour and this informed much of their engagement with the school. On the one hand they were clearly victims of racism and bullying, but on the other they were the perpetrators of similar behaviour. This in itself impacted on the views of some of the teaching staff and could perhaps be seen to offer further evidence of Gypsy children being accorded special status by the school's leadership. There was actually no evidence to suggest that any teaching staff allowed Gypsy children to get away with racist behaviour, but there was a clear perception amongst some staff that this was in fact the case. One reading of this evidence is that the sentiments of multiculturalism, which were very strong in the school, can be seen to be almost a reward or compensation for ethnic minority status, which status thus equates to victimhood. Within this understanding, the racist actions of Gypsy children towards other ethnic minority groups are read as a rejection of this reward. So an argument that sits quite comfortably within the pages of many national newspapers – that Gypsy culture is allowed to get away with behaviour that is not tolerated amongst the rest of the population and that this is the fault of misplaced liberalism – is effectively reproduced within the much more specific contexts of the school. Within the school, multiculturalism is responsible for some minor adaptations of school rules towards the needs of minority cultures (Gypsies and other groups) and at the same time Gypsy children are engaged in practices that do not sit comfortably within a liberal or multicultural stance. The Gypsy children are then viewed as not being worthy of the efforts being made on their behalf and as not fitting the stereotypical role assigned to them by parts of the school.

An alternative reading of the racist behaviour exhibited by

Gypsy children is that it very clearly reflected the racism and behaviour characteristic of the streets outside the school. Patterns of behaviour were transferred from understandings created outside the school and put into a new context within the school. In this context some more overt behaviour is seemingly hidden, especially from the eyes of staff, but, equally, much remains visible on the surface, particularly in circumstances such as a fight or an argument. It is apparent that racism reflects engagements with both the wider community and the multicultural institution.

Viewed in a very absolute, over-critical fashion, the multicultural institution is seen to fail on a number of accounts. Either it is associated with the reproduction of illiberal attitudes amongst its own staff that replicate intolerant understandings of Gypsy culture outside the school, or it is associated with simply reproducing the racisms endemic outside the school within its confines. A less critical viewpoint, one that we share, would note the seriousness with which the leadership of a school like Woodvale approach the task of delivering education in a multicultural fashion that is sensitive to the needs of all their pupils. The conditions in which the school functions, in particular in an environment in which many different types of racism are common currency, invariably influences what happens within the school.

A clash of cultures? Gypsy expectations and teacher expectations

From our interviews it was clear that many of the teachers and professional educators were sympathetic to the experiences of Gypsy families. A classroom teacher indicated that the Gypsy children she encountered were trying hard to fit in with the school culture, efforts for which they should be recognised and praised:

> I know it's hard for them because their home life is very different from what we do here. They have rules and they have a structure

here that they have to follow – just like all the other children – and most of them are able to do that and they get on with it. I think that we have to commend them for that, rather than just looking for the bad things they do and saying that they misbehave and have a problem with authority.

This was also echoed by a head of year:

I think when teachers first start to come and work here and they have never worked with Traveller kids before, they don't really know how to handle them and then they realise that we have to be tough with them. We can't let them just do what they want and because of that they realise this and so most of them do as they are told.

A small number of teachers, however, were not so positive about Gypsies. One teacher, a head of year who had been teaching at the school for five years, felt that the Gypsy children were just out to cause trouble. When asked about her relationship with the children and what she felt about them she was at first reluctant to respond and did so only when we assured her that she would remain anonymous:

To be honest, I don't really like them [Gypsy children]. They can't handle the fact that they have to do what we tell them and if they don't then they will get in trouble and be punished. I think they are allowed to get away with murder at home and so they think they can do this here. But they can't. We have rules here, it is a school and they have to follow the rules like everyone else, what makes them so different?

She then went on to describe how Gypsy children thought they could get away with 'doing what they want':

> I think they are very cocky. And I think a lot of the other kids are scared of them because they can be bullies. They can say things to other kids, but the kids can't say anything back to them. Because if they do, then all the other Traveller kids come and join in and they stick up for each other. Last year we had an incident here where one of the Traveller kids had a fight with a non-Traveller and threatened to bring her dad and cousins round and that's why people are scared of them. They think they can take things into their own hands and they do.

For some teachers there seemed to be a general lack of understanding of Gypsy culture and what that entailed. There also seemed to be an expectation that Gypsy parents did not want their children to get an education:

> I don't know why they have such a problem with coming to school. All the other kids do it, so why can't they do it? It has to be the parents, they don't want their kids to come to school and that to me shows that they don't care if their kids get an education or not.

As discussed, however, there has been a great deal of research looking at the reasons why some Gypsy families do not want to send their children to school, but there is also evidence of a cultural shift away from such standpoints towards a more positive perception of the value education can offer children (Bhopal 2004). These same themes emerged in the interviews with parents and were reflected by one mother who stressed the importance she placed on her children getting a good education:

> I think people don't know about us so they say things that aren't so. We do want our kids to get an education, they have to learn to read and write. They have to get a job. There's no jobs for them

now like there used to be, so they have to go out to work. I wants all of mine to get an education. I didn't get it, but they should.

Although some parents did not themselves have a formal education and in some cases were unable to read and write, this did not mean that they wanted their children to repeat their experiences. In a number of cases parents stressed the need for an education that merely taught their children to read and write:

I think as long as they can read and write that's all I want from them. The boys will get work anyway, but they must be able to read and write. The girls should do, but I don't think most of them will work. It depends what they do.

The children themselves, however, on the whole did not really like to be at school. For them, the structure and rules were hard to follow. Jack, a 12-year-old boy, indicated this:

Sometimes I don't want to get up and come to school. I hate it. I would rather stay at home. I don't like the teachers much, they tell us to do too many things and they don't like it if you answer them back. They always think they are right and we're not allowed to say anything about it.

When asked why he came to school, he responded:

To be honest, my mum doesn't really mind I think. It's because she thinks she's going to get into trouble if she doesn't tell me to come. I would like to go out with my dad and brother. He didn't go to school and nor did my brother and they both work now. People at the school don't understand this and when I try and talk to the teachers they think I'm back-chatting to them.

Julie, a 13-year-old girl, echoed this feeling:

> I don't think I need to come to school. I won't use it anyway. What I will do is get married and won't need any of this. So they are wasting my time. That's what Traveller girls do. We don't work like you do. We stay with our people and that's because they know us.

Within the diversity of these responses perhaps the only clear conclusion is that teachers, parents and children often failed to share similar expectations about the education of children. Although most of the teachers were sympathetic to the needs and cultural background of Gypsies and most were aware of their traditions and lifestyle, there were also some teachers who were not so positive. In a very few cases teachers displayed very negative attitudes towards Gypsy families, their cultural backgrounds and their values. The existence of teachers who were overtly hostile to Gypsy children was telling, as they worked within different types of schools, including those like Woodvale, which were considered to deliver a multicultural education that was generally sympathetic towards Gypsy needs. Where there was hostility it reflected both an understanding that Gypsy children did not engage with the values and processes of the school and a reflection of wider stereotyping about Gypsy engagement with the education process. What was evident within such responses was the lack of awareness on the teacher's part of some of the families' desire for their children to receive an education.

For many families it felt as though they were balancing a desire for education for their children against a desire to protect their children, their cultural identity and traditions. In a number of cases there was an identifiable conflict between expectations of what a school education might look like (just reading and writing, for example) and the realities of a school curriculum. Engagement with the multicultural ethos of some of the schools seemed limited to an understanding that Gypsy culture was recognised within the school gates. Whilst this was often an understandable reflection of historical engagements between parents and schools it reinforced a number of negative and stereotypical expectations of Gypsy families with some teachers.

Many of the children indicated that they did not enjoy school and the main reason for their attendance was the threat of sanctions faced by the parents for non-attendance, such as visits from Education Welfare Officers and the threat of legal procedures. Many children, particularly boys, felt their parents would be happy if they stayed at home. For girls schooling was often seen as a way in which they could embark on careers such as hairdressing or floristry (certainly being able to read and write was considered uniformly of value). At the same time, however, it was felt that formal schooling might threaten cultural erosion. Again, it was very clear from listening to the children that much of their understanding of the school was shaped by wider cultural reference points such as their families and the world outside the school gates.

Multiculturalism – inclusion or exclusion?

Woodvale School clearly demonstrated both its intent and ability to put 'good practice' into action in its relationship with Gypsy families. This was perhaps best highlighted in a photography exhibition that both recognised children's own knowledge and allowed an expression of their culture, demonstrated in ways that linked to the school curriculum. The exhibition included coursework developed by the school that examined the experience of the Gypsy diaspora in the Middle Ages and during the Holocaust. Here, the personal experience of the local Gypsy community was placed firmly within the culture and curriculum of the school. The approach of Woodvale School was, however, very different to that of other schools within the borough and beyond. In addition, the school inevitably remained engaged in the wider social trends of its locality. Racism expressed outside the school gates inevitably impacted on life within the school: Gypsies are subject to racism and this is reflected in the experiences of Gypsy children within the school. In general, incidents of racism towards Gypsies appeared to be dealt with effectively. Gypsy racism towards other groups, particularly Somali children, also reflected an unwelcome intrusion of attitudes from outside the school. There were hints from some teaching staff that incidents of racism by Gypsy children towards other children were treated less severely than was racism directed towards Gypsies. As no Somali children or children from other ethnic backgrounds were interviewed during this research, questions regarding this matter are left unanswered and specific interpretations cannot be reached. One reading might be that Gypsy children are in some way treated more favourably than other groups within the school; another would be that the portrayal of Gypsy children as being more favourably treated is in itself a misrecognition, possibly one motivated by racism, of these children. Given the context of some discussions of favouritism towards Gypsy children, such as the ten pence piece jewellery rule, there seems to be evidence of rule-bending in favour of Gypsy children.

If the school practises rule-bending it is seemingly within another context that is generated outside the school gates; that is, the difficulties of providing a multicultural experience of education. Traditionally multicultural approaches fall between two opposing poles: that of respecting and celebrating difference; or that of offering a difference-blind experience, treating all pupils exactly the same. Woodvale School would appear to fall firmly in the former camp in its attempts to both respect and celebrate the differences and difficulties of Gypsy families' culture. The immediate benefits are that Gypsy children are afforded opportunities to influence how the wider school perceives them and to have their culture respected within the school. This is undoubtedly a positive approach to the needs of Gypsy children and one that is sadly not generally reflected in many other schools with responsibility for educating Gypsy children. Questions of favouritism need to be considered, not least because there is an underlying suspicion that the engagement of Gypsy children with the education process would benefit from being within a context of equal respect for the cultures of their peers. This still needs to be read in the context of the excellent work of the teachers, pupils and the TES at Woodvale School.

Notes

1. The terms 'Gypsy' and 'Traveller' are used predominantly in this chapter to reflect the terminology used throughout much DfES literature. DfES concerns around Gypsy and Traveller education obviously reflect a wide remit of work with many different groups, including, for example, New Age Travellers. Since 2003/4 the categories 'Gypsy' and 'Traveller of Irish heritage' have been used in data collected for the Pupil Level Annual School Census (PLASC). Where appropriate these terms are also referred to in this chapter.
2. 'Woodvale School' is a pseudonym.
3. All names are pseudonyms.

6. Case study II: Media representations of Gypsy life in election year

For a brief period in March and April 2005 newspaper coverage of issues around the lives of Gypsies suddenly became a very hot topic. The immediate context for these stories was a virulently hostile campaign against Gypsy sites that was running across the pages of *The Sun* under the slogan 'Stamp on the Camps'. The newspaper outlined its role as standing up for the rights of its readers, who throughout this campaign were often described as being representative of 'Middle England'. This description seems slightly at odds with *The Sun*'s traditional image as the voice of a working-class readership. It may well, however, reflect a strategy to lure readers away from *The Daily Mail*, a newspaper whose readers have long been associated with descriptions of 'Middle England'. In this respect *The Daily Mail* has tapped into a lucrative market, as demonstrated by its standing as the second biggest selling UK national newspaper; only *The Sun* sells more copies.

If *The Sun* introduced a campaign about Gypsy issues solely as part of a marketing strategy, this would say something interesting about the engagement between Gypsy and non-Gypsy communities, in particular that representations of Gypsies are bound up in non-Gypsy society; that is to say, constructed ideas of Gypsies seemingly have a life of their own, and can play out within discourses of the dominant population including the economies of the newspaper marketplace. However, *The Sun*'s campaign was also driven by its ongoing spat with the then Deputy Prime Minister, John Prescott. His department, the Office of the Deputy Prime Minister (ODPM), was involved in promoting policy that would arguably make it easier for Gypsies to obtain planning permission to build permanent caravan sites. It was the effects of these policies upon the newspaper's readers that *The Sun* identified as the starting point of the stories it was to run with. *The Sun*'s coverage of stories focussing on specific issues around the lives of Gypsies seemed to be intensified in part, because it became entangled with more overtly political storylines and political agendas.

In political terms March 2005 was a tense time, with politicians and media all anticipating the long-awaited announcement of the next General Election and the start of official electioneering. Covert election campaigns were, inevitably, already in progress and the Gypsy stories being run by *The Sun* quickly became caught up with an intervention by the Conservative Party. Advertisements were placed in the Sunday newspapers of 20 March by the Conservatives carrying the text of a speech given by Michael Howard, then leader of the opposition, at Conservative Campaign Headquarters. In these advertisements Michael Howard flagged up his position under the personal statement 'I believe in fair play', and went on to argue that it was unfair that Gypsies were not subject to the same laws as the rest of the population. He suggested that Gypsies were being allowed greater leeway to build under planning law than would be afforded to the general population. New Labour was accused of kowtowing to the Human Rights Act, with the result that the ODPM effectively interpreted planning law in a more lenient fashion for Gypsies than for the rest of the population. Whilst the stories run by *The Sun* included a lot of collateral unpleasantness about the lives of Gypsies that Michael Howard, in his speech, did not make explicit, the nub of both arguments was the unfair interpretation of planning law.

Case study II: Media representations of Gypsy life

One fairly straightforward reading of the advertisement placed by the Conservative Party is that it was simply an opening salvo in the as yet undeclared, but imminent, election campaign, its focus being to engage and challenge ODPM policy and, by extension, the Deputy Prime Minister. The close links between Prescott and Tony Blair and the New Labour project were always going to ensure that the ODPM was targeted by its opponents on purely political grounds. In addition, Prescott's reputation for losing his temper publicly, mangling his vocal delivery and being an enforcer of New Labour discipline made him a target worth baiting. Such an attack on the ODPM also ensured that the Conservatives could adopt a wider stance opposing a perceived 'lefty-liberal' standpoint associated with the promotion of Human Rights legislation. Such legislation had resonances with a demonised European political agenda and as such made a comfortable target within a Conservative agenda that placed British interests at its heart. As a campaign position it sits amongst a diverse collection of affiliated platforms that may have little true ideological connection. Brought together, however, they supply a rallying cry – 'what about us?' – to another self-identifying group of Middle Englanders, namely the rump (in 2005, at any rate) of Conservative electoral support. The 'I believe in fair play' advertisement was part of an ongoing series that ran under another slogan, 'Are you thinking what we're thinking?' This seems to allude to a sense that the Conservative support was largely identified as a silent minority that needed to be roused in order to make its voice heard.

A second, but related, reading (whilst still acknowledging the empathic draw of these issues for a Conservative election campaign) might consider that this campaign was motivated more opportunistically. As *The Sun* was already running the stories about Gypsies, the Conservative press office was presented with a timely and simple opportunity involving little more than jumping onto *The Sun*'s bandwagon, allowing the party to make easy and literally cheap political capital out of the newspaper's campaign. The concern that should be raised about this second reading is the allegiance that is then brought into being between *The Sun*'s descriptions of Gypsy lives (explored in greater detail below, but generally situated around stereotypes of dirt, scrounging and violence) and a major political party. Contacting Michael Howard by email was encouraged by the Conservative Party at the time; however, when the authors attempted to pose some relatively innocuous questions through this channel to sound out the thinking behind the newspaper advertisement, they were met by a polite but unenlightening response; Michael 'welcomed our interest in this issue'.[1]

This chapter will look particularly at the newspaper coverage generated on a single day – Monday 21 March 2005 – across the pages of *The Sun* and *The Independent*, and at the wider political 'moment'. Both newspapers led with front-page spreads about Gypsies, *The Independent* unsurprisingly producing a far more sympathetic account than that of *The Sun*. This was the day *after* the Conservative Party placed advertisements in the Sunday newspapers and Michael Howard delivered his related speech (though the text of that speech, which closely followed that of the advertisements, had already been circulated to news desks in order to inform Monday's headlines and news stories). *The Sun* and *The Independent* have been chosen as the focus for this chapter for a number of reasons, not least because these newspapers assumed diametrically opposite standpoints. It is revealing to examine how such conflicting accounts also shared some common ground, particularly in their approach to the construction of a representation of Gypsies that would be understandable to their respective readerships. Two other important reasons for choosing these newspapers also stand out. Firstly, *The Sun* had been running what was to all intents and

Case study II: Media representations of Gypsy life

purposes an anti-Gypsy campaign under its 'Stamp on the Camps' slogan and so, in many respects, elect themselves for closer scrutiny. *The Independent*'s response was also pitched within a similar campaigning approach, one designed to oppose the work of *The Sun*, as highlighted by *The Independent*'s front page headline, 'Are These Britain's Most Demonised People?' Secondly, both newspapers used distinctive photographic imagery within their stories in ways that seemed to underscore the accounts given within the texts. This provides another, quite particular, point of comparison between these two newspapers.

The representations that are made about Gypsies in press coverage are important in understanding newspapers' relations with their readerships – those people willing to put their hands in their pockets and pay hard cash for the final product. Such representations also have wider resonances, as evidenced by the cross-cutting interests of *The Sun* and the Conservative Party, but perhaps more importantly in the relationships delineated between Gypsy communities and other groups of people summed up as 'Middle England' or similarly representative categories of readers. The process of pinning down such relationships and establishing the depth of meaning behind them is part and parcel of the production of an understanding of the nation state. The symbolic boundaries within which nationals must remain, if they are to be considered to belong within the state and the nation, are under construction within these discourses. There is also some sense of the strength of these boundaries being tested when they are ostensibly challenged, for example in *The Independent*'s coverage.

Apart from coverage in *The Sun* and *The Independent*, there were stories touching on Gypsy issues in nearly all the national newspapers that day. This was unsurprising in the light of the Howard speech and the Conservative newspaper advertisements, which generated many articles commenting on Gypsy issues with relation to Conservative election campaign strategies. However, it is also evident from the range of other coverage that appeared on the day that there was an ongoing media interest in Gypsies. *The Daily Mail*, for example, carried three pieces about Gypsies. The first was a news story based on the Howard speech and the advertisements in the Sunday papers, contextualised by reference to changes in Irish law that criminalised trespass primarily as it applies to Gypsies. According to *The Daily Mail*, 'The tough Irish laws are said to be one of the main reasons why so many travellers have moved to England' (Paul Eastham, 21 March 2005, p.1).

The Daily Mail also carried quotes from Keith Hill, the Minister for Planning, and Andrew Ryder, co-ordinator of the Gypsy and Traveller Law Reform Coalition, both of whom suggested that the Conservative Party was whipping up prejudice against Gypsies. This article specifically commented on the Conservative Party's successes at manipulating the media away from stories that the Government and the Labour Party were trying to promote. The second article was a reasonably long commentary piece entitled 'Travellers Tales: A Dossier of Despair', in which we learn that:

> For generations, country dwellers and travellers have lived amicably side by side. Their lifestyles were radically different but traditional British tolerance saw that there was a mutual respect for one another. (*The Daily Mail*, 21 March 2005, p.10)

Picking up on the earlier article suggesting an influx of Irish travellers, it was suggested that this state of amicable co-existence was under threat, and that 'since exposing the issue, *The Daily Mail* has been inundated with calls and emails from distraught readers whose lives have been made unbearable by these illegal sites' (21 March 2005, p.10). Eight readers' accounts then followed, detailing a number of consistent themes predictably centring on commonly held opinions about Gypsies, including

Case study II: Media representations of Gypsy life

their dirtiness and engagement in illegal activities. However, some other very specific issues also emerged including concerns about the desecration of beauty spots and disruption to local ecologies; repeated assertions that John Prescott would not be happy if he were to wake up one morning and find Gypsies living on his doorstep (often allied to threats that the reader in question would be happy to camp out in the Deputy Prime Minister's garden); falling house prices; and a sense that Gypsies were allowed to break the law, whereas non-Gypsies would be punished if they committed similar offences. Finally, there was a short piece in which a Gypsy and a non-Gypsy responded to the question 'can Gipsies live peacefully with neighbours?' This last piece was somewhat contrived and perhaps its biggest failing was that it did not allow the two opposing speakers to engage in a dialogue with each other. This is a shame and something of a missed opportunity; with these two voices in conversation the piece would have the potential to develop into something more interesting. However, on the Gypsy side there was discussion of the Holocaust, the role of Gypsies fighting in the Second World War and long-standing Gypsy engagements with the education system. On the non-Gypsy side the suggestion was made that most of the people calling themselves Gypsies are not 'proper gipsies', and that these are people who do not belong within commonly understood notions of 'community'.

The Daily Mail's coverage was, as would be anticipated, largely hostile to Gypsies. What seems surprising about its coverage is that it was quite detailed and reflected an engagement with its readers. Apart from the specifically news-based article there was a considerable involvement with reader's lives; what seems to drive these stories is not that they are about Gypsies, but rather that they are about another slice of Middle England, that is, *Daily Mail* readers. The question 'what about us?' is heard again and again in these stories; a Worcestershire teacher is quoted as saying:

> If I want to build a conservatory on my house without planning permission ... it would be pulled down because that is the law. The double standard is what upsets people in this area. Many of the farmers, for example, want to build houses for their families. (21 March 2005, p.11)

And in the same article a Wiltshire resident complains:

> With their dogs and children the travellers make a hell of a lot of noise. But what can I do? I've complained and complained but no one seems to be listening. (21 March 2005, p.10)

The tone of many of the stories is at times almost desperate, and the newspaper mines a rich seam of anxiety within these accounts, one that exposes real fears about the inner security not just of the people who are telling the stories, but also the wider readership. These stories recount popular stereotypes about Gypsy neighbours being responsible for creating mess and disruption in the lives of non-Gypsies, but they also go beyond this to paint a far bleaker picture. There is a suggestion in these stories that the meaning of people's lives is simply snatched away from them; their world and environment are desecrated and they can no longer feel safe in their homes. A businessman is quoted as saying: 'I'm so frightened of the camp I rarely go home any more. I would rather sleep in my van than return each night. It's an utter nightmare' (21 March 2005, p.10). And a graphic designer describes how:

> This lane used to feel like it was forgotten by time. We used to get horse riders, cyclists, ramblers not any more. It's just so noisy now, with lorries thundering past on the narrow road. The travellers have completely ruined the ecological balance of the village. (21 March 2005, p.11)

Case study II: Media representations of Gypsy life

He later notes that:

We bought this house for £163,000 and we expected to get £230,000 when we sold but we certainly wouldn't get that now. I'd be surprised if we could find a buyer who would want to live here. (21 March 2005, p.11)

There is almost a suggestion of homelessness in these accounts. The fear of falling house prices particularly compounds this by making the potential escape route of selling up and moving on impossible. The sense of belonging that seems to inform a vision of what it means to be a part of Middle England seems to have been lost. The emotional and financial investments made by Middle England and by *The Daily Mail*'s readers in their environments and homes are presented as being thoroughly undermined by the presence of Gypsies. The anger this arouses materialises in the regular calls for John Prescott to face the same demons, waking up one morning to find trailers parked in his back garden.

Prescott was luckier than Martin Greig, a Liberal Democrat councillor in Aberdeen, who suggested that there were parallels between apartheid in South Africa and the treatment of travellers in Scotland. On the same weekend that the Conservatives were running their newspaper advertisements, *The Aberdeen Evening Express* decided to test Councillor Greig's tolerance, according to Sally McDonald, a journalist working on the newspaper:

We rolled up outside the Aberdeen City Lib Dem councillor's home with a 4x4 pick-up truck and our very own trailer. Then we hung up washing and put out rubbish bags. (21 March 2005, p.4)

The appearance of this story on the same day as those in the national press gives a flavour of the *zeitgeist*, a sense of the importance being attached to the understandings of Gypsy lives and to the meanings they generated within a non-Gypsy world. These were stories that tapped into the dominant population's need to be confident in its own identity; the figure of the Gypsy that emerges seems to have a very troubling and disruptive impact on the wider world of readers' lives. The figure that comes across is, rather than an unidentified bogie man, more well known and at times almost mundane. It is a very recognisable figure, according to, in this case, *Daily Mail* readers, who comment on the technicalities of what it means to be a 'real' gypsy. The newspaper gives a distinct impression that Gypsies are well known to its readers and the figure that emerges seems close to that of the *stranger*, unsettling through a mixture of proximity and the association with an 'otherness' that defies imagination.

Two oppositional accounts of Gypsies

As discussed, *The Sun* and *The Independent* seemingly produced two very different figures of Gypsies and yet a distinct sense of 'otherness' is common to both. On Monday 21 March (2005) they both filled their front pages with content about Gypsies. *The Sun* ran another piece in its ongoing campaign against Gypsies under the headline:[2]

> **GIPSIES' £30M HANDOUT: taxpayers are funding camps**

whilst *The Independent* was more openly sympathetic, with:

> **Are these Britain's most demonised people?** Travellers' anger as Howard makes them an election issue.

Both newspapers picked up strongly on Michael Howard's (2005) speech and the 'I Believe in Fair Play' advertisement of the previous day.

Case study II: Media representations of Gypsy life

The Sun

The Sun originally began a 'campaign' against Gypsy manipulation of planning law on Thursday 10 March 2005 under the slogan 'Stamp on the Camps', in which the newspaper declared 'war on gipsy free-for-all' and warned of a Gypsy 'invasion'. This story was triggered by government advice sent to local authorities instructing them to take account of Gypsy families' needs and to consider earmarking land for Gypsies to purchase and develop. Throughout the following week and a half *The Sun* ran with a series of related stories targeting not only Gypsies, but also John Prescott and the ODPM. Although Gypsies as a body of people bore the brunt of these attacks, the Deputy Prime Minister was the individual singled out for personal abuse. On 21 March, in a particularly vitriolic piece, Richard Littlejohn describes how Prescott, referred to in this piece as 'Two Jags',[3] is destroying 'ancient fields and woodlands' in his housing plans:

> Picturesque Middle England is to be turned into a giant Soweto for Wealthy gipsies. Two Jags is doing to the people of Britain what 'travellers' are doing to the countryside. (Richard Littlejohn, *The Sun*, 11 March 2005)

This is accompanied by a cartoon of Prescott sitting on a toilet labelled 'Middle England' with his trousers round his ankles, the straightforward inference being that just as Gypsies defecate across the countryside without regard for decency or the values of Middle England, so the Deputy Prime Minister is using the power of his office to do the same thing to the long-suffering people who inhabit that countryside. Middle England, in the Littlejohn piece, seemingly transforms from a reference to a specific group of people with shared values into the physical reality of actual space: it is now 'Picturesque Middle England'. This is an extraordinary jump, but it allows for a physical materialisation of boundaries that previously might only have been imagined in the mind's eye. In the process it underlines an absolute understanding of belonging and, in the case of Gypsies, of *not* belonging within these boundaries. The unholy alliance of 'wealthy' gypsies and two-Jag-owning politicians seems to hint partly at illegality and/or corruption, but, even more damningly, it suggests that these are people who lack taste and do not know how to behave like decent, normal people even when they have acquired money and power. They are not like us and nor can they ever be. The linkage between the Deputy Prime Minister and Gypsies is made in such a way that they mutually damage each other enormously; it plays the 'otherness' of understandings of Gypsies off against the corrupt image of politics and attempts to create a ring-fenced notion of belonging. The use of 'Middle England' speaks volumes about the notion of a society in which certain behaviours are deemed socially acceptable and understood. As a boundary-making exercise it not only excludes the world of Gypsies but also any other native elements who are unable to understand the boundary lines.

In its lead story *The Sun* also stresses the strength of links between Gypsy groups and the ODPM in its analysis of government funding. In this piece it is claimed that £30 million (of taxpayers' money) has been spent on 'gipsy sites' and that this represents a trebling of spending by Prescott. It is quite hard to pin down *The Sun*'s figures, but the £30 million seems to comprise spending over a period of several years, and appears to conflate grant money from *The Big Lottery Fund* and local authority spending with other government money. *The Sun* argues that, despite a huge increase in spending on Gypsy sites, there is still a problem with illegal sites; its editorial comment says:

> *The Sun* has no quarrel with the settled gipsy community. The people causing trouble are those travellers who arrogantly think they can do what they like – while Mr Prescott encourages councils

Case study II: Media representations of Gypsy life

and police to turn a blind eye. (*The Sun*, 21 March 2005, p.8)

As with the breakdown of spending figures, it can be a little hard to pin down who exactly *The Sun* means by *those travellers who arrogantly think they can do what they like*. Such Travellers appear more clearly defined in earlier stories run by *The Sun* that describe two 'illegal' camps at Wickford and Crays Hill in Essex. The Wickford site is condemned on the following grounds:

> The sprawling EIGHTY-caravan camp boasts top of the range mobile homes and flash motors. But it is a squalid eyesore – blighting lives of villagers in Wickford, Essex. The 200 travellers squatting illegally in fields infuriate their law-abiding neighbours by roaring around in 4x4s, BMWs and Porsches. Shockingly there is even a £112,000 BENTLEY parked up. Yet each morning gallons of sewage overflows onto the roads. Stray dogs roam in packs, feasting on rats in the makeshift estate named locally as Hovefields. Just last Saturday a vicious fight broke out when a man with a samurai sword chased a teenager down the road. Two nights later a man was stabbed three times. (*The Sun*, 11 March 2005)

Plainly the most shocking aspect of the Gypsy site is their apparent wealth, presumably in comparison to their law-abiding neighbours. Whilst the references to dirt and illegality seem to articulate everyday shorthand for distinctions between Gypsies and non-Gypsies, the references to wealth add another dimension of difference. *The Sun* seems to suggest it is impossible for the behaviour of Gypsies to meet the standards of non-Gypsies; nothing, not even money, can encourage them into adopting a respectable way of life. Gypsies are differentiated in this way from other excluded groups who might loosely be thought of as the 'deserving poor'; people living in difficult or impoverished conditions whose lifestyle reflects a breadline existence. The account of ostentatious wealth marks Gypsy groups as belonging beyond society – more specifically, beyond the outlying parts of society that may well be largely excluded and regarded with some disdain, but are still felt to be entitled to a degree of communal support. Gypsy communities are not, for example, represented within the ranks of the 'deserving poor'.

The Sun argues that the Wickford site will receive retrospective planning permission on the say-so of John Prescott. Even disregarding the level of veracity in *The Sun*'s description of Gypsy life at Wickford, what is striking is how little of the description has any particular bearing on issues around planning law. Even if the description was an accurate one these are not planning issues, they are issues about difference and about distancing Gypsies from respectable society.

As noted above, Okely describes how Gypsies 'cannot escape the gaze of the Gorgio' (1983, 232), their lives are in part shaped by the representations that are made about them by the non-Gypsy world. The gaze of *The Sun* is driven by its agenda to sell newspapers, which, as is made clear in the linkages the newspaper makes to John Prescott, is also a politicised agenda. This agenda is not (yet) a straight party political agenda; at this time *The Sun* had not declared its support for either Labour or Conservatives in the election and its coverage of political issues (with the exception of baiting John Prescott), was fairly even-handed. If anything, the newspaper was painfully determined to be even-handed in the praise and criticism it handed out to both parties, perhaps suggesting a neutralised political agenda reflecting its best commercial interests. Within this context the 'Stamp on the Camps' slogan and related stories demonstrate that, if nothing else, in *The Sun*'s gaze Gypsy politics fall outside of party politics and into a wider arena of public approbation. The suspicion is that *The Sun* was not attempting to set an election agenda with these stories but was simply trying to sell newspapers by appealing to the commonly understood fears and prejudices of its readers. Whilst the Conservative Party's engagement is opportunistic and overtly politically motivated, it derives its momentum from the popularity of *The Sun*'s sentiments. *The Sun* understands itself to be aligned with a broad swathe of British opinion, hence the references to Middle England, the law-abiding neighbours and taxpayers. It is the newspaper with the highest circulation of all the daily national newspapers in the UK, selling nearly a million more copies than its nearest rival *The Daily Mail* (ABC Data, March 2005). *The Sun* represents and stands up for '*us*', the reader, and presents the Gypsy population as an alien 'other' or '*them*'.

The Independent

The tone of *The Independent* is undoubtedly more sympathetic to the Gypsies featured in its pages, but it is still interesting to examine the picture of Gypsy culture that emerges from its gaze. Many of the key themes in *The Sun*'s coverage are examined, in particular Michael Howard and the Conservative Party's attempts at staking a claim to the votes of Middle England, an examination of John Prescott and the ODPM's recent policy development in relation to Gypsies and planning law, and an examination of the historical failures of government to develop policies that allow sufficient sites for Travellers in the UK.

The Independent's front page story is built upon an interview with Bernadette Reilly, a Scottish-Irish Gypsy. The first paragraph of *The Independent* story states:

> Bernadette Reilly is furious. She pays for everything: her council tax, her road tax, her television licence. But, for as long as she can remember, she has endured abuse and hostility. Gypsies and travellers call it bigotry, and say they suffer it all over Britain.
> (*The Independent*, 21 March 2005)

The article continues with a sympathetic and fairly detailed account of the impacts of bigotry upon Mrs Reilly and her family's life. It examines issues around the lack of sites and the political manoeuvring of the major political parties around these. It also allows Mrs Reilly to discuss the changing nature of her life, from a more nomadic lifestyle to one that is more settled. The successes of this transition include registering with a GP, her children settling in well at school and the friendliness of neighbours, whilst the failures include difficulties establishing planning permission to build on her father's land.

What is most dramatic about *The Independent*'s coverage is the photograph of Bernadette Reilly with her daughter that runs on the front page; they both hold the camera's gaze, looking tired but defiant. In the background are other young girls and a woman, a caravan and pitch marked out by a two-brick wall, and a pram. It is a photograph that makes very specific visual representations of Gypsy lifestyle; the land around the van is barren, mostly dirt and stones, there is the hint of a large extended family in the unnamed women and children, and there are suggestions of poverty in the clothing worn. However, what is really striking is that if the caravan in the background is blocked out then the photograph could be used to represent very different figures. The formality of the setting gives a sense of resolve and strength to the woman and her daughter that resonates with a traditional idea of the matriarch battling against the odds to get the best for her family. In other circumstances and other times, the photograph could be of a family excluded from school by sectarian politics in Northern Ireland, a mother fighting drug crime on an estate in south London, or the wife and family of striking miners during the pit strikes. There is a generic quality to the image that, when it is wrested from its most specific point of reference, the caravan, seems to fall within an umbrella of white working-class archetypes. It recalls images of the 'deserving poor' that will

Case study II: Media representations of Gypsy life

generate a sympathetic response amongst *The Independent*'s readership. The gaze of *The Independent* is driven, as is *The Sun*'s, by a desire to sell newspapers to another, much smaller, swathe of British opinion (in this case liberal-minded opinion), and also creates a representation that is readily understood by their readers; by piggy-backing upon an image of a down-trodden white working class, the newspaper uses visual shorthand to evoke a response. Whilst *The Independent* seemingly works to produce boundaries that include Gypsies, they do so by constructing a Gypsy figure that sits comfortably within the wider areas of concern expected of the newspaper. There is a degree of misrepresentation dictated by the needs and desires of the newspaper and its readers.

In their representation of Gypsies *The Independent* presents a personal face, the face of the mother and daughter. In this respect the newspaper suggests it is engaged in a particular kind of honesty: it is willing to look the Gypsy woman in the eye. This approach is perhaps undermined by using an image that evokes wider stereotypes, which introduces a degree of distance between Independent readers and the world of Gypsies. *The Sun*, on the other hand, makes representations of Gypsies that are much more explicit in their approach to distancing Gypsies from their readers. Generally *The Sun* avoids any direct representation of Gypsies through photography; Gypsies do not appear in its pages individually. Instead the defining images for *The Sun* are aerial photographs of Gypsy sites. These work in at least a twofold manner to emphasise *The Sun*'s line on this story. Firstly they allow *The Sun* reader to maintain their distance from the Gypsy. Their gaze is safely beyond arm's length, looking in and down on the sites; there is no requirement to engage in the realities of any individual lives. *The Sun* reader glimpses an exotic world that is beyond his normal daily encounters. In this sense these photographs are read in a different visual language to that of *The*

Independent. 'We' (the readers) are invited to peek in and recoil in horror; via a telephoto lens, we are granted sight of a world in which we do not belong. By creating this physical distance *The Sun* is able to introduce a social distance between reader and the Gypsy subject. To a degree this reflects the social distance introduced by *The Independent* when they portray a stereotypical image for which the reader can feel sympathy. Secondly, and very much related to the physical distancing introduced by the use of a telephoto lens, the photographs used by *The Sun* make a specific connection to the language used in the accompanying articles, which describe Gypsy sites as 'Sowetos'. The sites appear in the same visual rhetoric as that associated with African townships or third-world shanty towns. In other circumstances, in another country for example, we might be asked to feel sympathy for their residents, but these sites are explained as intrusions into 'our' neighbourhoods. A consequence of distancing the lives of readers from the lives of Gypsies is that the newspaper's vitriolic and hate-filled messages are also placed at a significant remove. The lack of proximity distances the reader from a need to take a moral stand or, as Bauman suggests, 'the effects of human action reach far beyond the "vanishing point" of moral visibility' (Bauman 1989, 193).

The Gypsy as 'stranger'

Both *The Sun* and *The Independent* construct representations of Gypsies as 'others'. *The Sun* does this blatantly, by placing Gypsy communities in stark contrast to, and beyond the boundaries of respectability of, their neighbours. *The Independent* does something slightly different, concentrating on a personal story of a 'good' Gypsy who pays her taxes and who can perhaps be identified with other reclaimed figures of working-class resolve. In doing so *The Independent* is recognising the common currency of *The Sun*'s representation and, with a nod to liberal sensitivities, attempting to produce an opposite account. This representation is one that still implicitly acknowledges the existence, and the importance, of its alternative. The responses that are generated towards such representations of Gypsies also parallel some of the responses to the figure of the *stranger* discussed by Bauman.

Bauman (1991; 1997) underpins his analysis of the *stranger* and his representation within the modern nation state with two key concepts. Firstly, as discussed in earlier chapters, his *stranger* parallels Simmel's 'man who comes today and stays tomorrow' (Simmel 1971, 49); the *stranger* does not originate within the state or the community and there is an emphasis placed on his arrival from somewhere else. The *stranger*'s strangeness causes the state confusion: 'strangers exuded uncertainty, where certainty and clarity should have ruled' (Bauman 1997, 47). In response, Bauman suggests, the state can apply different strategies to eliminate or lessen such confusion, and, borrowing from Levi-Strauss, he characterises such strategies as being either *anthropophagic* or *anthropoemic* in nature. The anthropophagic approach suggests consumption of the *stranger*, transforming his flesh into the body of the natives; this is 'the strategy of *assimilation* – making the different similar; smothering cultural or linguistic distinctions; forbidding all loyalties except those meant to encourage conformity to the new and all-embracing order' (Bauman 1997, 47). The *anthropoemic* approach continues the theme of bodily functions, suggesting a vomiting out of *strangers* by the body of the state. It is a strategy of *exclusion*:

> Confining the strangers within the visible walls of the ghettos or behind the invisible yet no less tangible prohibitions of *commensality, connubium* and *commercium*; expelling the strangers beyond the frontiers of the managed and manageable territory; and, when neither of these two measures was feasible, destroying them physically. (Bauman 1997, 42, original emphasis)

Bauman clearly stresses the similarities behind these two differing approaches, both in the tone of his analysis of the state and the allusions he makes to bodily and scatological functioning. The references to food throughout both descriptions – the consumption of the stranger on the one hand, and the bar on *commensality*, the breaking of bread, on the other – suggest that prohibitions around strangers are fundamental, and represent aspects of the most basic human behaviour. This is underlined by the demarcation of boundaries suggested by the addition of *connubium* and *commercium*; sleeping with the *stranger* or trading with the *stranger* become indicative of falling outside of the understood boundaries of the state. Under these conditions the notion of a shared communal fellowship between natives and *strangers* is impossible. Most importantly, both strategies suggest that within modern nations there is a need to do something, to act, when faced by the figure of the *stranger*; there is not an option to ignore his presence.

It is in the duality of these approaches, Bauman argues, that the crux of the clash between liberal and nationalist/racist modern states lies, which at some very basic level seems to mirror the collision between *The Independent*'s 'liberal' positioning and *The Sun*'s 'nationalist/racist' standpoint. To some degree both newspapers would probably challenge such labelling, which creates categories that are too rigid to contain everything that appears within their pages. In the case of *The Sun* particularly there is a debate to be had about the limits of patriotism and Britishness in the context of nationalism. However, Bauman goes on to argue that the conditions of the modern state no longer hold true and that the postmodern state produces a different *stranger*. The desire for the state to rid itself of the *stranger* no longer holds; rather, both those on the right and left look to embrace difference and to effectively cope with the *stranger*. This is because for those on the political right difference is culturally produced and so

Case study II: Media representations of Gypsy life

there can be a sense of affirmation in the presence of the *stranger*, a sense that we are not like them. Meanwhile, for the liberal left there is community and the celebration of difference that materialises as multiculturalism.

Bauman (1991) argues that the figure of the *stranger* disrupts very clear-cut relationships that exist between friends and enemies; friends are natives in terms of the nation state and enemies are outsiders, beyond the tangible borderlines. Friends have responsibilities to each other; enemies do not. Crucially, the friends–enemies opposition allows society to take shape; friends can gather together to take responsibility for each other. Into this equation the *stranger* appears entirely unsettling; his presence within the tangible boundaries suggests the need to be responsible for him, but his allegiances beyond the intangible boundaries suggest the impossibility of eating, sleeping or trading with him. If, as Bauman suggests, 'All societies produce strangers, but each kind of society produces its own kind of strangers, and produces them in its own inimitable way' (Bauman 1997, 46), then the articles in both *The Sun* and *The Independent* need to be thought about in terms of the production of *strangers*. *The Independent* represents a multiculturalist approach and can be seen within a tradition of liberalism that spans both Bauman's modern and postmodern representations. The figure of the Gypsy is transformed into a 'good' Gypsy, one who is not only an acceptable white face but would also sit comfortably within the parameters of the dominant society, one who could share its food and bed. *The Sun*, however, is engaged in a perhaps more complex set of manoeuvres; like *The Independent* it presents (or produces) a new representation of the figure of the Gypsy, but this one is the figure of the 'wealthy' Gypsy. Ironically, this representation of the Gypsy could easily be read in terms of admiration; the flash cars, the top-of-the-range motor homes and the wads of cash used to buy up land have more than a hint of Thatcherite/Loadsamoney excess and perhaps a decade ago would have been celebrated by the newspaper. In *The Sun*'s unwillingness to embrace these aspects of Gypsy culture is perhaps the hint that Bauman is actually wrong to suggest that figures of the *stranger* are produced in a different fashion by different societies. *The Sun*'s account instead appears constrained by historic understandings of Gypsies. The newspaper reproduces a figure of the Gypsy as a *stranger* that seems strikingly familiar compared to many earlier representations. This Gypsy is again at once stigmatised and marked out as different and, in the representations of space that are shown to be the Gypsies' home (and labelled 'Gypsy City' or 'Soweto'), they are portrayed as a banished 'other'.

In this creation of a historical image of the Gypsy as *stranger*, even if it is placed within a new version such as the 'wealthy' Gypsy, what *The Sun* does is to recognise the figure of the *stranger*. The newspaper reacquaints itself with an existing figure and for good measure highlights the figure's unacceptability within a new register – that is, an association with unwarranted wealth. This is an unsurprising association as it links to another readymade 'figure' typified by a lack of taste and an inability to behave within acceptable social bounds. This figure, who appears within the pages of *The Sun*, is represented as the 'unworthy rich'. Sometimes it appears in the shape of minor aristocrats snorting cocaine and behaving badly in clubs, but more often it manifests itself in the shape of the 'trashy lottery winner', one such featured in fairly typical fashion in a story that follows under *The Sun*'s headline from 31 March 2005:

FURY AT LOTTO LOUT'S BANGERS 'N SMASH

In this story we learn about an ex-dustman lottery winner staging a demolition derby in his backyard and infuriating the neighbours. Both the figure of the Gypsy and that of the Lotto Lout (the materialisation of the 'unworthy rich') are recognisable

Case study II: Media representations of Gypsy life

figures within the vernacular of the paper. Ahmed makes the point that 'hailing constitutes the subject' and also:

> Constitutes the stranger in a relationship precisely to the Law of the subject (the stranger is constituted as the unlawful entry into the nation space, the stranger hence allows Law to mark out its terrain). To this extent, the act of hailing or recognising some-body as a stranger serves to constitute the lawful subject, the one who has the right to dwell, and the stranger at the very same time. (2000, 23)

In this respect *The Sun* acts by hailing the figure of the Gypsy (though it could equally be the lotto lout) and saying 'who the hell do you think you are? You're not like us – you do not belong amongst the respectable people'. It acts to police the boundaries of its readers by recognising both the reader and the Gypsy *stranger*. In recognising both parties *The Sun* acts to mark the boundaries of its society. As discussed earlier, *The Independent*'s representation of the 'good' Gypsy implicitly acknowledges the representation made by *The Sun*; thus *The Independent* also marks out and polices the boundaries of (liberal) society. Just as *The Sun* creates a figure of the 'wealthy Gypsy' to emphasise the nature of Gypsy communities, so too *The Independent* also produces a new figure of the Gypsy, one that resonates with other dispossessed white communities. Whilst historically Gypsies have tended to be misrecognised either as exotic and exciting 'others' or as dirty vagrants, *The Independent* seems to veer away from its assigned role in this dualism. The production of an exotic 'other' would perhaps fail dramatically within the context of dialogues with *The Sun*, in which the differences associated with Gypsy lifestyle are bound to other figures such as the 'lottery lout'. Instead, *The Independent* draws a more mundane picture of Gypsy lives, suggesting a tax-paying, TV licence-holding Gypsy that in some way epitomises the everyday respectability associated with parts of the non-Gypsy world that might loosely fall within a category of the 'deserving poor'. It undermines the value of such respectability partly through its engagement in a dialogue with the kind of representations being made by *The Sun*. By doing so both newspapers create new sets of dualisms designed to appeal more closely to their respective readerships, which, if they do not mirror exactly traditional dualist representations of Gypsies, seem to coexist in a similarly unhelpful fashion. What *The Independent* also does through the use of a particular visual rhetoric is to detail a clear distinguishing line between *The Independent*'s readers and Gypsy lives. Although it rethinks the figure of the Gypsy in a more mundane fashion, the ordinary life it summons into existence is an ordinary life that is distanced from the lives of its readers. *The Independent* reader can engage and empathise with figures such as the striking miner's wife or the Gypsy mother faced by a hostile community through the sense of burden associated with these categories or types of figures. The burdens by which they are categorised, however, also distinguish and differentiate their lives from those of the newspaper reader.

We have previously argued that perceptions of Gypsy communities are driven by a desire to:

> mark out a boundary between the acceptability of the dominant culture and the unacceptability of the subordinate culture. Where one is clean the other is dirty, one industrious the other idle, one is modern and urban the other is backward and rural. (Bhopal and Myers 2005, 8)

Both *The Sun* and *The Independent*, albeit in differing ways, perpetuate representations of the Gypsy as an 'other', a *stranger* within the dominant culture. In doing so they both perpetuate an imagination of the figure of the Gypsy that has been in currency since Gypsies first arrived in Britain. Bauman's argument that a

Case study II: Media representations of Gypsy life

shift occurs between modern and postmodern representations of the stranger rings at best only half true; the modern state's *anthropophagic* and *anthropoemic* strategies both persist into the realities of liberal and nationalistic responses to multiculturalism in the present. Bauman suggests that in postmodern responses to the *stranger* the desire to move them on has ceased, that both the nationalist right and the liberal left want, for differing reasons, to 'live with them – daily and permanently' (Bauman 1997, 55). This has a peculiarly unreal resonance within the Gypsy lifestyles in which the threat of being 'moved on' is for large numbers of Gypsies a daily and permanent threat as one of the state's responses to illegal encampment (Myers 2005). As discussed above, *The Sun* suggests they do not have a problem with the 'settled' Gypsy population, and again the use of the word settled has a peculiar resonance within the context of any discussion of Gypsy lifestyle. Many Gypsies may be described as settled in terms of their having been housed or having remained in static caravans on official sites for a long period of time. Even more fundamentally, many Gypsies may be settled within their communities and culture because they are comfortable with their lifestyle, be it more or less nomadic or more or less secure in terms of a *gaujo* gaze. The tone of *The Sun* piece, however, suggests they are using settled in a different way, perhaps as in sedimenting into the accepted norms of the dominant culture, rather than settled purely in terms of geographic and domestic arrangements.

Gypsies, strangers and the media

Both *The Sun* and *The Independent* produce representations of 'the Gypsy' that are designed to appeal to their readers and to sell newspapers. In many ways the need to sell newspapers, to provide an entertaining and engaging medium at the breakfast table or on a train on the way to work, is an inevitably powerful economic driver. These representations work in two distinctive ways, one seemingly based on a historical standpoint and the other reflecting current perspectives. Historically the Gypsy is cast in terms of Bauman's figure of the *stranger*, outside the boundaries of the dominant culture. This reflects misrecognitions of Gypsy culture that have been prevalent across many centuries and have materialised as differing means of oppression; at its worst this includes the deportations to slave colonies in the Americas and, in twentieth-century Europe, the Holocaust. On a more routine, mundane level the last twenty years have seen a succession of well-documented accounts of the state's failure to address Gypsy needs with regard to education, healthcare and accommodation. *The Sun* sustains traditional stereotypical attributes of Gypsy culture to do with dirt, vagrancy and idleness as one means of distancing its readers from the figure of the Gypsy. This distancing is compounded by the use of the telephoto lens so that Gypsy culture is firmly placed outside the norms of respectability. The Gypsy figure is portrayed as an 'other' and, in the specifics of the stories discussed, the Gypsy is a *stranger* who, through manipulation of the planning laws, has appeared literally amongst 'us', the readers. The accounts given by *The Sun* promote the dialogues that have resulted in the failures around issues such as health and education provision for Gypsy communities over long periods of time. Gypsy communities are portrayed as both undeserving and outside the nation state (and by default undeserving of the provision of the welfare state). In the rabidity of its portrayals *The Sun* at times seems frighteningly close to other, far worse, levels of oppression.

In *The Independent* there is an implicit understanding of this same figure of the 'Gypsy'; indeed, without this figure lurking in the cultural background it would be hard to make any logical sense out of *The Independent*'s story. *The Independent* needs the figure of *The Sun*'s Gypsy in order to build a story that will reflect back on

Case study II: Media representations of Gypsy life

its readers an agreeable sense of liberal, multicultural nationhood. They need the figure of the *stranger* so that they can accommodate his strangeness within the Liberal boundaries of the nation.

Reflecting their current perspectives, both newspapers also construct new Gypsy figures, the 'good Gypsy' in *The Independent* and the 'wealthy Gypsy' in *The Sun*. At some level economics are surely behind these novel creations – a simple need to provide readers with something different, something to talk about during a coffee break or in the queue at Tesco. Both figures are grounded in other figures produced by both newspapers; we have argued (Bhopal and Myers 2005) that within popular representations of Gypsy culture there have been repeated attempts to misrepresent Gypsies, often by an association with another despised group. The most recent of these attempts involves the cultural and geographic linkages made between Gypsies and so-called 'chavs', as discussed above. These representations are potent because they elaborate on themes that may be associated with a falling beyond the dominant culture's boundaries; often this seems to happen at implicitly understood although ill-defined areas such as the edges of respectability. *The Sun* provides an arena in which there is some conflation of representations of Gypsies and lotto louts, between Gypsy sites and Sowetos; both the representation of the personal conduct and the space inhabited is highlighted as outside the lived world of *The Sun*'s readership. *The Independent* plainly looks to provide a liberal insight into the difficulties of a Gypsy lifestyle but in their production of a figure of a 'good' Gypsy they are drawing the attention of their readers to an image of another heroic 'type'. In doing so *The Independent* also demarcates the personal experiences and the spaces occupied by their readers from those of Gypsies; the lives of Gypsies and *The Independent* readers are segregated from each other. Two things are happening in both accounts; firstly, the Gypsy subject is marked as an outsider, an 'other' or a *stranger*; and, secondly, misrecognition is involved in both representations. These are not reflections of Gypsy culture, they are constructions of newspaper readerships' imaginations of Gypsies.

Representations of Gypsy culture and the multicultural nation

For liberal societies and for the multicultural state it is readily acknowledged that there is a need for the dominant culture to recognise subaltern cultures. Such recognition is a marker of inclusive practices. However, in parallel to such inclusive practice there is a similar need on the part of nationalists on the right to also recognise 'others'. This second form of recognition is not concerned about establishing an inclusive approach but instead enables a sense of belonging to be maintained by the identification of difference, which is used to define what lies outside the boundaries of belonging. In establishing this boundary it is clear that the *stranger* who is created is the *stranger* described by Ahmed as somebody who is 'already recognised as not belonging' (Ahmed 2000, 21) or Bauman's stigmatised *stranger*. Representations of Gypsies work slightly tangentially to satisfy the different needs of both liberal and right-wing spectrums of dominant society to recognise 'otherness'. They are invariably misrecognised, either as an exotic 'other' or as dirty vagrants, but all these misrecognitions and, more importantly, the repetition of these misrecognitions suit the needs of the dominant population. Whilst it may be anticipated that the political right would demonise groups outside their national boundaries, it seems perhaps surprising that inclusive liberalism should also perpetuate such misrecognitions. Hesse's (1999) criticism of Taylor's 'politics of recognition' argues that liberal multiculturalism is founded within a western liberal mindset that struggles to look further than its own direct concerns. This seemingly plays out across the pages of *The Independent* in the creation of a figure that sits comfortably within its liberal outlook. The figure of the Gypsy here is transformed into a figure who, although marked as different and a *stranger* from beyond the reader's boundaries, is now found to be acceptable to the needs and desires of the liberal reader and his sense of an all-embracing multiculturalism. The figure is produced for the liberal reader out of a liberal imagination.

Both types of representation, that by the liberal left and that by the right, represent productions from within the specific political and cultural agendas of these parties. They neither reflect the perceptions of Gypsies of their engagement with the societies and nations they inhabit, nor do they reflect a representation in which Gypsies as a small, minority voice are heard within society. The ambiguous nature of representations of the figure of the Gypsy in the media is highlighted by the common linkages that exist between *The Sun* and *The Independent*'s portrayal of Gypsies. If *The Independent* implicitly recognises *The Sun*'s figure of the Gypsy, there is surely a suspicion that creations like that of *The Sun* are a response by its readers, or Middle England and its mouthpieces, to liberal multiculturalisms. Both *The Sun* and *The Independent* produce notions of the boundaries within which the nation is constituted and an important marker for these boundaries is the figure of the *stranger*, in this case the Gypsy. The presence of the *stranger* demarcates cultural boundaries within the geographic territory, producing an understanding of the allegiances and ties between people within the nation. Whilst at first sight it might feel that *The Sun* and *The Independent* in their differing representations suggest a schism within the nation, this is not really true. Both newspapers' representations of Gypsies are inextricably linked and this reflects a linkage between the cultural boundaries of the newspapers; it is a symbiotic relationship. The recognition of the relationships between divergent cultural boundaries and divergent representations of the *stranger* suggests at a deep level the makings of nation.

Notes

1. A rough translation of the polite but unenlightening email was that they were not interested in engaging in a dialogue.
2. Capitalisation and bold fonts of newspaper headlines all follow the published content of the newspapers quoted.
3. 'Two Jags' is a long-running jibe at the Deputy Prime Minister's supposedly lavish lifestyle, based upon his ownership of two Jaguar motorcars and several houses. He is noted for being easily riled by this nickname.

7. The outsider in multicultural society

Gypsies are represented in different contexts, times and places in different ways. Many of these representations have remained largely static across long periods of time and others seem more open to change. One context in which Gypsy representations should be more successfully negotiated between Gypsies and non-Gypsies is the multicultural spaces and institutions of the United Kingdom. By this, we mean state institutions such as schools and the civil service, where legislation promoting anti-racist agendas has been imposed and enacted. This is not to suggest that every school or every hospital has a perfect, or even adequate, track record in its dealings with people from ethnic minorities, let alone Gypsies; just that, in general, such institutions are governed in a manner that forces some engagement with multiculturalism, reflecting the influence of central and local government funding. The wider space that is occupied by multicultural society can be thought of in terms of the liberal understandings that shape much British culture; some of this may be seen in the work of some parts of the media and more can probably be identified through the everyday hopes and expectations of ordinary people. The foothold that multiculturalism has within British culture is to some degree a reflection of the behaviours people exhibit when going about their daily routines. Once again, it should be stressed that such liberalism is not the only shaping force on culture and, when looking at the attitudes and behaviours expressed towards Gypsies, it can be easy to conclude that such sentiments represent only a minority opinion. However, it is within multicultural practice that one would anticipate Gypsy culture may find itself recognised and treated with greater equity than in other parts of society.

The failure of liberal society to cope with Gypsy culture

Cultural differences between Gypsies and dominant British cultures are dramatic. As discussed, despite the adaptability of Gypsy culture's responses it has an ingrained and unchanging core. The experience of the education system's engagement with Gypsies tends to show that the most effective means of involving Gypsy communities is to recognise and celebrate their difference. This is not a liberal panacea that results in universal or unproblematic attendance in education, it simply creates an environment in which Gypsy culture may choose to derive value from what is on offer. This is reflected in some respects by Taylor's (1992) identification of two interlinked, although essentially irreconcilable, manifestations of the 'politics of recognition' in western democracies. On the one hand is a politics of dignity that is deliberately blind to the differences between cultures, while on the other is a politics of difference which seeks to recognise distinctness and difference between individuals. Both approaches reflect universal liberal-minded attempts to recognise different cultures, but both attract a liberal reproach towards their strategies. The most serious charge is that laid at the doors of advocates of the difference-blindness approach, which suggests that as the blindness is always directed by the hegemonic culture towards the minority culture it is a suppression of identity and an act of oppression. Schools that ignore differences in Gypsy culture fail to understand the different requirements of Gypsy children, the difference-blindness concealing a privileging of sedentary education and educational policies. Such an approach is also apparent in the media and the political shenanigans that surrounded coverage in the run-up to the 2005 general election. When *The Sun* suggested it 'has no quarrel with the settled gipsy community', and when Michael Howard declared 'I believe in fair play', they are latching on to a rhetoric that falls within a multicultural schema. Essentially this is the mouthing of a difference-blind multiculturalism through a particularly distorting language of oppression. Both arguments suggest that everyone should be treated exactly the same, that fairness and equity are determined by shaping a society in which everybody's behaviour is seen, judged and found wanting, or not, on a single set of criteria. It is a statement of reactionary political correctness that asserts the liberalism of the Conservative Party and *The Sun* newspaper by offering an across-the-board set of values to which everyone with taste and decency can subscribe. That these values are plainly constructed around the various constituencies, the different 'Middle Englands', that both newspaper and political party summon up is only the first hint of a problem with this approach. The level playing field is a fallacy for 'Middle Englanders' themselves and the leeway in interpretation of 'fair play' swings wildly depending upon what sort of 'Middle Englander' you are; the behaviours of Royals, company directors and dustbin men are judged differently, as are those of football fans and football hooligans, football players and football managers, or for that matter poets and policemen or stockbrokers or sausage-makers. There are endless distinctions in what constitutes accepted behaviour and accepted judgements of that behaviour and, by and large, none of these distinctions results in advertisements in the Sunday newspapers demanding fair play. When, for example, a large corporation decides to modernise a historic listed building and in its own commercial interests exceeds the agreed planning changes, irreparably damaging the building, it is likely that they will be castigated for their actions. They may incur some financial penalty, some harsh words of criticism in the press and, if the damage is serious enough, the issuing of a statement by English Heritage or the Commission for Architecture and the Built Environment. All of these actions will, however, be within an entirely different rhetoric to that used around Gypsies failing to secure planning permission for sites. Within this rhetoric is an understanding that the multinational corporation is within the boundaries of acceptable society; their actions may be deplorable, but they are understood. Difference blindness is used *against* Gypsies as a means of demarcating boundaries. Theoretically it is a blanket set of behaviours and standards against which everyone can be judged. In practice though, the difference blindness that is on offer is that of the dominant culture; it provides a backdrop against which the actions of the dominant culture, particularly at the margins of its acceptability, can be judged. If at its best it is a very constrained notion of liberalism (and one that would not be promoted by many who would actively describe themselves as liberals), at its worst it is a fabricated pretence at liberalism. At its worst, difference blindness is a process that recognises specific difference with a view to casting it as an 'other'. When the Conservatives launched the 'I believe in fair play' advertisement they appeared to be using a difference blind rhetoric, however, it was used in the context of deliberately recognising and highlighting the 'otherness' of Gypsies. In doing so the Gypsy community was not being judged against the same standards as everyone else, but rather was being selectively targeted.

Taylor (1992) argues that difference-blind liberalism assumes that it can offer a neutral ground in which different strands of a multicultural society can live together peaceably. It is debatable how true this might be of relations with Gypsy communities. The neutral ground on offer may simple be intended to salve consciences or apply a little gloss to reputations by demonstrating an adherence to a liberal set of values, which in fact merely continue and justify oppressive sets of behaviour. Such a judgement on *The Sun* or the Conservative Party might be a little harsh when both participate so directly in economies (selling newspapers; garnering votes) in which the need to tap into cultural mood swings is so critical. However, the notion of a 'neutral ground' flags itself up as almost oxymoronic within such economies; the specific loyalties being advertised in the process of subscribing to a daily newspaper or voting for a political party seem imbued with the marking of boundaries. These are self-elective cohorts of readers and voters who, when they hand their money across the newsagent's counter or place their mark on a ballot slip, are demonstrating signs of membership and of belonging within certain boundaries. These processes are also about re-stating the boundary lines to determine who does not belong within.

Using the example of *The Satanic Verses*, Taylor highlights another, different failing of difference-blind liberalism that originates more directly from the minority ethnic group than from hegemonic society. He identifies an inability to provide common, neutral ground where 'The awkwardness arises from the fact that there are substantial numbers of people who are citizens and also belong to the culture that calls into question our philosophical boundaries' (Taylor 1992, 63). The reconciliation of this 'awkwardness' is perhaps best described as the function of Bauman's (1991) modern nation(al) state. Here friends are reclassified as natives and the state legislates and propagandises a shared sense of community, cultural homogeneity and uniform value systems. To cope with the stranger the state may attempt various strategies to remove his anomalous nature, the most extreme being genocide, in which the state attempts to physically cut out the aberrant or strange parts of society. Different forms of ghettoisation, restricting either within a physical location or a limited sphere of communication, may also be employed. All of these can be found within the history of the Gypsy diaspora, Henry VIII's capital offence of being a Gypsy grimly foreshadowing Hitler's attempted genocide of European Gypsies (Acton 1997; Kenrick and Puxon 1972). They are manifested more recently in the physical restrictions placed on caravan sites, the number of local authority sites placed in poorly accessible and improbably unpleasant locations (Acton 2004) and the failure of schools and other state institutions to recognise fundamental elements of Gypsy culture and tradition (Bhopal 2004). Most commonly, the *stranger* is stigmatised: his differences are amplified and used to discredit his presence:

> An otherwise innocuous trait becomes a blemish, a sign of
> affliction, a cause of shame. The person bearing that trait is
> easily recognizable as less desirable, inferior, bad and dangerous.
> (Bauman 1991, 67)

The stigma is presented as being a fixed and unchangeable characteristic; it is therefore justification for exclusion. It also suggests a boundary to the effects of culture, to society's ability to shape itself; stigma is not subject to change, it is a natural fixed point. Bauman argues that the modern liberal state could reinterpret the signs of stigma as innocuous or neutral and, in doing so, assimilate the *stranger*, but this approach contradicts another role of the state, that of 'nation building' – the construction of collective identity within the state which inevitably involves building on traditional friend/enemy oppositions. It is in the shaping of this boundary between the collective limits of acceptability and the intolerance of 'otherness' that the role of the Gypsy figure becomes apparent within British culture; he is not just an 'other' on the outside, he is an 'other' who has made his home amongst the natives. The natives are torn between the desire to recognise themselves as a liberal society and the desire to distance themselves from the unacceptable *stranger*.

It is within the fixity of stigmatisation that difference-blind liberal strategies can perhaps best be understood to operate in highly oppressive ways. Difference blindness in which everyone is treated the same only works on the assumption that everyone behaves the same, or at least within an identifiable and close set of parameters. It assumes that the minority culture will exhibit the same behaviour patterns or acquiesce to those behaviour patterns that are preferred by the dominant society. The 'blindness' in question is actually not about ignoring different cultures' lifestyles but rather about assuming a pre-determined set of values that *everyone* can subscribe to (generally speaking those of the majority). If one group's culture is identified to behave in a different way, one that falls outside such parameters, then such behaviour needs to be treated differently. In the case of Gypsy communities different treatment is seen to materialise in, for example, the mustering of campaigns to enforce planning law in ways that do not adapt around the needs of these communities, unlike the adjustments that might commonly be made for other members of society.[1] More important is the fact that the identification of such difference is made in the first place, that stigmatisation should overtly appear within cultural dialogues. The work of *The Sun* and the Conservative press department in 2005 actively participated in the recognition and stigmatisation of Gypsy culture.

One purpose of the multicultural society is the materialisation of a liberal world view within the practical routines of everyday life. In the preceding two chapters some of those materialisations were examined in greater detail within the institution of a school and within the media (in the form of national newspapers). One obvious conclusion from both these examples is that multiculturalism is not universally regarded as the way forward and it is certainly not an approach that is unchallenged within British society. It also seems apparent that some representations of multiculturalism, such as the difference-blind approach, are used within frameworks that are themselves oppressive, although it is perhaps sought to cover this by a suggestion of liberalism. However, multiculturalism still plays an important role and one that perhaps needs to be examined rigorously within its more successful contexts; that is, within a context that celebrates difference and genuinely works towards liberal agendas. The assistant head at one of the schools in our research noted that:

> If you ask any school 'are you multicultural? Do you promote multiculturalism?' there's only one answer obviously, they get badges for it, charter marks. It doesn't mean much.

In such a light multiculturalism begins to sound like an industry in which institutions tick enough boxes and are rewarded with a small plaque declaring their political correctness. When conducting research in a school it is always a useful exercise to identify the different school policies in place; there will probably be a health and safety policy, policies on staff and pupil conduct, possibly policy on trips outside the school and, although it may not be labelled specifically or may be contained within other documents, there will be policy on the school's engagement with multiculturalism. It also appears in parts of the curriculum. Looking at the best work that was happening in schools (and looking at the thinking behind much of the liberal media, for that matter), it would seem apparent that a multicultural approach is understood as a moral and ethical starting point. Within these specific frameworks and within the wider worlds they create,

However, Gypsies continue to remain as outsiders. Even within the boundaries of a successful multicultural school with a proven track record of good relations with Gypsy families there is still a sharply drawn line between Gypsy pupils and non-Gypsy pupils. The notice boards celebrating Gypsy family culture are present, but as markers of commitment between school and community, not sites of dialogue between Gypsy and non-Gypsy pupils. At an exhibition of photographic work by Gypsy pupils and curriculum material based upon Gypsy experience there was a large attendance of pupils, non-school-age siblings, mothers, teachers, local agencies and representatives from local and national government departments; in principle, a mixed group, except that all the children and mothers were Gypsies and all the teachers, agencies and civil servants present had specific responsibilities for Gypsy issues. Now, we can be too cynical about this, and it may well be that if the exhibition had been about the achievements of the school's swimming club it would only have attracted a cohort of swimmers, their families and other parties interested in swimming. But it seems to hint that the celebration within the school of difference in Gypsy lives is distanced immeasurably from the lives of the majority, and other minorities. In the schools we visited celebrations of Diwali and Carnival seemed more inclusive of all pupils, including those without a directly related ethnic background. In primary schools, in particular, whole classes of children participated in producing displays of lights for Diwali. In the same schools the displays of work celebrating Gypsy culture were entirely produced by Gypsy children. It can almost be suggested that the culture is being distanced by the very act of celebrating Gypsy difference, the act reinforcing the importance of the space between cultures. This is quite different to the experience of celebration in many other cultures.

Elsewhere, the liberal representation of Gypsies in parts of the media such as *The Independent* seems well-intentioned but also draws out the same types of boundary line between the liberal readership and the figure of the Gypsy. Gypsies remain identifiable as an 'outsider' group despite, and in some respects because, of multiculturalism; *The Independent*'s representation of the Gypsy is certainly a response to the illiberal representations of its competitors, but it also distinguishes the lives of Gypsies from its own readers. Multiculturalism is itself one marker of the British nation (a marker of its liberalism and politics), but the creation of Gypsy identity suggests that this group falls outside the nation and therefore, to some degree, outside the multicultural remit. The Gypsy is seen as an 'outsider' or *stranger* from elsewhere, understood through boundaries of acceptance and non-acceptance. For some outsiders acceptance over a period of time indicates that recognition becomes a form of familiarity. However, the Gypsy experience suggests that recognition is always skewed towards imaginary understandings of Gypsies by the dominant population and any ongoing recognition is merely of unbridgeable difference.

As previously discussed, Taylor's analysis (1992) stresses the importance of identity as both a societal and an individual function. Identity is shaped and made secure at both the level of individual, loving relationships and at the level of an engagement with other people's culture and identity. Whilst Taylor's argument is surely intended to examine liberal politics within the nation state, it may also be (re-)read as the examination of the ways in which those who hold right-wing nationalist political views compose their notions of the nation. The sense of engagement described by Taylor could easily mesh with Bauman's suggestion that nationalists need to *cope* with the *strangers* amongst them and recognise their differences. The strategies for coping that appear in *The Sun* or in Conservative press campaigns, however, seem innately repressive. *The Sun,* having recognised the figure of the Gypsy as one that is constructed around difference, goes on to suggest that they do not have a 'quarrel' with the 'settled Gipsy' population. We never meet these 'settled' Gypsies in the pages of *The Sun*, however; the half-hearted hints at their existence suggests that they might be alternative, imaginary figures of Gypsies. Such Gypsies seem either to be created out of nowhere, in the very image of *The Sun*'s description of its readers, the all-embracing Middle Englanders, or, and this is perhaps where the importance of the newspaper's use of the word 'settled' comes into play, these are Gypsies who once would have been defined by their difference but are now subsumed within the values and lifestyles of *Sun* readers. For *The Sun* such Gypsies could be respectable neighbours and live next door to their readers without evoking any sense of threat or horror. Such a figure of the Gypsy is one that is entirely constructed within the newspaper's own rhetorical positioning, it is disconnected from the lives of real families who may or may not live in houses and may or may not consider their lives to be more or less settled as a result of being housed. The Gypsies that we do meet in the pages of *The Sun* are forever associated with dirt and illegality. They are shaped as living their lives irrevocably outside the values of *Sun* readers; the impossibility of living next door to such characters is absolute, their presence is an infringement into the lives of dominant society and they need to be cast out. Needless to say, this representation is also one that is constructed within the pages of the newspaper, rather than being a reflective account of individuals' actual lives.

Hesse (1999) argues that Taylor's analysis of multiculturalism is flawed by its foundation and immersion within European and American liberalism and the assumption that these concepts can be universally applied. Hesse suggests that a 'politics of interrogation' articulates other analyses of the role of western liberalisms, in particular its construction in terms of European and American colonialism. A 'politics of interrogation' both questions 'the relation of visible civilized grandeur to the invisibility of dehumanisation in constructions of Western culture' and its 'universal valorisations' (Hesse 1999, 213). This analysis of liberalism suggests that it conceals a dogmatism in which the liberal world view is only ever regarded in a positive light and any alternatives to this view become unacceptable – in Taylor's terms, for example, because we would then be 'compromising our basic political principles' (Taylor 1992, 63). Or, as Parekh notes (quoted by Hesse 1999):

> Liberals cannot consistently be dogmatic about their own beliefs and sceptical about all others, or talk about an open-minded dialogue yet both exclude some and conduct the dialogue on their own terms. They need to take a sustained critical look at their basic assumptions that both generate and prevent them from noticing and restraining, their illiberal and inegalitarian impulses. (Parekh 1995, 97)

Hesse's notion of a politics of interrogation suggests an understanding of multiculturalism which starts from somewhere other than the heart of western liberalism; 'it begins with an interrogation of the imperial construction of universal ideas like the West, Europe, 'non-Europe' and particularly the nation' (Hesse 1999, 214). Hesse's discussion of multiculturalism takes the experience of the black diaspora and the interpretation of this within liberal thinking as the basis for the analysis. There is, both within academic discourse and wider media, far less examination of the experiences of Gypsies than of the black experience. In part this undoubtedly reflects the smaller numbers of people involved but it is also a reflection of a different type of engagement (both culturally and politically) with hegemonic society. The concept of a Gypsy nation is made difficult by the different definitions that might be placed upon Gypsies, Travellers and Roma by themselves and by the communities they live amongst; by fluid and inexact psychological boundaries; by alliances and allegiances; and by extended understandings of family and community that do not closely tie with either the expectations or the apparent certainties that might be inferred from commonly held, expert or inexpert knowledge of the people concerned. This difficulty is compounded by the lack of a geographical grounding that could in other circumstances provide an understanding of how loosely associated groups might be connected despite a tumultuous diaspora; there is no equivalent to the role that Africa plays in the understanding of the black diaspora or that Israel can fulfil for Jewish people. Along with the lack of a tangible connection to India for modern Gypsy communities in the UK, as discussed above, there is a feeling that to construct a geographical Romanestan would be misguided in terms of its usefulness in addressing the existing engagements of many different Gypsy communities with countries across the world; in the early 1970s Gratton Puxon, Secretary of the Gypsy Council, argued for the creation of Romanestan but this was largely rejected by British Gypsy communities and politicians (Okely 1983).

This book primarily considers relatively local understandings of Gypsy identity and how these are constructed within ideas of the 'other' and the *stranger*. However, in addressing Hesse's concerns about multiculturalism and its rootedness in western white culture, questions are raised about how Gypsy culture is represented within a global liberalism. The 'otherness' of Gypsy culture remains apparent in the recognitions and representations that are made about Gypsies within the media; for example, Alvaro Gil-Robles, the European Commissioner of Human Rights, noted in 2005 that:

> to judge by the levels of invective that can regularly be read in the national press, Gypsies would appear to be the last ethnic

minority in respect of which openly racist views can still be acceptably expressed. (Gil-Robles 2005, 43)

Similarly, within education across the European Union, Liegeois (1988) has emphasised how Gypsies have been and remain socially excluded from education.

Simply recognising difference is not enough to tackle the problems associated with the racism and intolerance faced by Gypsy communities and there is a suspicion that even some of the attempts at celebrating difference merely act to mark out the borders of difference rather than actively generate engagement between different communities. However, if we are to rethink the means of generating successful multicultural societies in which an engagement does begin to take place, we might not wish to entirely dismiss the notion of a politics of recognition, but rather develop and extend the boundaries of its recognition. There is a weight of historical oppression of Gypsies that is neither understood nor acknowledged; indeed, this is essentially an unheard story for many, if not most, people in the UK. Some recognition of that history would add to an understanding of Gypsy culture in the present day. Just as societal understandings of Jewish and Afro-Caribbean culture are to some extent contextualised respectively by the Holocaust and the slave trade, it would be helpful if Gypsy culture was also understood more clearly against a backdrop of oppression. Understandings of the historic roots of Jewish and black communities do not provide an instant recipe for peace and harmony and good will to all men, but they do inform many of the sensitivities and perceptions we bring into our everyday lives, conversations and relationships. They inform understandings at the personal and the societal level. Yet if we look for comparable generalised understandings of Gypsy culture we might well conclude that the cupboard is very largely bare: the diaspora from India, genocides, transportation to plantations; all the great building blocks on which a cultural narrative might be constructed are hidden in the shadows. The impact of such an absence is felt in the everyday failures of misrecognition but perhaps more widely in society's inability to move forward and engage in more sophisticated understandings of culture and identity. Despite the ubiquitousness of television channels devoted to historical subject matter and the extraordinary breadth of human experience they find a market for, there seems little curiosity to develop understandings of Gypsy culture in this format. Hesse's politics of interrogation seems a long way distant when there is not even a commonly understood grasp of who Gypsies might be.

How willing or able British culture might be to adapt around different recognitions of Gypsy identity that would impact upon constructions of British nationhood and identity is highly debatable, not least because such change threatens the process of nation-building and of maintaining a sense of the security of national identities. The last half of the twentieth century saw an increasing interest in what Parekh (2000) calls the 'problem of British national identity'; many certainties have seemed to disintegrate and in their place British identity has increasingly found itself facing ambiguous and more fluid relationships. Following the steady loss of empire some of the conviction and assurance that might have been associated with British identity before and during the Second World War seems now to be severely tested. The post-war nation has in many ways become defined by the establishment of new social structures, such as the welfare state and entry into the European Community (now the EU), and also by changes to social composition resulting from increased black and Asian migration. Even more recently, British nationhood found itself again examining its own internal cohesions and the lack of them, which fed into the devolution of some political power to Scotland and Wales. There is a sense that the structures and constituent parts of British identity have had a rocky ride in the last sixty years; as a result, there are deeply embedded uncertainties about what it means to belong within the nation. In many ways this is an ironic process: the navel gazing and worries about identity that have ensued suggest in some ways a more insightful positioning than was perhaps apparent in the interwar period, yet at the same time the conclusions drawn from such reflections are defined by ambiguity and insecurity. The role of the Gypsy within this very unsettled moment seems to be to delineate some absolute notions of how far boundaries can be pushed. More than anything, the 500-year history of a Gypsy presence in the UK and the various representations that are made about them seem to present a historical reference point. However much we might care to argue that the representations of Gypsies are inaccurate, false or malicious, they have an enormous constancy about them and thus become a resource to be tapped into by the dominant population, a historical repercussive folk knowledge of where an absolute boundary line can be drawn; that is, the line between Gypsies and non-Gypsies. Parekh suggests that:

> Our identity is neither fixed and unalterable nor wholly fluid and amenable to unlimited reconstruction. We can alter it, but only within the constraints imposed by our inherited constitution and necessarily inadequate self-knowledge. (Parekh 2000, 5)

At a time when the constraints seem few and far between and the shape of a British identity seems almost at the point of either bursting apart into devolved nationalities or, alternatively, becoming subsumed within the wider political ambitions of Europe or the United States, Gypsies seem, ironically, to be capable of acting as a focus for a national sentiment. Despite Gypsies' own adaptations to different economic circumstances they are seemingly perceived as a fixed point within a changing world.

Parekh (2000, 5) argues that national identity should be defined in politico-institutional rather than ethno-cultural terms; it reflects the collective practices and institutions of the state. Whilst that makes sense, particularly when distinguishing individual identity from national identity, it feels uncomfortable when applied to a notion of a Gypsy nation, one that is not bounded by geographical boundaries and in which different communities are scattered and not necessarily bound by an institutionally coherent political framework. One interpretation would be to suggest that the idea of a Gypsy nation is actually unthinkable because it cannot exist within the parameters of nationhood, although this would undoubtedly be challenged by many Gypsy activist groups. Instead what seems more useful is to think of the body of people who may constitute a Gypsy nation as forming a different type of nation (one that does not sit comfortably within western academic thought, amongst other genres). Parekh argues that it is mistaken to conflate difference with identity, although difference is inevitably important in understanding identity; the process of understanding who we are and to which communities we belong also reveals who we are not and to which communities we do not belong. Communities or nations are different from each other because they have certain identities; it is not the case that because they have different identities they form into different communities. The national identity of Britain is something that is fluid; it changes over time and in the recent past such change has been more rapid. Despite this change, for most Britons, certainly for most Englanders (Middle or otherwise), the choice of leaving the nation, of putting your national identity to one side to become someone else is not a realistic option. The sense of national identity may have dramatically shifted but the need to remain within the national identity is largely unchanged (the obvious exceptions to this being those affected by devolution, who may feel that their identity is changing from being British to Scottish or Welsh). The situation of Gypsy communities within the British nation, as highlighted by the media coverage and the sense of social distance that exists between Gypsy and non-Gypsy communities, suggests that they are not a part of the national identity. The recognition of their difference, which quite possibly will not identify who or what constitutes the Gypsy nation, allows a simple distinction to be made between, on the one hand, natives belonging within the nation and, on the other, Gypsies falling outside that understanding.

White 'others' and the remoulding of multicultural Britain

The relationship between Gypsy communities and the nation state in post-war Britain indicates that British society has changed dramatically whilst its understandings of Gypsy culture have remained fixed. One identifiable change is the re-invention of a deprived white underclass, the existence of which also seems to determine where the further reaches of British nationhood might be found. As discussed in the previous chapter, one strategy employed by the media in their representations of Gypsies has been the conflation of their representation to some degree with that of a white underclass. There are obvious absurdities in this process, highlighted by some of the means by which many of the communities in question are represented[2] and by the vast cultural differences between those communities. Haylett (2001) outlines how, historically, there has been a white working-class poor who in their 'otherness' have marked out a boundary line in society; however, the reconstruction of post-imperial, post-Second World War Britain from welfare state to twenty-first-century welfare society (DEMOS 1999), with its emphasis on multiculturalism, needs to shift the language away from its emphasis on white working-class poverty or a white underclass. Haylett suggests that:

> The racialised discourse of 'underclass' does not sit well with the image of a modern, inclusive, multicultural nation; it suggests that

'things have gone too far'. The 'underclass' are therefore in the process of being renamed the 'excluded', their racialised otherness recast as a cultural otherness. The reference points of this discourse are not those of blood, race and nation, but of culture, ethnicity and a globalised place in the world. (Haylett 2001, 360)

Haylett's work primarily examines how the white working class are represented within political debate, but notes the similarities with academic and media engagements. Within academic debates, whilst certain 'others' are the subject of 'high symbolic status', this is not the case for representations of the white working class, which are all too often 'masked by silences which speak of disappointment, embarrassment and abandonment' (Haylett 2001, 353). The sentiment that the white working classes are the last group that can be openly abused in a way that would not be tolerated by other minority ethnic groups, and may have, in many ways, been left behind by the onset of a multicultural nation, is one that has found a populist position, for example in *The Likes Of Us* (Collins 2004). It is also a sentiment that echoes much that could and is said about Gypsies (see Gil-Robles 2005). That there might be subconsciously understood linkages between Gypsy and white working-class communities reflects the similarities that can be drawn out from understandings of their respective cultures and the representations made of them. Two connections, in particular, seem to speak volumes: the first centres on ambiguity and the second on skin colour. One consequence of the multicultural agenda has been to amplify understandings of the failings of poor white working-class cultures. The figures that are created – unemployed, welfare-reliant, uneducated loudmouths with big families and bigger dogs – are deeply unsettling and troubling figures within the nation. They do not hark back to the spirit of the Blitz, the Jarrow march or any sense of working-class resolve in the face of inordinate difficulties. Instead, the images that are conjured up are nothing to be proud of at all. These stereotypical images, which do not do justice to the lives of deprived white working-class communities, do, however, have a common currency. They are images that are understood to represent something that is British and, in doing so, they generate a feeling of ambiguity. Within the ambiguities prevalent in the construction of this group (for example, the use of symbols such as the England flag on the one hand, and a level of obnoxious behaviour on the other) is a level of uncertainty. In some ways this echoes the unsettling nature of the figure of the 'Gypsy', not as a reflection of the behaviours or the figures created but in the common currency of a national 'type'. The figure of the Gypsy that is created is one that is understood to be abhorrent.

Secondly, and related to the ambiguity described above, is the fact of whiteness; the shared skin colour in the face of diverse cultural and ethnic allegiances again seems to kindle a greater degree of ambiguity in the understandings of both groups. One consequence in some of our research in a deprived part of a metropolitan city was an acknowledgement by Gypsy communities of belonging within geographical spaces shared with poor white working-class communities and, to a degree, sharing values as well. These materialised, in particular, in shared racist attitudes towards non-white groups of immigrants. A germ of this shared geographical bonding was the sense of a common understanding of how the world saw them; the feeling that within deprived, run-down areas, white working-class and Gypsy communities were being effectively abandoned because of the type of people they were, and because they did not belong within the certainties of polite multicultural landscapes. The unfairness that was felt was directed back at the wider world but most specifically materialised in racist language that reflected locally held bigotries about newer immigrant groups. There was a considerable feeling of identification by Gypsy communities with the urban locality and their white neighbours.

The 'whiteness' of Gypsies (real or imaginary) impacts upon the position Gypsies are able to occupy within multicultural society. In many respects it acts as an enormous brake upon what becomes considered as an acceptable understanding of their culture. By not sitting comfortably amongst other recognisably non-white 'others' because of skin colour, the conflation with other white underclasses becomes acceptable, or at least it becomes the unthinking approach of multicultural institutions who have to deal or engage with Gypsy communities. This includes the Academy, which, despite the seeming progress of multiculturalism, remains to a large extent the preserve of white, middle-class people, and seeks to reflect and reproduce its white middle-class preoccupations (Fenton *et al.* 2000).

Within the Academy the importance of Gypsy research is limited almost entirely to very specific social ends; that is, policy-driven work aimed at improving education standards or healthcare. On the peripheries there is work about language and culture and occasionally there are more radical attempts at all-inclusive social, geographical and political understanding. But, on the whole, work that receives funding and is not a PhD thesis is directed by policy concerns. Whilst the student of identity who is interested in the black or Asian diasporas will find a shelf full of different and competing voices that take a myriad of different cultural moments as their starting point, there is significantly less on offer within Gypsy studies. In part this seems to reflect the ownership exercised by some academics producing work about Gypsies over 'their' subject matter, but it also seems to relate to the wider positioning of the Academy with regard to white 'others', including Gypsy communities. This privileging of non-white 'others' may in itself go some way towards explaining the insecurities of academics in taking their work forward about

Gypsies. Not only are their positions made precarious by lack of funding, but their work rarely registers interest comparable with that experienced by other colleagues. There is a hierarchy of importance for groups of 'others' in academic practice; within this pecking order work about Gypsies is close to the bottom. Any further threat to the standing of the group, and by association to academics working in this field, is therefore hugely amplified.

In our work we identified the linkages between white working-class communities and Gypsy communities in urban areas. Some conflation of these two groups is also seen to take place in the media representations of different types of people. Elsewhere Ray and Reed (2005) have identified the complex relationships that might be constructed between ethnicity, racism and identity in their work looking at the experiences of English Romany groups in rural parts of Kent. They identified both the strength of local identification to the immediate areas in which the Romanies lived and, transcending this, the importance of their identification to a wider 'imagined Romany community'. Some of these understandings were disrupted by the more recent appearance of asylum seekers in the locality, which raised questions about the meaning of 'whiteness' in a rural context. Different categories of desirable and undesirable whiteness (Neal 2002) seemingly surface within the ambiguities of these relationships.

Whiteness, or at least a recognisable 'degree' of whiteness, plays a part in the configuration of senses of belonging. It also acts as the marker of ambiguous and more tentative boundaries where belonging ceases to function or is no longer felt to be appropriate. For the Academy the challenge of interpreting such social constructions is made harder by the hazy set of associations between three different registers of academic investigation: firstly, there are the imprecise hierarchies of diasporic importance, often measured as the suffering associated with diaspora (how bad was the suffering, the different ways such suffering is experienced and the numbers of people involved in the suffering); secondly, there is a seeming conflation understood publicly and institutionally between Gypsy groups and other white deprived communities that a liberal, multicultural view of the world finds it exceptionally hard to be tolerant around; and finally, there is the interpretation of a certain kind of white 'other' that is made by the Academy, reflecting its white, liberal multiculturalism. This final strand, the understanding of white 'others', seems to unlock much of multiculturalism's failure to cope with Gypsy culture and also reflects something that is much more apparent in the mainstream, in the representation of 'Lotto Louts' or 'chavs' in *The Sun*, for example. Nash (2003, 640) argues that much work on race is extremely restrictive because it only ever addresses race in terms of non-white bodies and non-white spaces; such 'unreflexive whiteness' denudes much of the cultural content from understandings of whiteness and replaces it instead with a broadbrush understanding based on skin colour. This is, of course, the point at which it becomes so much harder for a society to formulate understandings of white groups who do not belong. It is the point at which white understandings of white 'others' become irreconcilable. If, on the one hand, there is a white hegemonic group who share broadly similar and fundamental cultural values, how can they construct an understanding of a lotto lout, a chav or a Gypsy that distinguishes themselves from the 'other'? The normalised understanding of who is white and who is not says these people are white; cultural instincts suggest the need to draw a distinct line and delineate a white 'other'. Within this process the 'other' that is produced is a racialised 'white other'. Nash underlines the cultural work that is undertaken here, stating that, 'In Britain, liberal multiculturalism that constructs and then condemns a reactionary and racist white English working class performs a complex form of cultural racism' (Nash 2003, 642). The construction of figures such as 'white trash' or 'chavs' is essentially a racist construction by the hegemonic white society. It sits comfortably with the types of understandings that have been generated over centuries about Gypsies, in which the overriding importance has been to establish a comfortable set of distinctions. That such distinctions do not necessarily reflect actual experiences of Gypsies inevitably leads to an unsettling understanding of the relationship between two different cultures. Something similar is reflected in the understandings of white working-class 'others' who may well exhibit elements of shared cultural heritage and who have been constructed within the same historic processes that have also seen the appearance of Middle Englanders or members of the Countryside Alliance. There is still a need to demarcate their 'otherness' and, once again, it is perhaps in the daily non-alignment of the understood image of a deprived working class and the reality of daily contacts that a similar sense of unease begins to materialise. The associations that exist between Gypsies and white working-class groups seem to operate both at the level on which understandings are constructed about them and also, in different ways, in the processes of responding to the understandings that are placed upon their shoulders. Unravelling the flows of influence and the respective impacts between these associations, and appreciating which drives the understandings of the other, are problems perhaps akin to the age-old conundrum of the chicken and the egg.

Notes

1. For example, commercial builders, property developers or local councils may be able to negotiate successfully around planning law. House builders wanting to develop greenfield sites or build luxury developments in inner-city areas may essentially be proposing work that falls entirely outside the remit of local plans. This does not thwart their ambitions, it just means they have to negotiate around other areas of planning gain: providing landscaped public

spaces, for example, or working elements of social housing into their initial plans. Similarly, developers of listed historic buildings may well agree plans in which the short-term development completely changes the character of a building but preserves the building in such a way that at some future date the changes can be reversed and the building returned to its original condition.

2. One striking distinction occurs in the photographic representations. Gypsy sites distanced by a long lens mounted on helicopters are the favoured representation of Gypsies. A typical 'chav', however, seems invariably to be shown up close and personal; zits and tattoos are all in close-cropped focus. It is almost as though the potency of the image of the Gypsy is reinforced by being half-seen, glimpsed somewhere in the shadows, thereby emphasising the role of the *stranger*. It is a figure that can be portrayed as being at large amongst the wider population without being fully seen or understood.

8. The outsider in racist society

In our suggestion that there is both a 'multicultural society' and a separate 'racist society' in which Gypsies and non-Gypsies might lead different lives there is a degree of ambiguity. To be quite clear, these understandings of society are, of course, not divergent and separate from each other. Rather they exist in tandem; more than that, they are superimposed upon and inform each other. Our understandings of behaviours and the accounts we give of ourselves seem at times to be fine-tuned by our understanding of where within society we are operating at any one time. So children might express a different range of attitudes within the classroom and at home, just as researchers might explain their work differently to potential respondents than they would to academic colleagues. During our research into 'good practice' in schools it was always apparent that, however distinctive we might understand the world of a multicultural school to be from a locality associated with long histories of racism and bigotry, the two worlds remained entwined. On occasion the materialisation of this engagement felt positive. We heard accounts of a morning when racist graffiti appeared on the walls of a building opposite the school gates and teaching staff from the school worked to clean it away before the children arrived for their morning lessons. On other occasions we were aware of racism within the school gates and of its wholly negative impacts: name-calling, bullying, fights, disrupted educations and lives. For the Gypsy children attending the school and for their families there is an engagement with both parts of this equation. Multiculturalism often feels as if it is a liberal response to racist society, a means of coping with the traditional and historic hostilities faced by Gypsies and other ethnic minorities. It is the means by which those not directly associated with racism, either as perpetrators or victims, can promote a design for society in which understanding of different cultures lessens the impacts of racist actions and attitudes. Whilst there is evident engagement between Gypsy communities and multicultural and liberal parts of society that has a bearing on the formation of Gypsy identity, it is perhaps within engagements with racist society over long periods of time that the deepest understandings of Gypsy identity are formed.

This final chapter will examine the role of Gypsy representations within parts of society that do not subscribe to a multicultural vision. This chapter will draw on strands of thinking from earlier chapters to provide an analysis of the particular role Gypsy representations have within society. It will consider the impact of 'whiteness', less in the sense of a racialised 'whiteness' that is attributed to certain groups in society in order to identify them as belonging at the bottom of social strata, but rather in a more direct fashion, in which an absence of 'whiteness' is constructed by linking Gypsy culture with dirt. Such characterisations carry with them alternative means of recognising Gypsy culture that also reinforce notions of Gypsies as 'others' or *strangers* within society.

For centuries Gypsies have been seen and portrayed in derogatory terms. All parts of society have associated them with negative connotations; we have used representations in the media and Gypsy children's experiences of racism in schools to highlight such practices. However, these form only a small part of the daily experiences that shape the lives and identities of Gypsy communities. The typical and immediate response from wider society to temporary Gypsy encampments is usually uproar from local residents, who do not want Gypsies anywhere near their land or their homes. Where Gypsies live in more permanent settings, on sites or in housing, they still face the same levels of hostility from non-Gypsy neighbours. They are identified as belonging outside normal society. These attitudes are prevalent both in urban and rural areas and have been consistently identified across many research projects. The racism and hostility that is experienced by Gypsies manifests itself in a range of ways, from basic one-to-one prejudice in everyday encounters to a reflection of racism and bias in policy initiatives. Sometimes policies that are intended to benefit Gypsy communities have had, in practice, the opposite effect.[1]

Racism in public

One noteworthy aspect of much of the racism experienced by Gypsies is its overt nature. It can be expressed openly within the public sphere in a way that would be considered entirely unacceptable if it was directed at other ethnic minority groups. In our own research it was clear that many non-Gypsy interviewees were not afraid to expose a degree of racism towards Gypsies that they would be extremely wary of revealing with regard to other minority groups (Bhopal and Myers 2005). This is not to suggest that the interviewees did not harbour similar racist views about other minority ethnic groups, simply that within specific contexts there is a clear understanding of the boundaries of acceptable attitudes (and this certainly includes the context of being interviewed as part of an academic research project). Such openness mirrored the expression of derogatory attitudes and use of the term 'white trash' by residents of Detroit, as discussed by Hartigan (1997); the same people were also careful not to use racist language about other ethnic minority groups while in his presence. In this sense multicultural society might well be seen as the public sphere, the world in which our public face can generally be judged. Within that public sphere we tend to expect that certain social etiquettes are followed, including a degree of political correctness when discussing issues around ethnic minorities. There is recognition, particularly in the presence of black or Asian researchers, of politically correct boundaries, and respondents often appear to silence racisms they might otherwise express in their private worlds (in other words, multicultural society is in the ascendancy and racist society is muted in such circumstances). There are obviously ways and means of testing such situations, including the building of longer-term relationships with respondents in order to create greater confidence and to enter more fully into their private worlds. However, throughout our research we constantly heard racist and derogatory names openly directed at Gypsies in the public sphere. What is more, this occurred within conversations between researchers and their interviewees; that is, within short-term relationships where a degree of circumspection on the part of the interviewee might be expected. It also materialised in marginal conversations conducted away from direct participants in the research:

> I've seen those Pikeys on traps round here and you have to watch out for them. I always keep my eyes open when they come down this road.

This was from a woman who lived in a rural village with a large population of Gypsies. The same sort of attitude was also expressed when researching in an urban area:

> I think they come here and stay and then they go and leave so much dirt and filth around and they get away it. That's the way they are and I think the law should be harder on them so that they are not allowed to do that and so that they don't get in our

way. Because we're trying to live a decent life and we are the ones who pay our taxes and we are the ones who work. They don't contribute to society at all.

That such attitudes are prevalent is not in doubt; they are frequently reported by Gypsies and by professionals working with Gypsy communities and are also plainly exhibited in many of the tabloids and other media. The public expression of such overt racism in an almost casual manner seems to suggest that it is a racism that works in a different way to that which might be expressed casually to close friends and family or within the confines of close-knit communities. If as researchers we had sought out groups of racists then we might expect the use of racist language in our presence, or, if we were reporting back on relationships with respondents that had been matured over long periods of time and in which great efforts had been expended in earning trust, then again we might be less surprised to hear such language. What is startling is the very ordinariness with which racist views are expressed without any possibility of knowing the listener's point of view; this seems to exceed the tolerances for exhibiting racist behaviour in public. There is a greater tolerance of racism towards Gypsies than towards other groups, when measured on a scale of how public such racism can be made.

The effect of racism expressing itself in private circumstances that were in fact a public arena was, unexpectedly, the most newsworthy story to emerge in the 2007 season of *Celebrity Big Brother*. Jade Goody fell from her position of well-liked celebrity to national disgrace within a few days because of her taunting and bullying behaviour towards the relatively unknown (in the UK) Bollywood superstar Shilpa Shetty. What seemed to trigger this unprecedented adverse reaction on the part of the public was the making public of some overt but mostly covertly held racist attitudes. Inside the *Big Brother* house Goody was seen having conversations with other housemates in which she made a number of offensive and seemingly racist remarks about the Indian actress. These comments were also aligned with taunting and bullying behaviour towards Shetty. It is apparent that, in her position inside the house, Goody was unable to make the judgement that she had crossed a specific boundary of acceptability. To all intents and purposes she seems to have been conducting these conversations within a private world, one that was only open to the scrutiny of her close confidantes within the house; this was obviously a gross misjudgement, bearing in mind that this was the seventh consecutive year in which every last detail of life inside the *Big Brother* house had been transmitted to the British public. Almost immediately upon leaving the *Big Brother* house the video footage of her behaviour was replayed to Goody; she immediately became aware of how far she had crossed acceptable boundaries and realised that she was open to being labelled a racist. Goody had described Shetty as 'Shilpa Poppadum, Shilpa Fuck-a-wallah', names which plainly carry racist overtones. It is instructive to consider whether there would have been the same uproar if Goody's victim had been a Gypsy; would there have been the same sense of revelation, when the video footage was replayed, that the celebrity bully had overstepped a boundary? The answer seems to be probably not. As discussed, the use of the derogatory term 'pikey' can often be heard on national TV, although generally in more ambiguous circumstances than Goody's full-frontal racism in the *Big Brother* house.

Something like Jade Goody's revelatory moment should have occurred in September 2007 on another celebrity reality TV show, *Hell's Kitchen*. The basic premise of this show is that a leading chef, in this case Marco Pierre White, trains a group of celebrities with little talent or aptitude for cooking to run a restaurant kitchen to Michelin standards. In one episode one of the contestants, Lee Ryan, a singer, asks to speak to White about some concerns he has.

White was apparently expecting Ryan to complain about the objectionable characteristics of one of Ryan's co-contestants, but instead found himself being challenged about his own use of the phrase 'a pikey's picnic' the previous evening. More than anything else the chef seems bewildered that anyone could take any offence away from his comment. Unlike Goody, he did not suddenly find himself considering the possibility of facing up to any public opprobrium, and with good reason: it never materialises. The offensive use of the word 'pikey' does not result in the same level of attention that comparably racist terms would undoubtedly attract.

> Marco Pierre White: What is wrong with being a pikey?
> Lee Ryan: Just the term 'pikey', it's not a nice word to say. I know my friends don't like being called pikeys. It's a derogatory term to a Traveller or Gypsy Roma.

Reaction to White's reference to 'a pikey's picnic' and his bewildered, disbelieving discussion of the inherent offensiveness of such comments was, to put it mildly, fairly muted. ITV broadcast the programme with a warning that it contained language that might offend some viewers. Lee Ryan walked off the show, but there was no apparent condemnation of White by the broadcasters and he continued in his role. In condemning White's comments the Commission for Racial Equality noted that the use of racist behaviours towards Gypsies seemed to register less than that about black or other minority groups. Perhaps ironically, the biggest storyline within the series was the homophobic bullying by comedian Jim Davidson of another contestant; this resulted in Davidson being thrown off the programme and led the Guardian Unlimited ArtsBlog to comment 'What's the exchange rate between homophobia and racism these days?' (12 September 2007).

Within the world of reality TV production there is a repeated and highly effective strategy of recruiting difficult or offensive characters to come on to programmes. In *Hell's Kitchen* this role was filled by Jim Davidson, a comedian whose material is often homophobic and racist. It seems likely he was recruited to the programme because of his potential to get under the skin of other contestants and, in doing so, to attract more viewers. Predictably, this did indeed happen. What was extraordinary, however, particularly in comparison to the Davidson homophobia story, which caused a great stir on and off the programme, was the degree to which the 'pikey's picnic' story simply fell flat. It was not that the programme producers would not have liked these comments to be at the centre of a racism row; however, for White, others taking part on the show and the watching public, there was no register of surprise or shock about what had happened. It was a moment that seemed to simply slip away amidst a million other television happenings that lacked noteworthiness.

The discrepancy in the importance attached to racism towards Gypsies compared to that towards other minority groups is reflected in many other areas. As academics we have both noticed the reluctance in some quarters to discuss racism in terms of Gypsies. At a recent national conference a session on 'race and racism' in which both audience and speakers came from a variety of ethnic backgrounds, the concept of racism was discussed and understood entirely within a simple and unchallenging binary. Racism was described as something that white people do to black people. Asked to comment on issues of racism towards Gypsies during the period allotted for questions, the speakers became hostile and angry. There was a debate in which the speakers challenged the very possibility that prejudice encountered by a white group could be compared to that suffered by black people. Afterwards, in conversation with other delegates in the margins of the conference, it was a relief to discover other voices who agreed that racism towards Gypsies was real and commonplace. The failure within parts of academia to acknowledge the power of racism that is faced by Gypsies highlights the wider framework within which Gypsies are understood. It speaks again of the failure of dominant society to grasp fundamental aspects of the historic and social conditions in which Gypsies have lived their lives for the last 500 years. It also raises ugly questions about how intellectual knowledge is produced; is there a pecking order for racisms and does this reflect levels of perceived suffering, for example? We would conclude that within academia, as in wider society, racisms are constructed in which different values are placed on the suffering inflicted on different groups of people. The suffering undergone by Gypsies registers very low on such intellectual scales. Just as the use of racist language or behaviour on reality TV programmes has a different resonance depending on whether it refers to Gypsies or other ethnic minorities, so within the liberal academic classes certain forms of racisms are legitimated and others are not. Within the Academy there are hierarchies of *acceptable* and *unacceptable* forms of racism.

The language used by *The Sun* in its campaign against Gypsies was certainly more provocative than the ranting of Jade Goody or the ill-informed comments of Marco Pierre White. In its readiness to mobilise a language of racism (if carefully avoiding the use of specific words), *The Sun* adopted an almost lynch mob mentality. The slogan 'Stamp on the Camps' has an almost incendiary quality about it, one that could be misread as active encouragement to their readers to march on Gypsy sites. We can only assume that *The Sun*'s rhetoric was intended to suggest a more intellectually orientated interpretation of 'stamping out' Gypsy sites, one enacted through political campaigning rather than direct action. Given the apparently blasé manner in which many of our respondents would describe Gypsies there appears to be a situation in which such racism is tolerated and unchallenged by much of society.

When diverse forms of evidence, including the accounts of Gypsy families, the statements of non-Gypsy interviewees, racisms expressed in newspapers and the media, and intellectual productions of knowledge about racism within the academy are brought together, a very bleak picture emerges. Gypsies are understood and defined by an overwhelmingly public racism; one that is not self-conscious, one that does not feel the need to hide itself away and one that is not exclusive to cultish right-wing organisations. It is a racism that suggests that the 'othering' of Gypsy communities and the associated intolerance expressed towards them is an unremarkable state of affairs.

Racism, Gypsies and the formation of boundaries

One moment that saw some very specific constructions of a racist account of Gypsies within a rural environment occurred amongst the discourses that emerged in the aftermath of Tony Martin's shooting of intruders who had broken into his home. One of the intruders, Fred Barras, a 16-year-old Gypsy boy, was shot dead. Vanderbeck suggests that the Martin affair was:

> emblematic of the state of current 'underclass' and 'social exclusion' discourses in contemporary Britain – discourses that emphasise the moral failings of the 'excluded' without any significant discussion of the sources of inequalities.
> (Vanderbeck 2003, 363)

Whilst the debate that ensued was framed by wider public concerns about out-of-control youth and the role of a dangerous and socially excluded underclass, there was also a specific interest generated around the importance of Fred Barras's Gypsy background. Vanderbeck notes how the media reiterate and reconstruct understandings of power relationships and spatial distances between Gypsies and non-Gypsies, on the one hand repeating enduring stereotypes about Gypsies and, on the other, relating these to newer social concerns such as problems with dispossessed youth. The Martin affair was used to effectively redefine ideas of rural crime within a definition of Gypsy crime and to suggest that Gypsy lifestyles are incompatible with other rural communities and life in the countryside. The Martin affair in many ways undermined more traditional constructions by non-Gypsies of what it means to be an authentic or 'real' Gypsy. Whereas 'real' Gypsies might well be imagined to have an acknowledged, albeit marginal, place in country life (Halfacree 1996; Sibley 1997), media accounts in this case suggest that even this role has been compromised.

The process of constructing real and fake Gypsies in a rural context echoes the comments made by James Paice MP around the appearance of Irish Travellers in his Cambridgeshire constituency. Paice distinguished the Irish Travellers as dirty in comparison to English Gypsies and suggested that the genuine English Gypsies at some time in the past were, unlike the recent Irish arrivals, engaged in real Gypsy employment such as crop picking. There was, however, an inherent suggestion in Paice's secondary, temporal distantiation that the real Gypsy in the countryside context has long since vanished due to changing rural economies. In his place is a fake, settled Gypsy who lives on a site or in housing and becomes associated with a new and dangerous social underclass. So even the English Gypsies that Paice seems at first sight to be slightly more sympathetic towards are also marked out as fake because they do not belong to a bygone age.

Levitas (1998) and Lister (1990) argue that groups can be positioned as 'socially excluded' to justify programmes of social inclusion and integration ultimately meant to (re)produce existing inequalities and relations of power. The representations of Gypsies in the Martin affair serve to further label and stigmatise Gypsies as undesirable, increasing the high levels of scrutiny, surveillance and suspicion to which they are already subject. Vanderbeck suggests that the process of linking traditional stereotypes of Gypsy involvement with criminality within discourses about the social exclusion of a newer underclass serves to bolster 'logistics for their increased control' (Vanderbeck 2003, 379).

Tapping into fears around personal safety and the invasion of the home, the Martin affair carried with it overtones of fear of *strangers* that were easily enflamed by their entanglement with representations of Gypsies. The images of Fred Barras's parents and associates that later emerged in much of the news coverage worked to portray a very negative impression of the type of people in his life. Reporting on his funeral in Newark, *The Daily Mail* (10 September 1999) adopts a slightly disconcerting tone, noting the scale of the funeral cortege, which included 'seven limousines and four lorries loaded with wreaths and bouquets' and brought the town to a stand-still. In these representations of the funeral there is an echo of East End gangster funerals, one that is undercut and situated within a Gypsy context by the references to flat-bed lorries. The funeral is also contextualised in descriptions of the grieving parents; Fred Barras's mother is described as 'wearing a black leather jacket' and his father as 'dressed in a scruffy jumper'. Other reports in the newspaper detail the criminal records of Fred Barras's associates on the night he was killed and those of his father. There seems to be a desire to stress both the potency and the danger associated with Fred Barras and those around him, but also to suggest, in the oddly specific details of dress, for example, that these are small-time, low-life criminals. The picture that emerges is of a marginal group of people, operating outside dominant society, who do not enjoy a lucrative or secure lifestyle. They are, in fact, a classical representation of an underclass group. The clear associations made with criminal activity identify them within state discourses as a group that can legitimately be targeted for anti-social behaviours.

It has been widely argued that the negative image of Gypsies in wider society is at the root of problems in establishing good relationships between Gypsies and non-Gypsies (see Hancock 1992; Liegeois 1987). Liegeois (1987) has argued that images that people have of Gypsies influence how they treat them and how they are viewed in society. Kenrick and Bakewell (1990) go further, pointing out that such negative images are damaging to Gypsies as they are a violation of their human rights as citizens. In particular, it is the images that have been created by non-Gypsies that are the most damaging to Gypsies. In their most current manifestations in the pages of *The Sun* and other newspapers, in the advertising campaigns of political parties or in parliamentary debates, these images are rooted in traditional stereotypes. They also reach out for newer representations such as the 'rich Gypsy' and associations with other underclass figures. The creation of new figures underlines that the very negative portrayals of Gypsies are a societal process, rather than one-off instances of bigotry. These are images that are summoned up by the dominant society to act on its behalf in situating where Gypsy communities fall within society. They are markers and reiterations of where the boundary lines lie between Gypsy and non-Gypsy society.

Sibley suggests that 'modern, negative reactions to Travellers often include the romantic observation that they formerly blended into the rural scene' and identifies this placing of Gypsies in the past as 'a common form of distantiation' (Sibley 2003, 224). This distancing from the figure of the Gypsy as a free rural spirit, a state assumed by modern commentators to have been characteristic of Gypsies in the nineteenth century, seems to work in a double-edged fashion. On the one hand it suggests that a true, 'authentic' ethnicity is no longer available to the vast majority of Gypsy communities, while on the other it identifies new contemporary ethnicities that can be occupied by Gypsies, which not only fail to reflect the realities of communities' lives, but also actively work to undermine their standing within society. Such newer positions can be seen to emerge within discourses around the underclass, refugees and asylum seekers, and media-created types such as the unworthy rich. The struggle between different non-Gypsies' accounts of Gypsy identity is reflected historically in alternative descriptions of criminality on the one hand and exoticism on the other, and also within newer discourses such as those within the media that make linkages between Gypsy communities and other underclass or excluded groups. In all these processes there is a tendency towards a name-calling that is little different to the earliest behaviours of primary school children. The use of offensive labels or racist name-calling becomes in many respects an acceptable and unquestioned practice, just as discriminatory practices become the acceptable norm. Throughout all these processes the expression of racism (through language and behaviour) becomes not just tolerated but, in practice, *acceptable*.

Perceptions of what constitutes a rural idyll in twenty-first-century Britain are vastly changed from what they might have been fifty or even twenty years ago. Tradition, within a rural context in particular, seems to have been shaken on many fronts, resulting in part in the increased politicisation of rural concerns through organisations such as Countryside Alliance. Whilst the immediate context of such political activity seems to be driven by specifically rural issues such as legislation prohibiting hunting or perceived government failures to support farming, there is also perhaps a background shift in what constitutes rural life. The increased availability of everything through the internet and the continuing move towards large out-of-town supermarkets speak of an increasing move towards an urban understanding of living in which even village life feels more suburban than rural. Within the Tony Martin affair, the figure of the Gypsy is negatively identified both within traditional rural discourses as a criminal element and within urban and suburban concerns as a threat to the safety and security of the home. Almost inevitably, the figure of Fred Barras was portrayed in the media as a representation of the Gypsy who is understood to be dangerous and criminal.[2]

Understandings of ethnicity and political organisation

Definitions of ethnicity are neither standardised nor generally agreed. This may well be a sign of the fluid nature of ethnicity itself and the different constructions that might result in different ethnicities. In the last ten years the concept of ethnicity has tended to replace ideas of race both within legal frameworks and the assignment of rights to groups of individuals, and also within work that has examined identity and culture. Miles's (1989) study of racism utilises a model of the concept of social construction that is based on ideas of selection and signification. Groups are formed, identified and defined by selecting from a range of criteria that are seen to be significant. A group can be formed according to characteristics such as skin colour, place of birth or religious beliefs. The idea of social construction is based on the idea that there is no consistency in the selection of significant differences and that these can vary over time and between different signifiers. So, for example, ethnic criteria have now replaced racial criteria as the primary characteristics used to distinguish groups.

The definitions and limitations of ethnicity or race become particularly important at junctures where legal designations are required, as without the categorisation and recognition of ethnicity there is a very possible danger of ethnic groups being denied civil rights. Under the Race Relations Act (1976) and its Amendment Act (2000), for example, there is a clear implication that individuals should not receive unequal treatment because of their racial and ethnic origin. In principle this is fine, but the question that cannot be easily answered by legislation is whether or not Gypsies can or should be seen as an ethnic group and how exactly that group should be defined. In order for Gypsies to achieve an equal status with other majority and minority groups they have to be seen as an ethnic group and given a shared ethnic status. Whilst there have historically been attempts to define Gypsies in terms of a pure blood-line, more recently accounts have tended to define Gypsy ethnicity and identity through cultural rather than biological characteristics. Often attempts at defining the characteristics of Gypsy ethnicity have been wholly negative and stereotypical; for example, in July 1999 the then Home Secretary Jack Straw made a number of comments about Gypsies which typified their ethnic characteristics in a very negative fashion. He said that many Travellers 'go burgling, thieving, breaking into vehicles, causing all kinds of trouble, including defecating in the doorways of firms', and that they were 'masquerading as law-abiding citizens when many are not' (BBC Radio West Midlands, 22 July 1999). Such statements legitimise the already negative attitudes that exist towards Gypsies. They also undermine some of the legal safeguards that might be anticipated to derive from culturally defined ethnicities. If the cultural characteristics are established in criminal terms by well-placed government ministers, then the assumption is that membership of such ethnic groups will not carry the same status in a court of law or on the streets as other identifiable groups.

There is an overriding impression that non-Gypsies, who are themselves engaged in processes around the construction and negotiation of ethnic boundaries, are often poorly placed to understand Gypsy culture both in the form of its historic foundations and in terms of the way it has adapted to contemporary economies. This is not unique to the UK; Clark (2002) describes how across Europe there is a lack of awareness of Gypsy communities adapting to post-industrial economies in order to prosper. Non-Gypsies continue to imagine that Gypsies remain engaged only within 'traditional' forms of economic activity. A different kind of discourse is apparent at Appleby, in

Cumbria, where historically there has been greater contact between Gypsies and local non-Gypsy residents as a result of the horse fair held every June. The fair, which dates back at least to the eighteenth century, is the biggest social gathering by far of Gypsies from across Britain. Holloway (2005) describes some of the flux in relations between Gypsies and non-Gypsies that can be found at Appleby, including the changing understanding of Gypsies who have moved away from more traditional elements of their culture, perhaps by engaging in full-time jobs. Such people found themselves normalised to a great degree in their relationships with the local population, in a way that was not apparent for other families still identified as living within more traditional cultural patterns. Holloway also notes distinctions made by Appleby residents between 'true' Gypsies and 'hangers on' who may not be regarded as belonging within an ethnic minority population (Holloway 2005, 356). Local residents tended to define categories of 'hangers on' as being associated instead with socially excluded urban groups. Crime in the area was often blamed on these 'hangers on', rather than the 'true' Gypsies, and via this apportionment of blame the residents avoided accusations of racism (Holloway 2005, 363). This obviously speaks of some of the routine distinctions made between 'authentic' and 'inauthentic' Gypsies within wider society. It is also a process that hints at the continuing flux that has always existed between Gypsy and non-Gypsy communities, some individuals becoming associated with Gypsy culture whilst others are distanced from it.

The idea of political organisation for Gypsies dates back to the 1940s and continues to the present day. The main driving forces for political organisation have been the promotion of Gypsy nationalism and identity, including the encouragement of a greater awareness of belonging to communities that have shared values and experiences, the fight against racism and discrimination, and the fight to obtain rights for Gypsy communities. Given a history associated with 'unremitting persecution and harassment, including executions, brandings, mutilations, whippings and rape' (Hancock 1998, 34), and a contemporary world in which Gypsy culture is regularly racially abused, there is great scope for a political organisation to harness the extreme reactions felt by Gypsy communities about such treatment, in order to bind disparate groups together. To some degree this has already occurred, and the existence of international organisations representing Gypsies as a distinctive ethnic group is one response to discrimination they have suffered. Such organisations also work to foster a sense of belonging within Gypsy communities and a sense of group solidarity when facing outsiders. Mayall argues that the 'discriminatory treatment by outsiders strengthens the group identity by creating a defensive response to such hostility' (Mayall 2004, 235).

In 1968 the history of and discrimination against Gypsies was first brought to the attention of international politics when a Swedish resolution ensured that their hostile treatment was passed for investigation by the Council of Europe's Social and Health Committee; it has remained a key area of concern both nationally and internationally since then. Within European politics one effect of increased political action has been to raise awareness about the Gypsy experience of the Holocaust and place these sufferings alongside the experiences of Jews and other persecuted groups.

We have noted elsewhere within this book that figures of community or political leaders rarely emerge in the discourses around Gypsies and their engagements with non-Gypsies with anything like the same visibility associated with other ethnic minority groups in Britain. Whilst this suggests an under-developed side to this activity it again provides some explanation of why clearly demarcated understandings of ethnicity are not ingrained within the British consciousness. More overt political representation from within communities would strengthen the response towards discriminatory behaviour and would also work to make non-Gypsies' understandings of Gypsy communities' sense of their ethnicity more clear.

At the grassroots of political involvement we encountered a strangely marginal account; when we asked schools for examples of 'good practice' around Gypsy education, one cited the example of a Gypsy parent who had been a school governor several years previously. This event had barely made an impact on the life of the school; when asked for further details about the parent's role as a governor, the school was unable to supply any detailed information. We were able to discover that the person in question had been a single parent and that they had been a governor for an unconfirmed period in the previous five years. We could find no account or recollection of anything they had done in the role. What was notable was that this low-profile occupation of a low-key political role had registered within the school because of the Gypsy ethnicity of the governor. It was presented as an example of 'best practice' because it was considered unusual and did not reflect the expected behaviour of Gypsy parents. As a happening within a specific time and place it bucked anticipated trends; the marker of Gypsy ethnicity within the spaces of the school carried with it specific assumptions not just about engagement of children with the education system but also about Gypsy communities' unwillingness to influence or shape the political organisation of schooling in the borough. This seemed to reflect a wider understanding of Gypsy communities as being outside mainstream political organisation and dialogues.

Ambiguity and the exaggerated stranger

Bauman's *stranger* (1991) is an interesting proposition in many ways because it is a construct that does not necessarily shed light on our understandings of society; instead, it works to muddy the waters. In a simple world we would be able easily to assimilate a knowledge of where boundaries are formed, so we would know unequivocally when we were at home and when we were abroad, when we were amongst friends and when amongst enemies, and we would have that sixth sense of knowing when we are about to step across the boundary markers of acceptability, good taste or safety. The *stranger*, however, disrupts these easily understood markers, acting to chip away at the confidence we might anticipate within our society. Instead of being able to look to a boundary and what lies beyond it we now have to look amongst ourselves; the *stranger* is in our company.

More than anything the *stranger* is a force for ambiguity, and an ambiguity that calls for a response. The figure of the Gypsy in popular imagination acts in this very troubling manner to create ambiguity that demands a response from society in order to lessen the tension caused by the *stranger*'s presence. Within multicultural expressions of society that response takes many different forms, often appearing in the guise of coping strategies that will ease the ambiguity by either celebrating or refusing to acknowledge difference. Unfortunately in many cases liberal good intentions are soured by mistakes and badly implemented social policy. At other times the response of multiculturalism seems simply to reflect the responses of racist society (the difference-blindness of, for example, *The Sun* or the Conservative Party). The need to dissipate ambiguity and lessen societal tension seems to be worked in such a way that the response is simply intended to make the dominant, hegemonic society feel better about itself. The racists in the *Big Brother* house constructed a picture of Shilpa Shetty that, with references to facial hair, suggested she was ugly and, with references to food hygiene, suggested she was unclean. One reading of this behaviour was that it was done simply to relieve the stress of these contestants by covering up insecurities that they were less beautiful or less sophisticated than the Indian actress. The images created around Gypsy culture are conveyed in such a way that there is a justification of the intolerant, racist attitudes and behaviours prevalent throughout society. In addition, they are images that work to bolster the confidence of white identities that are perhaps insecure and in need of reassurance about their dominant role.

The racism expressed towards Gypsies is a very particular racism and one that is expressed in a very consistent fashion: name-calling, misrecognition, assertions of impurity and associations with dirt feature prominently. These seem to reflect a desire on the part of the dominant population to define Gypsies in a very specific manner, regardless of any actual semblance to truthful accounts of their lifestyles. In this way, Gypsies are enclosed within an imaginary boundary, one that delineates again the clear markers of who in society can be a friend, who can be trusted, who is safe. There is a significant body of research which documents the vilification of Gypsies in Britain and elsewhere in Europe: what MacLaughlin (1999) describes as the 'historical geography of loathing' of Gypsies. The almost unchallenged historical construction of Gypsy identity is that it is associated with dirt, with criminality and with a sense of menace. In Britain today the same qualities routinely inform representations within the media and, as Turner (1999) notes, press accounts often employ a 'language used about enemies'. The misrepresentation of Gypsies in abhorrent terms reflects the longstanding discursive constructions that have been made around their identities; it seems unsurprising in this light that the Press Complaints Commission 'allows Gypsies in general to be referred to as scum, gyppos, parasites and so on with impunity' (Morris 2000, 218). The picture that emerges is an ugly one, in which the characterisation of Gypsies as a demonised group within popular culture is not regarded as being noteworthy. The abusive language can be endlessly repeated in any context without an expectation of censure. The expression of such public racism seems to have engrained itself so fully within the national psyche that it almost unconsciously leaks into even the more liberal parts of society.

Unlike other immigrant groups, Gypsies do not have a heritage that is well understood or available to the rest of society; very little of the cultural baggage of the Gypsy diaspora figures within insights into their culture or lifestyle. Instead, they are stigmatised with an imagined set of understandings summoned up within the fears of the dominant population. The ambiguity that surrounds their presence in British life is unsurprisingly exaggerated and heightened. In many ways this happens for entirely specious reasons caused by the racist characterisations of dominant society. As a result, society's experience of Gypsies becomes unintelligible because the false characterisations and their overtones of imaginary fears are not reflected in encounters with Gypsy communities. In the figure of the Gypsy, Bauman's *stranger* becomes exaggerated and distorted.

Geographies of racism

The social construction of Gypsy identity and perceptions of Gypsy ethnicity are shaped by a complex and fluid set of relations that do not easily lend themselves to a clear-cut analysis. It is not enough to simply assess how Gypsy communities construct their notions of identity, or how non-Gypsies seek to assign categorisations; it would also be mistaken to assume that a broad ethnicity can be drawn out of a melding of the two. There are manifold reasons for this, including disparities between different communities, misunderstandings and misrecognitions on the part of non-Gypsies, and the impact that other social constructions of marginalised or excluded groups have upon Gypsy identity (and perceptions of that identity). Theories of social construction have been important in the way in which we think about a range of identities (Bell and Valentine 1995; Laurie *et al.* 1999), but their influence on geographies of race and racism is most pertinent here. The adoption of this perspective marks a departure from empiricist mapping of the distribution of racial groups and the sociospatial processes that surround this towards a more critical examination of the meaning of the category 'race' and processes through which some groups are racialised (Jackson and Penrose 1993). Since the 1990s the emphasis placed upon racialised minorities has shifted considerably and more recently attention has been given to the white majority as well as to the study of antiracism (Bonnett 2000; Jackson 1998). These debates have shown that ideas of race are time- and space-specific.

Sibley's (1995) use of Freudian psychoanalysis to understand individuals' relationships to their social setting suggests that stereotypical ideas of good and bad objects and people are used to mediate their interaction with the world around them. These elements of good and bad can coexist in representations of the same social group, as demonstrated by the dualistic accounts of good and bad Gypsies. Often positive stereotypes are as distorting and as counter-productive as negative stereotypes, and may also work against the interests of communities (Sibley 1995; Sonneman 1999). This happens in the representations made by the dominant population about Gypsy lifestyle, which work to produce an idea of the Gypsy that clearly demarcates elements of the non-Gypsy identity. Nineteenth-century Romantics seeking succour in the face of modernity created an image of the Gypsy useful to them; for the same reason twenty-first-century newspapers have created different representations of Gypsies as a guide to defining their readers' identity. Whatever the stereotypes being produced, they have an impact on how definitions of the self and others are formed, hence the importance of space and place. These are definitions bound up within interactions between communities and individuals that are shaped in their cultural contexts: they don't just happen anywhere, they happen in specific places at specific times. Understanding the dominant discourses about 'otherness' in particular cultures is therefore crucial (Anderson 2000), as these discourses will be inextricably linked to the formation of those others.

The 'outsider' status of Gypsies predictably makes them the targets of harassment and abuse. What seems to intensify and in many ways work to reproduce this situation across long periods of time is the specific way in which misrecognitions are constructed around the culture by non-Gypsies, misrecognitions which are often matched by Gypsy wariness of becoming subsumed within non-Gypsy culture. The original misrecognitions, allied to the need for Gypsy communities to protect their culture and prosper within *gaujo* economies, conspire to create many shifts in understanding. These are largely designed by the non-Gypsy world to distance itself from Gypsies and reinforce boundary lines, and lead to a continuous discrepancy between the lived lives of Gypsies and the accounts that are constructed around their lives. These are situated within specific spatial understandings and misunderstandings, such as the different constructions of alienation within rural and urban contexts that work to suggest that the true Gypsy no longer belongs in either environment. Within urban or suburban geographies the Gypsy is a deviant intruder who rightfully belongs elsewhere in an imaginary and distant rurality. However, within the rural world they are situated within temporal misunderstandings, such as accounts that suggest that Gypsies belong to an earlier age when different economies were in place. In rural contexts too, therefore, Gypsy communities are seen as no longer belonging within contemporary economies and so they are marginalised into new understandings of dangerous criminal sub-classes. Such shifts in understanding work to complicate the construction of the figure of the Gypsy. Bauman's *stranger* becomes exaggerated, having arrived from elsewhere and having assumed some status of being amongst the natives, if not of them; the figure of the Gypsy then becomes more uncertain by not fulfilling the roles that would have been assigned to the *stranger*. The uncertainty and ambiguity that are associated with the figure of the *stranger* become intensified in the physical materialisation of Gypsies, who appear as recognisable as a stranger but are not the anticipated *stranger*.

If the Gypsy is an uncertain and ambiguously understood figure within British culture, the representation of Gypsies becomes further exaggerated by its contextualisation in parts of the media in terms of a 'Middle England' that itself seems unrepresentative and ill-defined. The use of 'Middle England' by newspapers and political parties seems to suggest another romanticised understanding, that of dominant white identity in the face of its own uncertainties. This context, with its 'othering' of additional, often white, socially excluded groups and its accounts of Britishness that seem to hark back to a time in the past understood to have been safer and more secure, does not ring true as an account of the dominant society. It is an account that fails to face up to the loss of empire, increased migration, the emergence of multiculturalism and the growing importance of a European sense of identity. Placing an account of the Gypsy within this uncertain world seems to add uncertainty to uncertainty, ambiguity to ambiguity, misrecognition to misunderstanding. In many ways it enflames the historic difficulties associated with Gypsy lives and British society.

Notes

1. Notably the 1968 Caravan Sites Act, which was arguably designed to reverse earlier policy designed to disrupt and move on Gypsy communities by requiring local authorities to provide sites. In practice it allowed councils to make a small amount of inadequate provision and legitimised the harassment and dispersal of large numbers of families who were not given a plot. Bhopal

(2004) also describes measures in schools designed to be inclusive, such as the creation of safe areas, that in practice have the effect of excluding Gypsy children within the education process.

2. Interestingly, in some of the newspaper reports of Fred Barras's funeral there were quotations from his friends and family that portrayed him in a light not dissimilar to that surrounding the romantic nineteenth-century free spirit (see *The Daily Mail*, 10 September 1999, 'Shotgun Farmer Jailed For His Own Safety').

Bibliography

Acton, T. (1974) *Gypsy politics and social change: the development of ethnic ideology and pressure politics among British Gypsies from Victorian reformism to Romani nationalism*, London, Routledge Kegan Paul

Acton, T. (1987) 'Foreword', in Hancock, I., *The pariah syndrome: an account of Gypsy slavery and persecution*, Ann Arbor, Karoma

Acton, T. (ed.) (1997) *Gypsy politics and Traveller identity*, Hatfield, University of Hertfordshire Press

Acton, T. (2004) 'The past, present and future of Traveller education', unpublished paper presented at Conference on Working Together: Raising the Educational Achievement of Gypsy and Traveller Children and Young People

Ahmed, S. (2000) *Strange encounters: embodied others in post-coloniality*, London, Routledge

Anderson, K. (2000) 'The beast within: race, humanity and animality', *Environment and Planning D: Society and Space*, 18, 301–20

Anthias, F. and Davis, N. (1992) *Racialised boundaries*, London, Routledge

Banton, M. (1997) *Ethnic and racial consciousness*, Harlow, Addison, Wesley Longman

Barany, Z. (2002) *The East European Gypsies: regime change, marginality and ethnopolitics*, Cambridge, Cambridge University Press

Barth, F. (1969) 'Introduction', in Barth, F. (ed.), *Ethnic groups and boundaries: the social organisation of cultural difference*, Boston, Waveland Press

Bauman, Z. (1989) *Modernity and the holocaust*, Cambridge, Polity

Bauman, Z. (1991) *Modernity and ambivalence*, Cambridge, Polity

Bauman, Z. (1997) 'The making and unmaking of strangers', in Werbner, P. and Modood, T. (eds), *Debating cultural hybridity*, London, Zed Books

Bauman, Z. (2001) *Community*, Cambridge, Polity

Bell, D. and Valentine, G. (1995) 'Queer country: rural lesbian and gay lives', *Journal of Rural Studies*, 11, 113-22

Belton, B. (2005) *Gypsy and Traveller ethnicity: the social construction of an ethnic phenomenon*, London, Routledge

Bercovici, K. (1929) *The story of the Gypsies*, London, Allen Lane

Bhopal, K. (2004) 'Gypsy Travellers and education: changing needs and changing perceptions', *British Journal of Educational Studies*, 52.1, 47-64

Bhopal, K. (2005) 'Who are you and what do you want? An Asian woman researching Gypsy Travellers', unpublished paper presented at The International Institute of Sociology 37th World Congress, Sweden, July 2005

Bhopal, K. with Gundara, J., Jones, C. and Owen, C. (2000) *Working towards inclusive education: aspects of good practice for Gypsy Traveller pupils*, London, Department for Education and Employment Research Report RR238

Bhopal, K. and Myers, M. (2005) '"Because they're black, they're better off than us" – Gypsy Travellers, social exclusion and marginalisation', unpublished paper presented at the British Sociological Conference, York, 2005

Bhopal, K. and Myers, M. (2006) *Gypsy Traveller pupils in schools in the London Borough of Greenwich: a report on good practice*, London Borough of Greenwich, Education and Inspectorate Advisory Council

Binchy, A. (2000) 'Shelta/Gammon in Dublin', in Acton, T. and Dalphinis, M. (eds), *Language, blacks and Gypsies*, London, Whiting & Birch

Bonnett, A. (2000) *White identities*, Harlow, Prentice Hall

Bulmer, M. (1986) 'Race and ethnicity', in Burgess, R. (ed.), *Key variables in social investigation*, London, Routledge, Kegan Paul

Clark, C. (2002) 'Not just lucky white heather and clothes pegs: putting European Gypsy and Traveller economic niches in context', in Fenton, S. and Bradley, H. (eds), *Ethnicity and economy: race and class revisited*, Basingstoke, Macmillan

Clark, C. and Greenfields, M. (2006) *Here to stay: the Gypsies and Travellers of Britain*, Hertfordshire, University of Hertfordshire Press

Clebert, J. (1963) *The Gypsies*, London, Red Union Ltd

Clifford, J. and Marcus, G. (eds) (1986) *Writing culture: the poetics and politics of ethnography*, Berkeley, University of California Press

Collins, M. (2004) *The likes of us*, London, Granta

Bibliography

Commission for Racial Equality (2000) *Race relations (amendment) act 2000*. London, CRE

Commission for Racial Equality (2006) *Gypsies and Travellers: a strategy for the CRE, 2004-2007*, London, CRE

Cornell, S. and Hartmann, D. (1998) *Ethnicity and race*, Thousand Oaks, CA, Sage

DEMOS (1999) *The welfare society lectures*, London, DEMOS.

Denzin, N. (1997) *Interpretive ethnography*, London, Sage

Denzin, N. (2001) 'The seventh moment: qualitative inquiry and the practices of a more radical consumer research', *Journal of Consumer Research*, 28, 324-30

Department for Communities and Local Government (2004) *Community cohesion education standards for schools*, http://www.communities.gov.uk/publications/communities/cohesioneducationstandards

Derrington, C. and Kendall, S. (2004) *Gypsy Traveller children in secondary schools: culture, identity and achievement*, Stoke on Trent, Trentham Books

DfEE (1999) *Raising the attainment of minority ethnic pupils*, London, DfEE

DfES (2003) *Aiming high: raising the achievement of Gypsy and Traveller pupils*, London, DfES

DfES (2005) *Aiming high: partnerships between schools and Traveller education support services in raising the attainment of Gypsy Traveller pupils*, London, DfES

DfES (2006) *Ethnicity and education*, London, DFES

Dyer, R. (1997) *White*, London, Routledge

Fenton, S., Carter, J. and Modood, T. (2000) 'Ethnicity and academia: closure models, racism models and market models', *Sociological Research Online*, 5.2, http://www.socresonline.org.uk/5/2/fenton.html

Fraser, A. (1992) *The Gypsies*, Oxford, Blackwell

Gil-Robles, A. (2005) *Report by Mr Alvaro Gil-Robles, Commissioner for Human Rights, on his visit to the United Kingdom*, Strasbourg, Council of Europe

Halfacree, K. (1996) 'Out of place in the country: Travellers and the rural idyll', *Antipode*, 28, 42-72

Hall, S. (1990) 'Cultural identity and diaspora', in Rutherford, J. (ed.), *Identity: community, culture, difference*, London, Lawrence and Wishart

Hancock, I. (1987) *The pariah syndrome: an account of Gypsy slavery and persecution*, Ann Arbor, Karoma

Hancock, I. (1992) 'The roots of inequity: Romani cultural rights in their historical and social context', *Immigrants and Minorities*, 11.1, 6–16

Hancock, I. (1998) 'Introduction', in Hancock, I., Dowd, S. and Djuriç, R. (eds), *The roads of the Roma*, Hatfield, University of Hatfield

Hancock, I. (2000) 'Standardisation and ethnic defence in emergent non-literate societies: the Gypsy and Caribbean cases', in Acton, T. and Dalphinis, M. (eds), *Language, blacks and Gypsies*, London, Whiting & Birch

Hartigan, J. (1997) 'Name-calling', in Wray, M. and Newitz, A. (eds), *White trash*, New York, Routledge

Haylett, C. (2001) 'Illegitimate subjects? Abject whites, neoliberal modernisation, and middle class multiculturalism', *Environment and Planning D: Society and Space*, 19, 351–70

Herder, J.G. (1877-1913) Ideen, ch. 7, sec. 1, in Suphan, B. (ed.), *Herders Samtliche Werke*, Berlin, Weidmann

Hesse, B. (1999) 'It's your world: discrepant M/multiculturalisms', in Cohen, P. (ed.), *New ethnicities, old racisms*, London, Zed Books

Holloway, S. (2003) 'Rural roots, rural routes: discourses of rural self and travelling other in debates about the future of Appleby New Fair, 1945–1969', *Journal of Rural Studies*, 20.2, 143–56

Holloway, S. (2005) 'Articulating otherness? White rural residents talk about Gypsy-Travellers', *Transactions*, 30, 361–76

Home Office (2005) *Improving opportunity, strengthening society: the government's strategy to increase race equality and community cohesion*, London, Home Office

hooks, b. (1997) 'Representing whiteness in the black imagination', in Frankenberg, R. (ed.), *Displacing whiteness*, Durham DC, Duke University Press

Jackson, P. (1998) 'Street life: the politics of carnival', *Environment and Planning D: Society and Space*, 6, 213–27

Jackson, P. and Penrose, J. (1993) *Constructions of race, place and nation*, London, UCL

Jarosz, L. and Lawson, V. (2002) 'Sophisticated people versus rednecks: economic restructuring and class difference in America's West', *Antipode*, 34, 8–27

Jenkins, R. (1994) 'Rethinking ethnicity: identity, categorisation and power', *Ethnic and Racial Studies*, 17.2, 189–201

Kenrick, D. and Bakewell, S. (1990) *On the verge: the Gypsies of England*, Hatfield, University of Hertfordshire Press

Bibliography

Kenrick, D. and Puxon, G. (1972) *The destiny of Europe's Gypsies*, London, Heinemann

Laurie, N., Dwyer, C., Holloway, S. and Smith, F. (1999) *Geographies of new femininities*, Harlow, Prentice Hall

Levitas, R. (1998) *The inclusive society? Social exclusion and New Labour*, London, Macmillan

Liegeois, J.P. (1987) *School provision for ethnic minorities: the Gypsy paradigm*, Hatfield, University of Hertfordshire Press

Liegeois, J.P. (1988) *Gypsies and Travellers, Council of Europe – dossiers for the intercultural training of teachers*, Strasbourg, Council for Cultural Co-operation

Lister, R. (1990) *The exclusive society: citizenship and the poor*, London, CPAG

McGhee, D. (2005) *Intolerant Britain? Hate, citizenship and difference*, Berkshire, Open University Press

MacLaughlin, J. (1999) 'European Gypsies and the historical geography of loathing', Review-Fernand Braudel Center for the Study of Economies, Historical Systems and Civilisations, 22.1, 31–59

Mason, D. (1994) 'On the dangers of disconnecting race and racism', *Sociology*, 28.4, pp.845–58

Mason, D. (1995) *Race and ethnicity in modern Britain*, Oxford, Oxford University Press

Mayall, D. (2004) *Gypsy identities 1500–2000: from Egipcyans and Moon-Men to the ethnic Romany*, London, Routledge

Mead, G.H. (1934) *Mind, self and society*, Chicago, University of Chicago Press

Miles, R. (1989) *Racism*, London, Routledge

Morris, R. (2000) 'Gypsies, Travellers and the media', *Tolley's Communications Law*, 5.6, 213–19

Myers, M. (2005) 'The education of Gypsy children in south-east London', unpublished paper presented at the University of Greenwich

Myers, M. (2006) 'The imaginary Gypsy', paper presented at the 2006 British Sociological Conference, North Yorkshire, Harrogate International Centre

Nash, C. (2003) 'Cultural geography: anti-racist geographies', *Progress in Human Geography*, 25.5, 637–48

Nayak, A. (2003) '"Last of the real Geordies?" White masculinities and the subcultural response to deindustrialisation', *Environment and Planning D, Society and Space*, 21, 7–25

Neal, S. (2002) 'Rural landscapes, representations and racism: examining multicultural citizenship and policy-making in the English countryside', *Ethnic and Racial Studies*, 25.3, 442–61

Ofsted (2001) [*Woodvale*] *Inspection Report*, London, Ofsted

Ofsted (2003) *Provision and support for Gypsy Traveller pupils*, London, Ofsted

Okely, J. (1983) *The Traveller-Gypsies*, Cambridge, Cambridge University Press

Okely, J. (1992) 'Anthropology and autobiography: participatory experience and embodied knowledge', in Okely, J. and Callaway, H. (eds), *Anthropology and autobiography*, London, Routledge

Okely, J. (1997) 'Non-territorial culture as the rationale for the assimilation of Gypsy children', *Childhood*, 4.1, 63–80

Paice, J. (2006) 'Trespass with a vehicle (offences) debate', in *Hansard*, 28 February 2006, http://www.publications.parliament.uk/pa/cm/cmhansrd.htm

Parekh, B. (1995) 'Liberalism and colonialism: a critique of Locke and Mill', in Pieterse, J. and Parekh, B. (eds), *The decolonization of imagination*, London, Zed Books

Parekh, B. (2000) 'Defining British national identity', *The Political Quarterly*, 71.1, 4–14

Pilkington, A. (2003) *Racial disadvantage and ethnic diversity in Britain*, Basingstoke, Palgrave

Plowden Report (1967) *Children and their primary schools*, London, HMSO

Ratcliffe, P. (2004) *'Race', ethnicity and difference*, Berkshire, Open University Press

Ray, L. and Reed, K. (2005) 'Community, mobility and racism in a semi-rural area: comparing minority experience in east Kent', *Ethnic and Racial Studies*, 28.2, 212–34

Redfield, R. (1971) *The little community*, Chicago, University of Chicago Press

Reynolds, R., McCarten, D. and Knipe, D. (2003) 'Traveller culture and lifestyle as factors influencing children's integration into mainstream secondary schools in west Belfast', *International Journal of Inclusive Education*, 7.4, 403–14

Rousseau, J-J. (1959) 'Les rêveries du promeneur solitaire, "Cinquième Promenade",' in *Oeuvres Complètes*, Paris, Gallimard

Scraton, P. (1976) 'Images of deviance and the politics of assimilation', MA thesis, University of Liverpool

Sennett, R. and Cobb, J. (1972) *The hidden injuries of class*, Cambridge, Cambridge University Press

Sibley, D. (1995) *Geographies of exclusion*, London, Routledge

Sibley, D. (1997) 'Endangering the sacred: nomads, youth cultures and the English countryside', in Cloke, P. and Little, J. (eds), *Contested countryside cultures: otherness, marginalisation and rurality*, London, Routledge

Sibley, D. (2003) 'Psychogeographies of rural space and practices of exclusion', in Cloke, P. (ed.), *Country visions*, Harlow, Pearson

Simmel, G. trans., ed. and with an introduction by Kurt Wolff (1950) *The sociology of George Simmel*, New York, Free Press

Simmel, G. ed. and with an introduction by D.N. Levine (1971) *On individuality and social forms: selected writings of Georg Simmel*, Chicago, University of Chicago Press

Smith, M. (1986) 'Pluralism, race and ethnicity in selected African countries', in Rex, J. and Mason, D. (eds), *Theories of race and ethnic relations*, Cambridge, Cambridge University Press

Song, M. (2003) *Choosing ethnic identity*, Cambridge, Polity

Sonneman, T. (1999) 'Dark mysterious wanderers: the migrating metaphor of the Gypsy', *Journal of Popular Culture*, 32, 119–39

Strauss, A. and Corbin, J. (1990) *Basics of qualitative research*, London, Sage

Swann Report (1985) *Education for all: the report of the Committee of Enquiry into the Education of Children from Minority Ethnic Groups*, London, HMSO

Sway, M. (1981) 'Simmel's concept of the stranger and the Gypsies', *Social Science Journal*, 18.1, 41–50

Taylor, C. (1992) 'The politics of recognition', in Taylor, C. and Gutmann, A. (eds), *Multiculturalism and "the politics of recognition"*, New Jersey, Princeton University Press

Turner, R. (1999) 'Fellow travellers: Jack Straw is alone in his certainty about who a Gypsy is', *The Guardian*, 24 August

Vanderbeck, R. (2003) 'Youth, racism and place in the Tony Martin affair', *Antipode*, 35, 363–84

Webber, J. (1997) 'Jews and Judaism in contemporary Europe: religious or ethnic group', *Ethnic and Racial Studies*, 29.2, 271–90

Weeks, J. (2000) *Making sexual history*, Cambridge, Polity

Winders, J. (2003) 'White in all the wrong places: white rural poverty in the postbellum US South', *Cultural Geographies*, 10, 45–63

Websites

http://www.chavscum.com

Newspapers

The Aberdeen Evening Express (22 March 2005)

The Daily Mail (10 September 1999) 'Shotgun farmer jailed for his own safety'

The Daily Mail (21 March 2005) Paul Eastham

The Daily Mail (21 March 2005) 'Travellers tales: a dossier of despair'

The Independent (21 March 2005) 'Are these Britain's most demonised people?'

The Sun (11 March 2003) Richard Littlejohn

The Sun (21 March 2005) 'Gipsies' 30M handout'

The Sun (23 December 2005) 'British Comedy Awards'

The Sun (16 April 2002) Fatima Bholah, 'Get the gipsy look'

Other

BBC News (16 September 2004) 'Rural England, Gypsies and land reform', http://www.news.bbc.co.uk/1/hi/uk/3635672

BBC Radio West Midlands (22 July 1999) Jack Straw

Celebrity Big Brother (2007) Channel 4, Endemol Productions

Guardian Unlimited ArtsBlog http://www.blogs.guardian.co.uk/arts/

Jack Dee Live at the Apollo (2004) BBC1, Open Mike Productions

The Frank Skinner Show (24 December 2004) ITV1, Avalon Productions

Index

Aberdeen Evening Express, The 153

Acton, T. 4, 7, 23, 30, 31, 32
  diaspora 16, 17
  education 78–9, 125
  inadequate sites 180

Ahmed, S. 167, 172

Aiming High: Raising the Achievement of Gypsy and Traveller Pupils 118

Anderson, K. 224

Anthias, F. 12

Appleby horse fair 216–17

Assimilation 109–111

Baddiel, David 92

Bakewell, S. 213

Banton, M. 11

Barany, Z. 23

Barras, Fred 210, 212, 214, 226n

Barth, F. 104–105

Bauman, Zygmunt 2, 15, 25, 76
  community 113
  and distancing 162
  friends and enemies 98–9, 102, 165, 179–80
  nation-building 110, 164, 179–81
  postmodernism 164, 168–9
  stigmatisation 180–1
  see also Strangers

BBC News 60

BBC Radio West Midlands 216

Bell, D. 223

Belton, B. 7, 15

Bercovici, K. 105

Bholah, Fatima 63–4

Bhopal, K. 7, 42, 43, 49, 226n
  association of Gypsies with white underclass 171
  changing attitudes to education 119, 138
  demarcation of boundaries 20, 168
  DfEE report *Working Towards Inclusive Education* 118
  difference 98, 109
  geography 103
  gypsy culture in schools 180
  name-calling 79
  racism of respondents 203

Big Brother see Celebrity Big Brother

Big Lottery Fund, The 156

Binchy, A. 16

Blair MP, Tony 3, 147

Bollywood 205

Bonnett, A. 91, 223

Boundaries 12, 14, 18–21, 25
  between 'good' and 'bad' Gypsies 66–8
  and difference 106–107

235

disruption by *strangers* 165, 184
ethnic boundaries 105–106
formation within academia 50, 209
imaginary 221
labelling 106, 166, 214
national identity 69, 76, 184
produced by media 161, 167, 183–4
racism 209, 210–11
real and imaginary 103
society 87–8, 100
'white' boundaries 103
see also Middle England; Taylor, C.

British National Party 132

Britishness
multiculturalism 184
national identity 189–90, 225
nationalism 164
white working class 192–4, 196

Bulmer, M. 12, 13

Cambridgeshire 60, 66–9, 211

Caravan Sites Act 225n

Celebrity Big Brother 115n, 205–206, 220–1

'Chavs' 90, 92, 94, 171, 197–8, 199n

Chavscum website 115n

Citizenship 100

Clark, C. 7, 33, 46, 216

Cleanliness *see* Dirtiness 32

Clebert, J. 16

Clifford, J. 43

Collins, M. 193

Commission for Architecture and the Built Environment (CABE) 178

Commission for Racial Equality (CRE) 46, 122, 207

Community 110, 113, 164, 191

Conservative Party 66, 146–8, 150, 159
multiculturalism 177, 179

Corbin, J. 127

Cornell, S. 12

Cottenham 60

Council of Europe's Social and Health Committee 218

Countryside Alliance 198, 214

Crays Hill 157

Daily Mail, The 3, 150–3, 159, 212

Davidson, Jim 207, 208

Davis, N. 12

Dee, Jack 92

DEMOS 192

Denzin, N. 41–2, 43–4

Department for Communities and Local Government 123

Department for Education and Schools 118, 119, 122–3, 143n

Department for Education and the Environment 42, 122

Derrington, C, 119

'Deserving poor' 157, 160, 168

Dirtiness 19, 28, 32, 54, 72, 97
cleanliness rituals 79
media representation 185
name-calling 79, 80, 91, 95
see also Whiteness

Dyer, R. 96

Eastenders 71

Eastham, P. 150

Education 21, 41, 42, 78, 100, 170
Active Citizens in Schools 123

Index

bullying 119, 124, 138, 201
see also Name-calling, in schools
celebrating difference 176
children not registered with school 118
child safety 119
Community Cohesion Standards for Schools 123
curriculum materials 141, 183
Education Welfare Officers 124
elective home education 118–121
Every Child Matters 118, 120
exclusion 107–109, 188, 226n
favouritism in schools 117, 129–32, 135, 142
Improving Opportunity Report 123
multiculturalism in schools 140, 141–3
Pupil Level Annual School Census (PLASC) 118
racism in schools 132–6
school funding 121
Special Educational Needs (SEN) 123
Vulnerable Children's Grant 121
see also Plowden Report; Traveller Education Service

English Heritage 178

Ethnography 37, 38–44, 203–205
gatekeepers 47–9, 125

European Commission 187–8

European Commissioner for Human Rights *see* Gil-Robles, Alvaro

European Community *see* European Union (EU)

European Parliament 122

European Union (EU) 188, 189

Every Child Matters see Education

Exclusion 91, 106, 107–109, 110, 111–115, 211
recognised by European Parliament 122
in schools 141–3

Exoticisation *see* Gypsies, as exotic

Fashion 63

Favouritism *see* Education, favouritism in schools

Fenton, S. 195

Frank Skinner Show, The 92

Fraser, A. 16

Funerals *see* Gypsies, social functions

Gammon 16

'Gaze' 75, 96, 97, 158, 159
camera's 'gaze' 160
media 'gaze' 161
see also Okely, J,

General election (2005) 26, 132, 146, 177

Gil-Robles, Alvaro 187–8

Goody, Jade 115n, 205–206, 207, 209

Greenfields, M. 7, 33, 36

Greig, Martin 153

Gypsies
adapting to new economies 216
and community 76, 78, 81, 83, 113–14
diaspora 4–6, 14, 29, 188–9, 222
see also Acton. T.
ethnic boundaries 15
ethnicity 13–18, 32
ethnic minority status 18, 135
as exotic 62, 64, 79, 80, 96, 105, 167
gender roles 35–6
Gypsy Council 187
Gypsy studies 23–4
holocaust 170, 180, 188, 218
idealised representation 79, 154, 211, 217

inadequate sites 180
nation 31, 102, 186–7, 191
out of time 68, 77
policy 21
politics 22, 187, 215, 217–19
pressure groups
see Gypsies, politics
racism displayed by 48–9, 52–4, 133–6
social functions 32–6, 212
slavery 30, 170, 188
Traveller Law Reform Coalition 150
in the UK 30–6

Halfacree, K. 211
Hall, Stuart 5–6, 14
Hancock, I. 7, 20, 30, 213, 218
Harder They Come, The 71
Hartigan, J. 91–2, 93
  Name-calling 95, 203
Hartmann, D. 12
Haylett, C. 91, 192–3
Headley, Victor 71
Healthcare 21, 41, 100, 170
Hell's Kitchen 206–208
Henry VIII 30, 180
Herder, J.G. 75
Hesse, B. 172, 185–6, 187
Hill MP, Keith 150
Holloway, S. 32, 90, 217
Hollywood 65
Home Office 123
hooks, b. 96
Housing 21, 41, 170
Howard MP, Michael 146, 148, 154, 159, 177

Human Rights Act 132, 146–7

Immigration 70, 189, 194
Independent, The 27, 159–62
  liberal representations 183–4
India 4–5, 14, 187, 188
Inter-marriage *see* Marriage
Irish Travellers 16, 19, 54, 66–7, 211
  anti-trespass laws 150

Jackson, P. 223
Jarosz, L. 91
Jenkins, R. 107
Kendall, S. 119
Kenrick, D. 4, 30, 180, 213

La Gitana 61–2, 67, 79
Labour Party *see* New Labour
Language 4, 13, 16
Laurie, N. 223
Lawson, V. 91
Levi-Strauss, Claude 163
Levitas, R. 211
Liberal Democrats 153
Liegeois, J.-P. 15, 16, 20, 188, 213
Likes Of Us, The 193
Linguistics *see* Language
Lister, R. 211
Littlejohn, Richard 155
Live at the Apollo 92
'Lotto louts' 166, 197

Index

McDonald, S. 153

McGhee, D. 13

MacLaughlin, J. 221

Major, John 3

Marcus, G. 43

Marriage 35, 38

Martin, Tony 210, 212, 214

Mason, D. 11

Mayall, D. 7, 18–19, 21, 22, 25, 218

Mead, G.H. 85n

Media representations 21, 55, 57, 63, 65
 planning 103
 stereotypes 29, 33, 72, 75
 visual representation 160, 161–2, 168, 199n

'Middle England' 145, 147, 151, 156, 177, 198, 225
 see also The Sun

Miles, R. 11, 215

Morris, R. 221

Myers, M. 42, 79
 association of Gypsies with white underclass 171
 demarcation of boundaries 20, 168
 difference 98, 109
 geography 103
 racism of respondents 203
 use of term 'settled' 169

Name-calling 7, 45, 92, 206, 214, 221
 by the media 93
 in schools 79, 124, 133–4, 201
 see also White trash; Dirtiness; Education, bullying

Nash, C. 197

National Farmer's Union 115n

Nationalism 164, 184

Natives see Strangers

Nayak, A. 91

Neal, S. 196

New Labour 146–7, 150

Newspaper circulations 145, 159

Nomadism 13, 16–17, 30, 32, 102

Nomenclature 6–11, 143n, 186–7

Office of the Deputy Prime Minister 146–7, 155, 156, 159
 see also Prescott, John

Ofsted 118, 119, 122

Okely, J. 4–5, 7, 8, 31, 32,
 cultural values 85
 ethnicity 8, 15, 17
 ethnography 40
 Gorgio 'gaze' 95, 97, 158
 Romanestan 187

Operation Trident 71

'Otherness' 3, 15, 30, 69, 76
 construction of 25, 89, 156, 162–3
 Gypsies historic 'otherness' 105
 Gypsies in the UK 73, 88, 91
 stigmatisation 166
 'white other' 81, 89, 90–8

Others *see* 'Otherness'

Outsiders *see* 'Otherness'

Paice MP, James 66–9, 77, 211

Parekh, B. 186, 189, 190, 191

Penrose, J. 223

Pilkington, A. 12, 13

Planning 103, 146, 150, 170, 178
 enforced differently for Gypsies 181, 198n

Plowden Report 22, 117

Policy work   41, 195, 225n

Prescott, John   146–7, 151, 155
see also Office of the Deputy Prime Minister

Press Complaints Commission   221

Puxon, Gratton   4, 30, 180, 187

Race Relations Act see Race Relations (Amendment) Act 2000

Race Relations (Amendment) Act 2000   118, 215

Racist names see Name-calling

Raising the Attainment of Minority Ethnic Pupils   121–2

Ratcliffe, P.   13

Ray, L.   196

Reality TV   115n

Redfield, R.   100

Reed, K.   196

Reputation   34

Reynolds, R.   119

Romanestan   187

Romani studies see Gypsy studies

Romanticisation   20–1, 61, 65, 79, 80, 213, 223, 226n

Rousseau, J.-J.   74

Rurality   210–11, 214

Rushdie, Salman   179

Ryan, Lee   206–207

Ryder, A.   150

Satanic Verses, The   179

Schools see Education

Scraton, P.   36

Self-employment   31, 82

Self-exclusion see Exclusion

Selvon, Sam   71

Sennett, R.   83–5

Shetty, Shilpa   115n, 205–206, 220–1

Sibley, D.   211, 213, 223

Simmel, Georg   2, 76, 99–100, 163
see also Strangers

Smith, M.   13

Song, M.   12

Sonneman, T.   223

Stereotypes   72–3, 83, 152, 211
British   193–4
and distancing   106, 161, 162
positive stereotypes   223
The Sun   148, 170
see also Media representations; 'Wealthy Gypsy'

Strangers   2–3, 15, 77–8, 81
ambiguity   219–20
coping with   164, 179, 184
exaggerated stranger   101–102, 219, 225
fear of   212
hostility towards   104
media representations of   162–3
otherness and the s*tranger*   88, 163–6
recognisability of   25, 76–7, 172
spatial belonging   104
stigmatisation   180
see also Boundaries

Strauss, A.   127

Straw MP, Jack   216

Sun, The   10, 26–7, 63–4, 67,
'chavs'   92
'Middle England'   145, 149, 185
multiculturalism   177, 179
Stamp on the Camps campaign   145, 149, 155–8, 209
see also Stereotypes

Index

Swann Report 118, 122

Sway, M. 100

Taylor, C. 73–5, 79
   difference-blind liberalism 176–7, 178–9
   identity 184
   uncrossable boundaries 179

Thatcher, Margaret 3, 165

Traveller Education Service 47–50, 54, 108
   acting as gatekeepers 47–8, 125
   legislation 124
   school attendance 118

Turner, R. 221

Underclass 91

Valentine, G. 223

Vanderbeck, R. 210, 211–12

'Wealthy Gypsy' 165, 166, 167, 171, 213

Webber, J. 13

Weddings *see* Gypsy, social functions

Weeks, J. 110

Wells, Roy 37–8, 39, 40, 58–9

'White other' 81, 197

White, Marco Pierre 206–207, 209

Whiteness 3, 25, 91, 93
   associated with goodness 96, 196
   and dirt 28, 202
   underclass 192, 194–5
   unreflexive 197
   see also 'Chavs'; 'White other'; White trash'

'White trash' 25, 90, 92, 197, 203

Wickford 157, 158

Winders, J. 91

Windrush 70, 71

Writing Culture 43

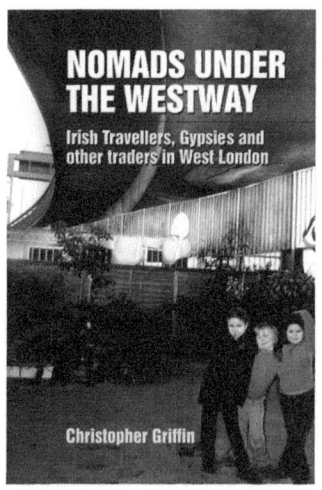

ALSO OF INTEREST

As warden of the Westway site, social anthropologist Christopher Griffin had a rare opportunity to immerse himself in Traveller culture. Dr Griffin observed and listened to the Gypsies at the site as he carried out his duties as caretaker. Lasting friendships were established which deepened his knowledge of Gypsy society.

The author of this scholarly yet personal account combines social anthropology with the author's direct experience as site warden of the Gypsy encampment under London's Westway.

Reflexive and partly autobiographical, *Nomads Under The Westway* is a history of West London's Gypsies and Travellers set in a broader context of immigration and race relations.

ISBN: 978-1-902806-54-9
Publication due in Autumn 2008
Paperback £14.99 / US$29.95 / Canadian$40.95
(+p&p UK £2.75, Europe £5.00, rest of world £8.00)

To order direct
Email: UHPress@herts.ac.uk
Tel: +44 (0)1707 284654
Fax: +44 (0)1707 284666
Website: www.herts.ac.uk/UHPress